Sanctuary School

Sanctuary School

Innovating to Empower Immigrant Youth

CHANDLER PATTON MIRANDA

Harvard Education Press
Cambridge, Massachusetts

Paperback ISBN 9798895570098

Library of Congress Cataloging-in-Publication Data

Names: Miranda, Chandler Patton, author.
Title: Sanctuary school : innovating to empower immigrant youth / Chandler Patton Miranda.
Description: Cambridge, Massachusetts : Harvard Education Press, [2025] | Includes bibliographical references and index. | Summary: "This book examines the concept of sanctuary, its cultural and historical roots, and evolution to policies affecting the lives and experiences of immigrant youth"—Provided by publisher.
Identifiers: LCCN 2025013537 | ISBN 9798895570098 (paperback)
Subjects: LCSH: Immigrant youth—United States—Social conditions. | Education—Social aspects—United States. | Safe spaces—United States. | Educational leadership—United States. | Educational innovations—United States. | Education and state—United States.
Classification: LCC LC3719 .M57 2025 | DDC 371.826/9120973—dc23/eng/20250528
LC record available at https://lccn.loc.gov/2025013537

Published by Harvard Education Press,
an imprint of the Harvard Education Publishing Group

Harvard Education Press
8 Story Street
Cambridge, MA 02138

Cover Design: Abigail Coyle
Cover Image: Angel Garcia, www.angelgarcia-art.com

The typefaces in this book are Carrara and Gotham.

Para mi querida familia, Luis, Gabriel y Martina. Los amo con todo mi corazón, y hasta la luna.

To my parents, Mary and Mike, who taught me to take risks and let me explore the world.

And to Gustavo, who lives on in our memories.

CONTENTS

Introduction

A Turning Point for Immigrant-Serving Schools

"IT'S DISRESPECTFUL," LAUREN reminded the students in her twelfth-grade social studies class. "It's not even about him; it is about me. I made that bulletin board to teach you about the election," she explained. "But Miss. He hates immigrants," a student responded.

It was one of my first days of fieldwork at International High School (IHS), and I had expected to see students beginning a new humanities project with Lauren.[1] Instead, I found myself in a conversation about the serial vandalization of a bulletin board. Half of the board was covered in blue butcher paper, and the other half was covered in red with a CSPAN map of the United States in the middle explaining the electoral college. On the blue side of the board was a picture of Hillary Clinton, and on the red side, Donald Trump. Question bubbles on white paper floated around the map asking: *Who can vote in the United States? What is the Electoral College? What are the issues?* Lauren scolded the students because Donald Trump's face had disappeared from the board and ended up in the boy's urinal . . . again.

I first heard about the urinal incident in the assistant principal's office, where the teachers snickered with each other about the students' antics when there were no students around. Even as I watched Lauren reprimand the students, I noticed her fighting not to let the corner of her lips turn into a smile. In this New York City high school for recently arrived immigrant teenagers, Trump was a joke they were all in on.[2] The educators at IHS were annoyed by the anti-immigrant rhetoric but assured their students that he could never win. Election forecasters were on their side, predicting that Hillary Clinton had an 85 percent chance of winning on election night.

Like many educators in New York City and across the country, I watched the *New York Times* election needle descend the interactive speedometer from royal blue to bright red with despair.[3] What would Trump's election mean for students at IHS and their families? What would it mean for my family as we muddled through our own immigration case? November 9, 2016, was a scary day for many people in the United States, but it was particularly jarring for immigrant communities given that Trump's campaign promised mass deportations and closed borders. It has become apparent in the years that followed that this moment was a turning point in global politics that had an immediate and lasting impact on schools' ability to serve immigrant youth.

It was shortly after the election that local governments nationwide began drafting resolutions to protect and reassure immigrant communities, using *sanctuary* as a descriptor for the new policies, often for the first time. In 2010, only two dozen cities across the United States were sanctuary cities. By the end of 2017, over six hundred municipalities had adopted sanctuary policies.[4] Sanctuary schools, those that adopted and implemented policies to support and protect immigrant students, emerged during this time as well. Local papers began reporting on sanctuary school policies in cities like Eugene, Palo Alto, Des Moines, Pittsburgh, and New York City.[5] At IHS, a Sanctuary City poster was hung in the main office, and the Department of Education's statement of support for immigrant families was posted in the hallways. The concept of sanctuary was rapidly evolving into a significant tool for political intervention in both school and city contexts. However, each policy had its unique local characteristics and vague legal implications. While some contend that sanctuary school policies are largely symbolic, others argue that schools cannot serve as sanctuaries due to legal restrictions and their historical ties to state-driven assimilation efforts. Nevertheless, the concept of sanctuary remains insufficiently explored as an educational policy.

SANCTUARY: A POWERFUL CONCEPT WITH FLEXIBLE MEANINGS

Sanctuary is a word with many meanings and interpretations. Over time, it has been associated with organized religion, human rights law, and progressive politics. The word originated in ancient times as a practice of providing shelter to the unhoused, nomadic, and persecuted. It has come to describe practices in cities worldwide that intend to receive migrants in more welcoming ways than the nation or state. In this book, I use the word "sanctuary" to describe schooling practices that I observed at IHS. My definition draws from historical and contemporary understandings of sanctuary politics and policies to offer a new way of thinking about school spaces for immigrant youth.

Providing refuge from persecution is an ancient practice developed by the Greeks and Romans and emanates from thousands of years of Christianity, Islam, Judaism, Buddhism, Baha'i, Sikhism, and Hinduism. World wars in the early twentieth century displaced people globally, and the United States became a place that offered refuge and sanctuary to some. In 1948, following World War II and the "barbarous acts which . . . outraged the conscience of mankind," the newly formed United Nations drafted the Universal Declaration of Human Rights, proclaiming the right to seek asylum without persecution a fundamental human right.[6] Recognizing the right to locate sanctuary as fundamental legitimated seeking asylum beyond the actions of a particular country or institution.[7]

Despite the concept's roots in religious doctrine and human rights rules, the modern interpretation of sanctuary has been denigrated as anarchical by the political right since the 1980s. During the American Sanctuary Movement, John Fife, a Presbyterian minister, and Jim Corbett, a Quaker, organized a national movement to defy the Reagan administration's position that Central Americans attempting to cross the border were economic refugees and not genuine asylum seekers.[8] Supporters of the Sanctuary Movement argued that migrants fleeing the violence of American-backed regimes in El Salvador and Guatemala were entitled to asylum in the United States under immigration law.[9] In this era, sanctuary began to mean a public practice of protecting migrants from the state and holding the state accountable for human rights violations.[10] In studying this movement, scholars outlined a new framing of sanctuary as the civil initiative of people who nonviolently protect human rights.[11]

What I found interesting about the Sanctuary Movement is that it largely remained decentralized and informal but depended on hundreds of churches nationwide declaring themselves sanctuaries and offering undocumented immigrants services, including counseling, legal defense, housing, and transportation.[12] Sanctuary was, in part, a place and, in part, a practice. The church became a local epicenter of services, and the community members became the service providers and recipients. While reading about this movement, I started to see that IHS was responding to the Trump administration in a more robust way than other school districts across the country who were also using sanctuary as a descriptor of their policy approach.

Based on what I read in the news, district policy documents, and public statements from school leaders across the country, it became clear to me that the concept of sanctuary in the United States only really meant that local police could not cooperate with Immigration and Customs Enforcement (ICE) agents.[13] In other words, school districts that used the word sanctuary were pledging to be uncooperative and noncompliant with ICE if they were to try to come onto a school campus. These were critical protective measures with legal precedent.[14] Nevertheless, studies of sanctuary policies on education outcomes suggest that while policies may reduce immigration enforcement, they are largely symbolic and may not go far enough in reducing uncertainty and increasing educational outcomes.[15]

Although ensuring students were safe on and off campus was a priority at IHS, what I observed went far beyond protectionism and noncompliance. Educators at IHS were innovating daily in response to the moment to ensure that what they were teaching was relevant and helpful to their students, that the social and emotional needs of students were being met, and that all school actors were critical of how both information and misinformation were being relayed and interpreted within the school community. It required risk-taking and rule-breaking, organizing within and outside the school community to be a voice for immigrant communities, and shifting what, when, and how concepts related to civil duty, fundamental rights, and racioethnic identity were taught to empower students most marginalized by the state.

The remarkable response to hostile policy moments by school actors at IHS was an interpretation of sanctuary in line with the ideology of the Sanctuary Movement.[16] Still, in 2017, it seemed out of sync with school and university interpretations of the concept as a protective measure supported by legal precedent.[17] While swift actions proved important for keeping students and their families coming to school during a particularly challenging moment in time, there was much more to the school's approach to sanctuary that was deeply rooted in its culture. How the school had institutionalized care, belonging, activism, and community in other immigration policy moments made it possible for the educators at IHS to move beyond protection toward innovation in response to hostile national politics.

I eventually found a policy parallel to what I was observing. In Europe, Sanctuary Cities, Solidarity Cities, Cities of Refuge, Integrating Cities, and Fearless Cities emerged beginning in 2015 as a consequence of national governments' insufficient responses to the migration of asylum seekers from Syria, Afghanistan, Nigeria, Pakistan, Iraq, Eritrea, and the Balkans.[18] It was from these cities that a reconceptualization of sanctuary through localized citizenship rights and services emerged. In learning about these policy initiatives of radical welcoming, I began to ask what a school would have to be and do to go beyond the protective sanctuary. Could my observations at IHS serve as a model for educators of immigrant youth who want to do more than keep ICE out of schools?

Drawing on both the history and contemporary interpretations of sanctuary, I developed a twofold definition of sanctuary schooling. First, it is a responsiveness to immigrant students' immediate needs for safety and protection in an increasingly polarized political environment. Protective sanctuary allows schools to respond to acute needs and rapidly changing politics and policies. However, I also use sanctuary to describe innovations that can create an adaptable culture of empowerment and radical welcoming. Both factors are critical when trying to create sanctuary schools for immigrant youth. Therefore, the term "sanctuary school" as used throughout this book will refer to schools that offer not only protective sanctuary, but innovative practices and policies that empower, welcome, and uplift immigrant students, thus creating true sanctuary.

TURNING POINTS IN US SANCTUARY POLITICS

The US government has a long history of hostility toward immigrant communities, particularly those that do not advance America's foreign policy agenda. Despite the long history of border theatrics, many see the Trump presidency, particularly his first term from 2016–2020, as a turning point in immigration enforcement. In addition to dehumanizing migrants to a great degree, the Trump administration left little in immigration policy untouched. The Immigration Policy Tracking Project logged over a thousand changes to the immigration system in just four years.[19] In the years since, the Biden administration was unwilling or unable to reverse many policies that harm immigrant children and their families, and conservative state legislatures are quietly passing laws to defund or make sanctuary cities illegal. The 2024 presidential election centered immigration in even more violent, vulgar, and racist terms than in 2016. Democrats shifted to the right, supporting more militarization on the border, and Republicans rallied their base through fearmongering, telling them that immigrants take their jobs and their affordable housing and eat their pets.[20] More than half of Americans support some form of mass deportation of unauthorized immigrants and avenues to asylum have been blocked from every direction.[21]

Trump has promised to go even further to target, scapegoat, and traumatize immigrant communities in his second term. In the coming years, schools will feel the direct impact of the hateful rhetoric toward immigrants. It was such hostility that prompted the creation of school sanctuary policies, and I anticipate that the resistance to such deplorable treatment of children will fuel the fire of the sanctuary school movement.

Recent scholarship has documented through surveys and *testimonios* how the political climate of the United States has become more hostile toward immigrant youth who are experiencing increases in hate speech, violence outside of school, bullying in school, and raids, resulting in long-term trauma.[22] Sanctuary school policies that emerged for the first time during the first Trump administration have become even more critical as more newly arrived immigrants live in limbo, and Congress fails to make meaningful immigration reform.[23] Urban centers and immigrant-serving schools are critical institutions at the forefront of the response to globalization and changing migration patterns.

Newly arrived immigrant families in cities like New York and Chicago may be the most at risk in a second Trump term. These sanctuary cities have evolved into contested spaces that epitomize the political divisions in the United States—as exemplified by actions such as transporting migrants from conservative states to sanctuary cities like New York City, Chicago, Washington, DC, and Los Angeles. This means that schools, as public institutions, will continue to play an essential role in determining who can go to school safely and how youth and their families will be received in the front office, hallway, classroom, gym, and cafeteria. We need sanctuary schools now more than ever.

This book asks, *What makes a school a sanctuary?* It asks you, the reader, to think beyond current understanding of sanctuary schools as protective spaces of noncooperation. Instead, it asks you to imagine a whole school approach to sanctuary that protects and empowers immigrant youth through radical welcoming and innovation. Schools need to be prepared, now more than ever, to protect new immigrant students as the political environment becomes even more polarized and comprehensive immigration reform looks less and less likely. The next generation of educators and school leaders must be prepared to move beyond crisis management and toward innovation to create school spaces where immigrant youth can thrive in an era of increased surveillance and xenophobia.

THE INTERNATIONALS NETWORK OF PUBLIC SCHOOLS

In the early 1980s, educators Janet Lieberman, Cecilia Cunningham, and Eric Nadelstern initiated a collaboration between the NYC Board of Education and the City University of New York to address the educational challenges faced by immigrant students in New York City. Eventually, they founded the first International High School at LaGuardia Community College in 1985, which served sixty recently arrived immigrant high school students. Their model integrated English language instruction within all subjects. This approach expanded to two more schools in the 1990s: Brooklyn and Manhattan International High Schools. Bounded by a philosophical approach, the leaders of the schools supported the evolution of the Internationals Network for Public Schools, a 501(c)(3) nonprofit that currently supports thirty-one innovative public schools and academies serving almost ten thousand students nationwide.

What sets the Internationals Network apart from other schools serving immigrant youth is its unifying vision for instruction, assessment, school design, and growth. They call their unifying instructional framework the "HELLO Principles." These guiding ideas represent a holistic approach to education that prioritizes collaboration, experiential learning, and shared responsibility across the entire school community. The HELLO acronym is described as follows:

- **Heterogeneity and Collaboration** ensure that schools and classrooms are diverse and use collaborative structures that build on the strengths of each member of the school community to optimize learning. By embracing the unique perspectives and skills of everyone, schools create an environment where students and teachers work together to achieve common goals.
- **Experiential and Project Learning** takes education beyond the traditional classroom setting. This expansion of the school environment motivates students by connecting learning to the real world. Engaging in project-based learning enhances students' ability to apply knowledge in meaningful ways.
- **Language and Content Integration** emphasizes that students develop strong language skills best in context. When language is taught in an interdisciplinary and experiential way, learning emerges naturally and purposefully. This approach ensures that students acquire language and content knowledge simultaneously.
- **Localized Autonomy and Responsibility** links autonomy with accountability at every level within the school. It empowers all members of the learning community to take ownership of their roles and responsibilities, allowing them to contribute to their fullest potential.
- **One Learning Model for All** ensures that all members of the school community work together in diverse, collaborative groups. Student and adult learning is continuous and collaborative and structures for collaboration designed for students are also used by the adults in the school.

These HELLO Principles form the foundation for a school environment that fosters deep, meaningful learning and ensures that all members of the community are engaged, empowered, and able to thrive. This book will help illustrate what this framework looks like in practice.

INTERNATIONAL HIGH SCHOOL

I selected one school in the network, International High School (IHS), as the site of this study because, like its sister schools, it surpasses other immigrant-serving schools in terms of measurable outcomes and reputation. Most high schools with large populations of recently arrived immigrant teenagers are unsuccessful at helping students feel like they belong in school, learn English, pass state exit exams, and ultimately graduate. However, schools in the Internationals Network serve only the highest-need immigrant students yet consistently report positive outcomes on almost every traditional measure of student achievement.

Students at IHS have been in the country for fewer than four years when they begin high school, and all are learning English.[24] Over 95 percent of students live in low-income households, and approximately half of the four hundred students in the school are undocumented. When this study took place, 47 percent of students identified as Latinx, 27 percent as Asian/Pacific Islander, 4 percent as white, and 1 percent as Native American. Many students start ninth grade at fifteen, sixteen, or seventeen years of age, and at least a fifth have had interruptions in their formal education.[25] Despite the many challenges that students face, 80 percent graduate from high school within six years.

IHS successfully educated students throughout multiple crises following the 2016 election. Even after the COVID-19 pandemic, 82 percent of the class of 2022 graduated within four years, 89 percent of the class of 2020 graduated within six years, and 45 percent of students enrolled in college within six months. In most New York City schools, fewer than half of English learners graduate within four years. While this is only one metric for success, a recent impact analysis found that IHS was much more successful in ninth-grade credit accumulation, attendance, engagement, dropout rates, and post-secondary opportunities than schools serving a comparable newcomer population. For these reasons, I chose International High School as an exceptional case for examining the potential of schools to be sites of possibilities for immigrant youth.

IHS and the network of schools like it in New York City have been responding and adapting to global migration patterns and their impact on young people living in urban areas for decades. I have followed in the footsteps of researchers who understand these schools as sites of possibility for immigrant youth.[26] The initial data for this study was gathered over two academic years between September 2016 and June 2018. I spent over two hundred hours as a participant observer, conducting in-depth interviews and gathering and analyzing school documents. While visiting the school, I observed what was posted in the hallway, interacted with students in classrooms, chatted with teachers during lunch, and watched student presentations, talent shows, and sporting events. I participated in the daily lives of school actors for many years to watch what they did, listen to what they said, and collect documents and artifacts. I initially spent several days a week at the school and built lasting relationships with many teachers and students, most of whom I am still in contact with today. I formally interviewed twenty-one teachers, two counselors, the social worker, the parent coordinator, the assistant principal and the principal, and two paraprofessionals. Nine students participated in in-depth interviews, and five students participated in a focus group. I audio-recorded formal interviews and focus groups with teachers and students, committee meetings, and other professional gatherings. Each audio recording was transcribed along with fieldnotes that detailed the unspoken gestures and interactions of participants. I attended twenty student presentations in which I recorded one-on-one interactions between students and their mentor teachers and asked students questions about their experiences learning in the school. Informal interviews and group discussions took place in the classroom setting to generate cohesive and complete narratives. I photographed the hallways and collected teaching materials and student work to understand what was taught and learned in classroom spaces. I detail how I got access to the school and built relationships with educators and students in the appendix of this book.

I spent an additional semester visiting the school once a week in 2023 to ensure that my findings reflect recent events and social shifts following the pandemic and the racial reckoning that the country went through after the murder of George Floyd. I continue to maintain contact with educators and school leaders at schools across New York City as the country watches how this beacon of a sanctuary city responds to large numbers of migrants under the Eric Adams administration and another election cycle focused on immigration begins.

I continue to visit this IHS and the other thirty-one International High Schools that are part of the Internationals Network of Public Schools because I believe they are living laboratories, often ahead of the research in how to best serve a highly diverse set of students in a constantly changing political environment. I think of these schools as successfully serving students who are not well served in almost any other setting in the country. The stories I tell in the following chapters reflect a deep understanding of how educators and students at IHS engaged with one another, articulated their experiences and perceptions of their interpersonal relationships, and documented their beliefs in public school documents and private correspondence.

THE POTENTIAL AND LIMITATIONS OF SANCTUARY SCHOOLS

As a professor of education, I teach my students that schools can be amazing places of change, reform, and innovation but that they cannot fix society's problems alone. Schools are important fixtures in a web of social support for children and families but cannot solve poverty, cure racism, or banish xenophobia in our society. They can, however, be sites of resistance and possibility. Educational anthropologists often write about schools where immigrant youth are marginalized, and little is done to combat societal ills. They tell powerful stories about how politics and policies at every level of government impact children's school lives and how schools often maintain the status quo, particularly when it comes to the marginalization of non-white, non-English speaking, and undocumented youth.[27]

I wanted to write a book about IHS because it is disrupting the status quo. As one of the most impactful immigrant-serving high schools in the country, it was an appropriate site to uncover the cultural practices that support student belonging, learning, and social–emotional well-being. I wrote *Sanctuary School* to provide a roadmap for educators, activists, school leaders, and policy makers who want equitable schools and increased opportunities for immigrant youth. This book details a comprehensive, whole-school approach to sanctuary that considers students' safety as well as their agency, identity, and futures. Through innovative approaches to design, socialization, educator development, and advocacy, sanctuary schools can be empowering places for immigrant students that move beyond protection to challenge the norms, values, and power structures that often limit schools' capacities to serve immigrant youth well.

ORGANIZATION OF *SANCTUARY SCHOOL*

This book begins by transporting us to the start of the 2016–2017 school year at International High School because this timeframe coincided with a significant juncture in US history—the election season featuring contenders Hillary Clinton and Donald Trump vying for the presidency. The urinal vignette is intended to be comical but also to illustrate the pivotal nature of the election. The chapter introduces the powerful concept of sanctuary and outlines how its meaning has been interpreted over time in distinct locations. In the following chapters, divided into two parts, I argue for the future utility of sanctuary schools by telling the stories of teachers, students, and school leaders at IHS as they navigated protective sanctuary and radical welcoming.

PART I: SANCTUARY AS PROTECTION

Part I of *Sanctuary School* provides rich ethnographic evidence of how sanctuary schools can provide protection to immigrant students. Chapter 1 argues that protection can be understood as legally supported noncompliance and advocacy. Chapter 2 makes the case for understanding protective sanctuary as a way to ensure students' bodily safety and social well-being.

In chapter 1, I illustrate how the school reacted to events related to the election of President Donald Trump. What began as a joke to most school actors quickly accelerated into efforts to protect immigrant students living in a sanctuary city from a hostile political environment. Creating a sanctuary for students in this time involved thoughtful shifts in the curriculum, social–emotional support during instructional time, and explicit teaching of constitutional rights. The chapter details how educators who initially taught the election in a "fair and balanced way," choosing to keep their own political orientations a secret, evolved in the following months. Between the election in November and the inauguration in January, teachers often referenced the systems of "checks and balances" but stopped assuring students that they would be safe in a sanctuary city after the first so-called Muslim ban immediately impacted students from Yemen in January 2017. In the months following, educators adapted formally established practices, like Know Your Rights workshops, to the changing political environment. They developed accompaniment plans with undocumented and mix-status families to ensure students could stay in school and have a safe place to live, even if their parents were deported. Teachers began to talk openly about their political views because "to stay silent was to betray" students.

This chapter argues that the school took a protective turn in a way that was reactive to the moment and in line with shifts made by other US schools, universities, and municipalities that adopted sanctuary policies in this era. In sanctuary cities, police departments were prevented from sharing information with immigration agents. In sanctuary schools and districts, *Plyler v. Doe* and the Family Educational Rights and Privacy Act (FERPA) provided a legal basis for keeping student data private and immigration agents off campus. Sanctuary as protection at the cultural level of the school was enacted through noncompliance with immigration authorities and explicit gestures of support and allyship from school staff.

Chapter 2 begins with Milagros' story. Milagros traveled from Guatemala to cross the Mexican border in the southernmost part of Texas, eventually arriving at IHS. Her story highlights how many students come to the school and the challenges they face along the way. I ask my reader not to question why Milagros made the journey but to consider what happens to her when she gets to school. I address both the legal and social aspects of schooling that impact immigrant communities. Schools are often the first point of contact that immigrant families have with public institutions in the United States, particularly those who are undocumented and undetected. While all children in the United States have a constitutional right to attend public schools, older teenagers like Milagros are often turned away. At IHS, they are received with open arms, and their safety and well-being are the school's first priority. Where other schools rush to assess a newly arrived student's English proficiency, educators at IHS worried about Milagros' legal status, abusive home life, food insecurity, loneliness, and lack of winter clothes.

The school provided a protective sanctuary for Milagros by helping her move into a safe living situation, securing legal representation for her asylum case, and taking her shopping for winter boots and a coat.

This interpretation of protection goes beyond the legal responsibilities of sanctuary schooling but is still focused on acute challenges that must be addressed before a young person can be reasonably expected to learn and prioritize schoolwork.

PART II: SANCTUARY AS INNOVATION

The three chapters in Part II examine the culture of the school that existed long before the election and continues to evolve today. Rather than rapidly responding to a crisis, the practices detailed in these chapters are thoughtful, comprehensive, and holistic. They took time to build and can be difficult to maintain. While most of the data in these chapters was collected between 2016 and 2018, I returned to the school in 2022 and 2023 to see how the pandemic, change in administration, and migration patterns had impacted the school's culture. While the protective aspects of the school culture had changed dramatically, mostly in response to being in the epicenter of the pandemic, the cultural elements and essence of the school largely remained the same. The chapters focus on how school actors think about the built environment, ways of knowing, and policy impact.

In chapter 3, I paint a picture of IHS and its culture, traditions, rituals, and norms. I tell Gonzalo's story to demonstrate how a sense of belonging is cultivated in students' daily lives through the school's built environment, institutional structures, and social interaction. Students feel seen and heard because they can't disappear in the single hallway that makes up the school. I reveal how structures at IHS empower immigrant students and affirm their belonging in both the country and the school. Further, I show how a culture of belonging has been embedded in official and unofficial school rules, rituals, and pedagogical practices. The chapter begins with Gonzalo's first day in which he glares at his new teachers and classmates from under his hoodie. He learned in middle school that school was not a safe place after watching daily fights and one particularly traumatic bathroom stabbing. It ends with his graduation from high school six years later. Gonzalo's evolution, told to me over the course of several interviews, shows how the school's size, what was hanging on the wall, and how class cohorts were structured impacted his ability to stay in school.

This chapter introduces the concept of sanctuary as an innovative practice and argues that the traditional ways in which schools are constructed and structured exclude recently arrived immigrant youth as well as other marginalized youth. I ask readers to imagine the walls and trophy cases ubiquitous in most US high schools. Who do the trophies, honor rolls, and perfect attendance bulletin boards celebrate? Who do they exclude? The meaning that humans assign to symbols orients them in their social worlds.[28] What educators paint on their walls and staple to their bulletin boards are symbols of what a school community values. Students who do not see their trophies in the cases, their pictures on the wall, or their work being celebrated may feel invisible in the school. They may feel like they do not belong. This is a common occurrence for immigrants and students who often feel unimportant, insignificant, and invisible in public schools where they are the minority—and social isolation within a school can prevent students from thriving in the classroom. Gonzalo felt the difference on his first day of high school. When he walked into the school, he saw bulletin boards showcasing student work with multilingual annotations, drafts with peer and teacher feedback, and artwork of students' interpretations of their cultures and identities. By doing this, educators indicate to students that they value the learning process more than the polished outcome. This chapter argues that creating a space that counters anti-immigrant discourses really begins with easily overlooked environmental factors that signal belonging and inclusion.

Chapter 4 argues for innovative sanctuary practices to be extended to teachers of immigrant youth as well. Considering teacher identity in hiring practices, distributing decision-making power to increase buy-in, focusing on teacher and leader retention, and growing-your-own approaches to building school culture are well-researched practices that can make schools more welcoming places for marginalized youth. These practices are innovative when combined and given time to evolve.

For example, Carolina, a young math teacher, was hired because she was a child of immigrants, a proud Cuban-Colombian American, and bilingual in Spanish and English. In her interview, she took risks and showed a willingness to learn from her mistakes. She had recently graduated from a traditional secondary math program that valued efficiency over engagement. Her student-teacher mentor would spend the entire class enthusiastically completing a problem set on the board. At the end of the class, sweaty and excited, he would declare, "We did so much work today!" Meanwhile, she could see students were disengaged. Carolina knew she wanted to teach differently but didn't know how. Over the next five years, she received mentoring and support from veteran teachers to learn about project-based learning, teaching literacy in the math classroom, and how to take care of her own mental health. Had the principal hired Carolina based on her identity alone and without the input of a committee of peers, would she have remained in teaching? Had she been left to "shut the door and teach" would she have been able to learn the art of designing math projects that consider both content and literacy? This chapter challenges the notion that a silver bullet, delivered through consultancy or professional development, can dramatically impact the culture of a school or its ability to serve marginalized youth. Rather, it argues that innovative schools evolve when committed educators are given the time, support, and care necessary to develop into change agents for immigrant youth.

In chapter 5, I discuss how educators at IHS contend with state and local accountability policies that disproportionately disadvantage their students. Specifically, I examine how educators at the school contend with exit exams given in English that are required for graduation and the pressure to ensure that students graduate within four years. School leaders at IHS have joined forces with other networks of educators in New York to advocate for using Performance-Based Assessment Tasks (PBATs) as graduation requirements to replace problematic exit exams that disproportionately disadvantaged immigrant English learners. They have also advocated for using a five- and six-year graduate rate to evaluate high schools and for the state to acknowledge the strengths of immigrant and immigrant-origin students with the Seal of Biliteracy.

This chapter argues that advocating for just policies for immigrant youth is a crucial act of sanctuary schools. School leaders at immigrant-serving high schools are under incredible pressure from local and state education departments to focus on test scores and four-year graduation rates. Leaders may know that these statistics do not represent what their students need to succeed in school, but they may feel that compliance is their only recourse. To be sure, compliance can protect immigrant students when test scores are prioritized, and schools remain safe from scrutiny, but these impulses often fail immigrant students who need more support, time, and care. Instead, leaders of immigrant-serving schools should see their work as inherently political and work to build coalitions with other leaders who want to better serve immigrant students in their schools. Networking to share strategies and coalition building to influence policy decisions are innovative practices that combat exclusionary actions by the state and create space for practices that empower students to see their skills and contributions as valuable.

The conclusion suggests critical mindset shifts necessary for nurturing sanctuary schooling and examines the potential policy implications of these shifts. These include recognizing the flaws in the social contract and the failures of state and district policies and urging educators to critically challenge the systems that shape schooling, encouraging educators to fully know students beyond data points or test scores by embracing their full identities, asking educators to move toward valuing stability and long-term well-being in students' lives rather than prioritizing short-term outcomes. Last, it asks educators to reconsider how they measure student success and honor their contributions. Together, these shifts set the stage for reimagining sanctuary schooling as spaces of radical welcome, protection, and empowerment.

Finally, I include an appendix for novice ethnographers to illustrate how this study was done. The appendix serves the dual purpose of increasing the transparency, trustworthiness, and rigor of the book and makes the book an appropriate teaching tool for undergraduate methods classes and advanced classes in the anthropology and sociology of education.

POSITIONALITY

When I moved to Brooklyn in June 2014, I was entangled with the immigration system on behalf of my husband, Luis, whom I met in 2010 in Barranquilla, Colombia, and married in a courthouse in Fort Worth, Texas, eighteen months later. Luis and I had learned while we were dating that my US passport allowed for nearly unrestricted global travel, while his ability to travel was severely restricted as a Colombian citizen. We understood that marriage and eventually pursuing residency for Luis was our only possibility if we wanted to eventually live anywhere outside of Colombia together.

In 2012, Colombian citizens faced significant barriers to mobility across borders, with long and costly application processes for visas to travel, work, or study abroad. As a young man from a low-income background with few family connections, we knew he was unlikely to get a tourist visa, but we applied anyway, and he was given an interview date. I emailed an unpublished embassy address that a friend had used to successfully reverse an embassy decision after her partner's visa was denied, explaining that I worked at a well-known international school where many embassy workers sent their children and that I wanted Luis to get the visa. I never received a response and felt uncomfortable engaging in what Colombians call *palanca*, using my privilege and position to potentially influence Luis' fate.[29] Luis went to his interview in his Avianca uniform, an easily recognizable navy-blue suit with a yellow and orange striped tie. We still do not know if it was my scheming, Luis's charm, or a sympathetic embassy employee, but he secured a tourist visa on his first attempt, a rare success at that time.

Luis flew to Texas on a Thursday in July 2012, and we were married by Monday afternoon. We navigated the immigration process meticulously in the years that followed. After our courthouse wedding, we continued to live in Bogotá for two more years to shorten the time Luis would have to wait to work in the United States legally and the number of years he would have to wait to apply for citizenship. In June 2014, we flew into New York's John F. Kennedy Airport with an enormous binder of Luis's documents, including college transcripts and vaccination records, all translated and notarized, as well as a dozen notarized letters from friends and families attesting to the legitimacy of our relationship. I would not let the binder out of my sight since it had taken me years to compile. I still have it nestled in the bookshelf with our family photo albums. Luis entered the United States on a tourist visa, and I immediately began the change of status process, submitting extensive documentation to support my petition for him as my spouse.

Despite our best efforts, we faced numerous delays and bureaucratic obstacles. After spending hours on hold with the United States Customs and Immigration Services (USCIS) offices, we eventually resolved each issue. By October 2014, Luis received advance parole and work authorization, and he obtained his green card in March 2015. He became a US citizen in March 2018 in a somber ceremony devoid of the typical fanfare—no cheers, little flags, or video messages from the sitting president. The judge administering the oath emphasized the importance of exercising civic duty and voting, adding gravity to the occasion. For many in the room, the decision to seek citizenship was driven by concern that a green card alone offered insufficient protection, reflecting the broader climate of uncertainty and apprehension at that time in immigrant communities. Our first child, Gabriel, was born seven months later.

Luis's journey from foreign spouse to US citizen within six years is notably swift within the immigration system. Although we did not hire a lawyer, the process still cost us approximately $10,000 in application fees and lost wages during the periods that Luis could not legally work. Most of my US-born friends are astonished by how burdensome and costly it is to navigate legal immigration. Those familiar with the system know our experience was unusually quick and inexpensive.

Supporting Luis as he navigated living, working, and studying in a new country deepened my understanding of the varied and often harsh realities that new immigrants face. In my fieldwork, these experiences gave me a much more nuanced understanding of what many students and teachers at IHS had experienced in coming to the United States and why so many people make the difficult decision to come to the country using any avenue possible since legal immigration is almost impossible for most of the people who would like to migrate. For instance, Prasana, a science teacher from Nepal, was a permanent resident married to an undocumented partner who faced the agonizing choice between self-deportation to "parole" in Nepal for five to ten years away from his family or remaining undocumented in the United States indefinitely.[30] Similarly, Walter, a student from Barranquilla, initially came to the United States believing that his family had planned to visit Disney World but found himself unable to work or apply for federal loans for college since overstaying his six-month tourist visa meant that he was now undocumented. Or Jesus, who had been separated from his mother for sixteen years while she tried everything in her power to get him residency. Navigating the process of immigration helped me learn the complex and often punitive nature of the immigration system on young people and mixed-status families. While our case was much different than most because of my privileged position as a highly educated white woman with helpful connections, interacting with USCIS, preparing for interviews at Federal Plaza, and listening to Luis's challenges and frustrations about immigration and life in the United States gave me context.

Luis and I moved into a studio apartment in Brooklyn and I began my doctoral studies at New York University (NYU). I had applied for graduate school as a high school teacher with seven years of classroom experience in public and private schools in two countries and three cities. However, I was a total outsider in the vast and complex education system of New York City and in academia. Having attended public schools in Texas and most of my teaching career outside the United States, I had little understanding of New York's Department of Education, its scale, and its intricacies. I was unfamiliar with the sheer number of students it served, the socioeconomic and racial diversity of these students, and the complexities of school choice, including zones, admissions, and charter schools. This lack of local insight left me excited but overwhelmed. How would I ever be able to write about schools in this massive bureaucracy with any authority? When I started my coursework as a doctoral student at NYU that fall, I began earnestly studying US education policy and became profoundly interested in the plight of immigrant teenagers in New York.

My outsider status in New York City, combined with my intense insider experience as a high school teacher and a wife navigating the immigration system on behalf of my immigrant husband, put me in a unique position to study IHS and try to understand the school at a cultural level. Since becoming a mother and a public school parent of Latinx, Spanish-speaking children in Brooklyn, my commitment to sharing the story of this high school community has deepened. I am convinced that everyone can learn from this remarkable place. This book is essential not only for those who educate immigrant youth but for any educator—present or future—who is dedicated to radically welcoming all children into public schools, especially the most marginalized and minoritized. Many educators want to make a difference but may not know where to start in creating sanctuary for children and young people.

I hope this book will serve as a guide for educators and school leaders striving to better meet the needs of recently arrived immigrant students.

It is not a workbook with simple steps for creating a sanctuary school; instead, it shares stories meant to inspire educators to consider new possibilities and change mindsets. As a professor, I frequently meet educators from newcomer schools across the country and inquire about their school designs. Typically, these schools and English as a New Language programs focus on identifying students who need to learn English, quickly teaching them, and then integrating them into the general population. I challenge this approach by asking provocative questions such as, "Do your students actually need to learn English immediately?" and "Will the tests you prepare them for improve their lives?" By sharing stories from IHS, I hope that this book will guide the creation of sanctuary schools where the primary focus is on the holistic well-being and empowerment of immigrant students rather than merely on student privacy and rapid English acquisition, which are often the focus of immigrant students' transition to schooling in the United States. The following chapters illuminate the time, care, and mindsets that educators and leaders must adopt to change the status quo and create true sanctuaries for their immigrant students.

I

Sanctuary as Protection

1

The 2016 Election and the Reemergence of Sanctuary as a Protective Movement

ON A COLD SUNDAY MORNING *in February 2017, Lara, the principal of International High School, stands on a park bench with a friend to better view the speaker. Lara is part of a group of women organizing a post-election rally to celebrate and advocate for immigrant communities. She holds a sign that reads "Immigrants Welcome Here," while her friend has one that says, "A Proud Immigrant." I greet Lara as her young sons return from buying snacks at the nearby farmers' market. Amid scolding them for buying chocolate instead of juice and the chants of "no ban, no wall" and "no hate, no fear, refugees are welcome here," Lara confides that she is unsure how to protect her immigrant students both physically and emotionally. She worries, "I am not sure what I will do if I get arrested for refusing to let ICE into the school." Lara wonders what she would do if ICE tried to take her students. "I know I have some students with active deportation orders," she tells us. Her friend reassures her that ICE has said they will not enter schools and that deportation orders are not arrest warrants. Lara shakes her head, still skeptical, having heard that ICE agents have detained parents just outside schools in other cities when they drop off their kids. It feels so unpredictable. Lara needs a plan to feel prepared and to understand the consequences if the unthinkable happens.*[1]

Lara has been an educator for over twenty years in New York City. She was a student teacher at an International High School (IHS) with a view of downtown Manhattan, just steps from the Brooklyn Bridge on September 11, 2001. At the time, the school served a large population of Arab and Muslim students, and she remembers how she and other teachers walked each student home to ensure their safety. She was a founding teacher at IHS and then served as the assistant principal for many years before becoming principal. In 2019, she became a deputy superintendent in the New York City Department of Education and guided seventy schools through the COVID-19 era. She is no stranger to the challenges that US schools have faced in the twenty-first century. Over the years, we have become good friends, and I have watched her approach challenges in her professional and personal life with unshakable confidence and steadfastness. She is not easily rattled and is someone that people trust and look to when times are hard.

On the morning of the rally described in the opening vignette, Lara was beginning to draft an action plan to protect her students and teachers. Lara knew that her role had changed in the weeks since the presidential inauguration. Previously, Lara believed that the mission of her school was to offer her immigrant students the opportunity to pursue an excellent and equitable education—after the election, she felt forced into a more protective role, one that extended beyond the confines of the school walls. She became an even more active organizer in the community and fervently investigated what she could legally do to protect her students and their families from isolation, deportation, and separation. She recognized that her students were, or soon could be, in real and immediate danger.

In the introduction of this book, I began with a story of how students moved a cut-out of Donald Trump's face from a hallway bulletin board to the boy's bathroom urinal throughout the election season. This was a small act of resistance by students to call attention to the fact that the 2016 presidential campaign was defined by anti-immigrant rhetoric. For months, chants of "build a wall" at Republican rallies were broadcast on the nightly news, accompanied by the candidate's campaign promise to oversee mass deportations of millions of undocumented immigrants. Immigrants and refugees were continually framed by Trump as dangerous and destructive criminals when the future president referred to immigrants as "bad hombres," "rapists," and "animals" who were supposedly making America less safe. Republican events featured guests and speakers who were family members of people hurt or killed by "illegals," and right-wing media using thinly veiled tropes to conjure images of dark-skinned drug dealers, gang members, and radical Islamic terrorists.[2] During the campaign, bombast overshadowed truths, obscuring the fact that most immigrants are law-abiding citizens.[3]

Before November 8, 2016, despite the anti-immigrant rhetoric, teachers at IHS were attempting to teach about the election in a fair and balanced way. Several teachers reported feeling it was their responsibility to teach students about US democracy, help them access reliable information about political issues, and allow them to formulate their own opinions. In providing students with a holistic look at election norms and governmental structures, teachers hoped students would make their own judgments of US politics. Teachers regularly explained to students that it was their civic duty to be informed about issues of the time and take advantage of the right to vote if they could.

Even teachers with strong political views felt pressure to appear impartial. When asked by students about their political orientation, most teachers refused to disclose to students whom they were voting for and responded to questions about US politics with retorts like, "Well, what do you think about X issue?" Teachers increasingly felt unsure about what they were legally permitted to say about politics in the classroom.[4]

Teaching the election in an unbiased way was not always easy. In October, for example, the technology teacher who often used current events to plan her lesson tried to have a nonpartisan conversation with her class about the release of a video in which the Republican candidate described sexually assaulting women in graphic detail. She introduced the video in class as part of a human rights–focused graphic design project. The teacher intended the video to be a jumping-off point for a debate on women's rights. However, the discussion derailed as the teacher tried to explain the vocabulary used in the video to students who were all learning English and describe the mechanics of groping and forcible kissing to students in clear terms. As the tape's content became clear to students, some giggled uncomfortably, and others looked shocked as the teacher muddled through the lesson.

I was still new to the school during the first few months of classes in the fall of 2016. While I had volunteered in the school the previous school year, I was still unknown to many teachers. Some thought I was a college student who needed fieldwork hours; others knew I was a doctoral student but were not sure why I was doing a study of the school. In these first few weeks of fieldwork, I spent lots of time quietly observing in classrooms and the assistant principal's office. I, like many of the educators I was observing, was appalled by how Donald Trump talked about immigrants but believed that he was unelectable. Away from students, there was more conversation, anticipation, and excitement around the election of the country's first woman president than fear about the election of the most anti-immigrant president in generations. When attempting to teach the election by giving equal credence to both sides of every debate, it seemed that the teachers were fulfilling what they saw as a duty of their profession. As election day approached, teachers looked forward to the relief of not having to answer any more student questions about Trump. But that relief never came.

On November 9, 2016, educators across the country returned to work at public schools where one in every four students is an immigrant or has an immigrant parent.[5] At IHS, where all students and many teachers come from immigrant households, the election's impact was immediately evident. This chapter chronicles how teachers and leaders at IHS engaged students in political discourse following the election and their political and pedagogical evolution in the following months.

"WE JUST KEEP TALKING ABOUT CHECKS AND BALANCES": REACTING TO AN UNEXPECTED OUTCOME

Two days after the election, I sat with a student who told me, "All the teachers came to school crying yesterday, and they made us do [Restorative Justice] circles. Students are worried, but the teachers are way more upset than us." When I asked Bryan, the school's assistant principal at the time, what he thought about the student's comment, he replied, "That is probably true because we understand the implications so much better than they do." Another teacher suggested that because many of the students at the school had already been let down or disenfranchised by the federal government, their baseline was to expect very little from elected officials. One of the school's counselors explained that teachers were upset because of the election's implications and because they felt like they had misled their students.

> I think that, initially, when the election results were in, so many of us had assured the kids, "There's no way Trump is ever going to win. There's no way." We were stunned into silence after the election, we had to come together as a community and hold circles for ourselves so we could start our healing and start moving forward. [We asked ourselves], how are we going to work with our students? How are we going to reassure them that this is a safe space for them?

In conversations with teachers and students, I found that teachers encouraged students not to be upset or scared by the election. I overheard one teacher tell a student that we "live in a democracy, and our government has checks and balances that keep a president from having too much power." Teachers continually referenced rules and procedures in US politics that distribute power in lessons and informal conversations. One teacher explained to her students, "We have checks and balances to keep things from changing too quickly. He can't come in and change things overnight." Several teachers also spoke about living in a "sanctuary city" where "immigrants have always been safe and welcome." Teachers hoped that the city government could prevent the "mass deportations" that were openly discussed during the presidential campaign. Finally, teachers reminded students that the school cared about them and would do everything possible to keep them safe.

Teachers did not know if what they were saying to students would turn out to be true. Overwhelmingly, teachers hoped to pacify student's fears, make them feel safe, and answer their questions optimistically. One teacher explained:

> Kids are really resilient. For the most part, I think that it bothers us more than it bothers them . . . whether they understand the whole issue or not. I feel like if you make a big deal out of something they are going to make a bigger deal out of something as well. Obviously, you are there to support them if there is an issue but, me personally, I try to make light of things. I mean, we were talking about the current situation in advisory and I just said, "these things take time, there is a process. You live in a democracy . . . things are not immediate. This is not a dictatorship. Checks and balances. Yes, it is important to be aware, but the world isn't going to stop tomorrow." I think that you have to show a strong face that way.

The school also attempted to console parents and retain their trust by holding seminars about immigrant rights. Shortly after the election, a private doctor's office called the school to offer students free healthcare services. Bryan thanked the doctor and agreed to disseminate the information to students and families. He warned, however, that families might not sign up for the service because they would be worried about giving out their personal information. He explained, "We spent lots of time trying to get them to sign up for the city ID program—telling them it was safe—and now we are unsure if that was true. People are really scared, you know, with the new presidency, about giving their information."

Teachers and school leaders attempted to address student concerns without causing unnecessary alarm. Helping students feel safe at school was important for the teachers because so much was still unknown. "We will just have to wait and see what happens," one teacher told me. He explained that he did not think it was productive to alarm students before the new president took office. Teachers were more inclined to encourage passive acceptance than active resistance between the election in November 2016 and the inauguration in January 2017. However, in the weeks following the presidential inauguration, that stance began to change again.

"AFTER THE MUSLIM BAN, WE STOPPED SAYING 'CHECKS AND BALANCES'": EVOLVING SANCTUARY SCHOOLING PRACTICES

Educators' perspectives began to change after it became clear that executive actions and policy shifts on immigration would directly impact the students and their families. Teachers and school leaders began questioning whether they could continue reassuring students of their safety. For example, the school leadership team planned workshops for parents so they could ask questions about their rights as immigrants or as undocumented parents of American citizen children. Parent workshops had always been well attended, even in the months after the election, but in the first workshop after the inauguration, only two parents showed up. The guidance counselor explained:

> We would have meetings for families, and they just weren't showing up. At one meeting one father told me, "Well I sat in the lobby for a half-hour to see who was going to show up [and then left]." Then I spoke to other families and they are afraid that if they all get together, there's a place for immigration [officials] to come and get them. So, reassuring families that our school is a safe place isn't working.

The fact that parents were too fearful to gather in their own public school indicated to school leaders and teachers that they would have to rethink how they engaged their community in political discussions inside and outside the classroom.

Events like the poorly attended workshops began to shift educators' rhetoric and reaction to the election. While some teachers opposed the new president in the days after the inauguration, others were more hesitant. Over time, however, most teachers in the school became more open to engaging in political conversations with their students and revealing their political positions in the process.

On January 21, the Saturday after the new president was sworn into office, two students decided to attend the Women's March with their teachers and four hundred thousand other New Yorkers. The students came back from the protest feeling empowered and optimistic. Similarly, the school's atmosphere shifted from nervous anticipation to careful solidarity. "Know Your Rights!" posters went up in the bathrooms. On classroom doors, teachers hung signs that read, "In this classroom, you are safe. In this classroom, you are respected. In this classroom, you are loved" in three different languages. The school's mood seemed to reflect the attitude of the city and country, as it was portrayed in the media. When mayors across the United States declared their cities to be "sanctuaries" and vowed not to help federal agents apprehend undocumented immigrants, it seemed like the protective promises made to students in the weeks following the election might be sustainable. New York City's mayor released a message to the city's immigrants declaring that the city was prepared to "defend and protect our immigrant brothers and sisters." This message was posted along with a list of resources for immigrants in the school's hallway.

The feeling of empowerment in the school rapidly deflated just a week later when, on a Friday afternoon, President Trump issued an executive order immediately suspending travel from seven primarily Muslim countries. One teacher recalled, "After the Muslim Ban, we all stopped saying 'checks and balances' and started talking about what we really thought and felt." This transition was evident in how the school reacted to a national "Day Without an Immigrant" boycott, in how teachers demonstrated at a protest on International Women's Day, and in the ongoing curricular choices across all grade levels.

On February 15, the school began receiving calls from parents planning to keep their children home from school the next day to participate in the "A Day Without an Immigrant" boycott. The school leadership and counseling team had just a few hours to decide how to respond. First, they gathered information about the boycott and determined that it was indeed a national call for Latinx "immigrants not to work, purchase goods, or send their kids to school." In an email, the school leadership team asked teachers to communicate that the school would "support students and families choosing to join this national action" but also remind students that it would be a regular school day. They wanted teachers to encourage students to be "mindful about missing school and doing it in a responsible way." I observed how one teacher approached this topic with her students. She began the class by saying:

> There are rumors about there not being school tomorrow. If your family is staying home to protest together, we support you. I ask that if you are staying home, you do it for the right reasons and in the right way. We really worry about you skipping school and being out on the streets. It is still a school day, and we don't want the police picking you up out on the streets.

After answering a few questions about the goals of the boycott, she continued:

> Striking is a good way to put economic pressure on NYC leaders and the president. It makes sense to not go to work, or not shop at the deli. I am all for it. I support economic boycotts. Just imagine if no one bought anything tomorrow. That would have a big impact.

This teacher was able to convey the message from the leadership team but also took the opportunity to share her perspective rather than remaining apolitical.

The school leadership team agreed that they needed to recognize the reasons for the boycott and show solidarity with the students who came to school instead of participating in the boycott. They hung a twelve-foot sheet of paper outside one classroom on the wall with the hashtags #heretostay and #toimmigrantswithlove printed in large bubble letters across the middle of the page. Students were encouraged to draw on the make-shift mural and add pictures, poems, images, drawings, and quotes "affirming and celebrating immigrants." They also asked all school community members to wear red as a "sign of power and support." Many families chose to be part of the protest; over 25 percent of students were absent for the boycott, versus a typical day where only 10 percent of students were absent. The mural was filled with beautiful passages and drawings from students in many different languages throughout the day.

The school's leadership council believed that one way to show solidarity with students was through schoolwide actions like creating the mural. However, at grade-level team meetings the afternoon before the boycott, teachers expressed some frustration at missing class time; for example, taking all the students in the school outside to take a picture of everyone wearing red shirts. One teacher questioned the benefit of the schoolwide actions, saying, "I mean, I am all about solidarity, but is this the way to spend our class time?" Ultimately, a few weeks later, even the teachers who were most unsure how best to show solidarity opted to participate in an International Women's Day walkout. They invited students to join them outside, where they made a circle and talked about the calls for a national general strike by women, the benefits of boycotting, and the experiences of being a woman and a teacher.

Teachers also began to include material about the election and other current events in class projects that reflected a shift from the fair and balanced teaching of US politics to a more pro-immigrant approach to teaching and learning about current events, US history, and politics. "We are teaching them to know their constitutional rights," explained the assistant principal. In an advisory period, students learned about their rights as immigrants and as students in public schools. The school also held workshops for parents that explained how to assert those rights if Immigration and Customs Enforcement (ICE) agents showed up at their door. When parents were too scared to show up, students were sent home with laminated red cards that explained their rights in Spanish on one side and provided a script of what to say to immigration officials on the other. Class assignments included a task that raised awareness about Syrian refugees, an essay that used a quote by Pakistani activist and Nobel Laureate Malala Yousafzai on the US president as a prompt, and a research project in which each group focused on a different contemporary protest movement.

"WHOA! THIS IS REAL": PROTECTING UNDOCUMENTED AND MIXED-STATUS FAMILIES

The most profound shift in the school's reaction to the election took place after an ICE raid of an IHS student's house in March 2017 that displaced the entire family and resulted in the deportation of the student's father. In the middle of the night, ICE agents began banging on the door of the student's apartment. Terrified, the family fled and went into hiding. When the student did not come to school for several days after the raid, his team of teachers and counselors enlisted his friends to contact the family so the school could offer support. Eventually, teachers were able to help convince the student that he would be safe in school and that the school could help him find housing and legal aid for his mother.

The counselors and social worker were able to help the student return to school within a week and help his family find a new place to live. While the school was able to help alleviate some of the immediate stress of their encounter with immigration officials, they knew that the student and his family would now face new challenges. The father, who was also the breadwinner, was ultimately deported, and the family faced homelessness and financial instability. One counselor recalled:

> They're living in a different place. Kids are back in school, but it's not over. The man was deported because he had gotten a citation, three, five years ago, something like that. He was found sleeping in his car. The car was parked, and he was sleeping in his car. That's the only part of the story that we know. We don't know if there's anything else to the story, but he was deported.

Because the school was so involved and the student told his friends, news of the raid and deportation quickly spread throughout the school. Teachers responded by holding restorative circles with their students to allow them to ask questions and work through their fears.[6] In one classroom, teachers and students formed a small circle of chairs, lowered the lights, and spread blankets on the floor. A talking piece was passed around to those who wanted to speak. Students were encouraged by their teacher and each other to share their feelings and concerns. When I asked about conversations in these circles, one student recalled that in one of these gatherings, she was surprised to learn that one of her close friends was undocumented and that another classmate from Yemen had been worried about her family and future after the travel ban was put in place.

The school also began to pay more attention to the social media information circling in the immigrant communities. For example, the school took this seriously and followed up when there were Twitter reports of immigration officials at a particular subway stop or street corner. Before the election, they may have dismissed these rumors as false information. Now, they began to investigate them to help their students differentiate between the fear-mongering fake rumors and the legitimate reports of threats to their safety. At this moment, teachers reported feeling like their fears were not unfounded. One teacher recalled, "I mean, I think that before [the ICE raid], we felt it. But I think after that happened, it suddenly was like, 'Whoa! This is real.'"

In May, after ICE officers were spotted outside a nearby elementary school, Lara wrote in an email to teachers that these incidents "should remind us of the incredibly stressful and fearful times all of us, especially our immigrant students, are living in. Please remember to continue to check in with your students as they may have heard about these events and remind them that we will always do everything in our power to protect [them]." But what was their power really? Schools receive little guidance on how to support undocumented students and their families, and educators at IHS were devising new approaches in real-time.

Students from mixed-status families, like the family who experienced the ICE raid, began to fear separation by deportation. School leaders estimate that the majority of students were either undocumented themselves or living in a household with an undocumented parent, caretaker, family member, or friend. While educators at IHS wanted to do everything in their power to protect mixed-status families, students were often secretive about their status until they were in crisis. Some undocumented students went to great lengths not to share their status with the school until there was no other option.

Educators at IHS often have to guess if a student is undocumented because they are prohibited by law from asking. One staff member explained that when a student does not have immunization records, it is a telltale sign that they are undocumented.

> It is just an assumption because most of them will have some type of immunization to give to me when they are . . . in the intake process. If they don't have it, I immediately refer them to one of the free clinics. I know a place that gives out free immunizations, the initial ones, and fill out the forms for the schools.

Similarly, the college counselor assumes the same when students do not fill out a Free Application for Federal Student Aid (FAFSA) form during the college application. Supporting un- or under-documented students who are secretive about their status can be challenging, particularly when their status becomes known in a crisis, and the school must respond rapidly in order to support or protect the student or the student's family.

For students who are vocal about their status, the challenges are different. For example, Chandrakant was living alone in New York City when his math teacher learned that he was undocumented and emancipated from his parents. She learned that the reason he was coming to school tired was because he was staying up to all hours of the night to talk with loved ones in India before waking up to face the realities of life without a social security number. She became a mother figure in his life and helped him navigate choosing a college. Early in his senior year, he made it to the third round of interviews for a full college scholarship and felt hopeful. When he got the rejection letter, he was devastated, and seeing no path forward, he stopped coming to school. His teachers and friends called and visited him at home, urging him to return to school. When he did eventually return, he slumped around the school, depressed and hopeless. It was not until he was accepted into a different scholarship program, earning a full four-year scholarship, that Chandrakant began to engage in school again.

Chandrakant, who graduated in 2017 as the valedictorian of the senior class, told the story of his family's return to India and the resulting isolation in his graduation speech. "It felt like a complete dream because I started to lose the physical presence of loved ones in my life. First, my dad moved back to India and then my sister had to go back. And, then my mother too." Chandrakant began to sob as he described this struggle, his shoulders heaving as he tried to catch his breath. "I chose this life. To be honest, at the beginning it was fun and all, but as time passed by, I began feeling lonely. Sometimes I would cry when I was alone at home because I missed my family. . . . I stumbled; I broke, and dropped to the bottom of the ocean. At one point during this school year I was even ready to give up, to drop out." Chandrakant's declaration that he considered dropping out during his senior year is not what one would typically expect to hear from a class valedictorian.

Chandrakant believes that he made it to graduation because of the persistence of his teachers at IHS but they could not convince every student to stay. The election was so disruptive to the school in 2016 that they lost many students despite valiant efforts. For example, in February, Lucho, a highly motivated and popular eleventh grader, walked into Lara's office, hugged her, and informed her that he was dropping out.

Lucho had been detained at the border in 2014 and spent a few months in detention before being reunited with his family. He had only attended school until the sixth grade in El Salvador, so he started at IHS as a ninth grader even though he was seventeen. He came to the school as a formal requirement of his detention, planning to stay until his eighteenth birthday and then go to work as a day laborer. As a ninth grader, Lara recalled that Lucho had initially been approached by gang members in the community surrounding the school who hung out in front of a deli a few blocks away, but he would have nothing to do with them. He left El Salvador to escape the gangs in his town. He was in the United States to work.

Lucho's plans changed when he fell in love with the school and began to thrive academically and socially. Three years later, he was in eleventh grade and at the top of his class. He was one year away from graduation and would have likely earned a college scholarship. Instead, three months after the inauguration, he retreated to the shadows, working dangerous construction jobs before what he believed was imminent deportation. Lara recalled:

> He ended up dropping out this year. He was one of the top eleventh-grade students but decided to drop out because Donald Trump was elected. He came into the office and said, "I cannot go back to my country with no money in my hands." He told me, "I need to leave money for my child here if I get deported. If I go back, I will be ashamed to show up with no money—like the whole point was for me was to work here. If I get deported, I need to have money so my child can stay here because I don't want to bring my child back to El Salvador."
>
> We all cried. We begged. We were like, "Please, Lucho. Please stay." He's a great student, great kid . . . really great kid. But I couldn't tell him it's not going to happen. I couldn't tell him, "You're not going to get deported." I couldn't say that.

The school responded to each student differently based on the individual needs of their students. They tried to provide support when they could but felt that they were also limited in what they could do and unable to ensure the safety of their most vulnerable students.

Teachers reported that they felt confident that they could protect their students within the four walls of the school by preventing immigration officials from having physical access to them but felt powerless to protect them once they left campus. To help students learn to defend themselves and their families outside of school, teachers began to engage students in projects that focused on themes related to universal human rights, constitutional rights, and local sanctuary policies. For example, in a digital media art class, students chose one right from the United Nation's Universal Declaration of Human Rights to use as inspiration for a stop-gap animation sequence. The teacher explained:

> We had already done some things that were very directly related to the election, and I had the sense that I needed to pull back from direct politics just in terms of what I was sensing from the students and at the

> same time, I felt like there was an urgency about addressing something that related in some way to basic human rights and so, it just emerged from that—both wanting it to be connected and not wanting it to be necessarily super overtly related to Trump.

During the project's duration, the teacher had many political conversations with her students about the freedom of speech, the freedom to migrate, and the right to food and shelter, helping students differentiate between sanctuary city assertions, constitutional rights, universal human rights, and the debates between the two. One student reflected on her perceptions of this teacher's choice to share her political views during these conversations.

> She is an American . . . like . . . she's white. And I was like, why is she [concerned]? I mean, it isn't going to affect her the same way it's going to affect us because we're immigrants. But she made us feel like she was part of us, like she was with us. Why can't the rest of America think like her?

This student initially believed that the teacher was not as concerned about current politics because she, as a white, middle-class woman, would not be as impacted as non-white immigrants. These conversations helped the student experience a sense of solidarity with her teacher and made her question her assumptions about race, class, political views, and affiliations.

CREATING PROTECTIVE SANCTUARY AT A TURNING POINT

During the transition from teaching about the election in a fair and balanced way, to becoming more vocally opposed to the politics of the Trump administration, a Sanctuary Cities Now poster was hung in the main office. The print, originally designed by Pete Railand for the immigrant and worker rights activist group Voces De La Frontera, has a white background and large blue letters framing a city skyline, a row of houses, and a crowd of people representing different immigrant groups being embraced by two large arms.[7] Each day, when I signed in, seeing the poster left me with more questions than answers. What exactly did a call for sanctuary entail? What was the legal basis for resolutions calling for creating sanctuary schools and cities? And how could sanctuary be understood and interpreted at the cultural level?

This book is not about Donald Trump or a single presidential election but about understanding the events that led to a movement's resurgence. I begin this book with stories about the 2016 election because it was a turning point for the country, for the school, and for my research. After the 2016 presidential election, schools and districts attempted to reassure their immigrant students and families nationwide. For example, the Fresno Unified School District in California passed a resolution allowing schools to invite legal professionals to campus and distribute literature in multiple languages to families to educate them about their immigration rights.[8] Similar resolutions were passed in districts in Florida, Illinois, Minnesota, New York, and Texas.[9] In Chicago, teachers attended workshops to learn about what it means to be undocumented, how sanctuary schools can support students, and what rights undocumented immigrant children and their families have.[10] And in Seattle, a celebrated US history teacher hosted a town hall meeting to help teachers understand their rights when it comes to protecting students.[11]

In her 2018 book *Bans, Walls, Raids, Sanctuary,* A. Naomi Paik points out that while only a dozen US municipalities were considered sanctuaries before the 2016 election, over six hundred declared themselves sanctuaries in 2017—a similar pattern emerged in school districts.[12] She argues that the concept of sanctuary has deep roots that remain unbounded by a legal definition, arguing:

> Its capacious meaning has adapted over time and space, with each iteration adjusting its scope according to particular conditions. The contemporary sanctuary movement in the United States began in the

1980s to challenge the government's refusal to grant asylum to Central American refugees and has been revived as the New Sanctuary Movement (NSM) in response to escalating deportations in the 21st century. Even within these two iterations sanctuary has encompassed a range of meanings and modes of organizing. It has included faith-based and secular movements that provide safe harbor to immigrants threatened with deportation as well as lobbying for policies that shield immigrants from federal enforcement agencies. Grassroots mobilizations undergird all these efforts.[13]

In 2016, there was little theoretical or practical guidance for educators on what happens after these commitments are made. In the years following, groups like Immigrants Rising began to publish guides for educators about the sanctuary school movement.[14] What became clear to me was that most of the guidance was drawn from legal theory and carceral policy. For example, in sanctuary cities, police departments were prevented from sharing information with immigration agents. In sanctuary school resolutions, *Plyler v. Doe* and the Family Educational Rights and Privacy Act (FERPA) were often cited because they provided a legal basis for keeping student data private and immigration agents off campus. The language used to describe sanctuary focused on how best to protect immigrant families, particularly those with undocumented loved ones.

This first chapter illustrates how IHS took a protective turn in the months following the election, which was reactive to the moment and in line with shifts made by other US schools, universities, and municipalities that adopted sanctuary policies in this era. Sanctuary as protection at the cultural level of the school was enacted through noncompliance with immigration authorities and promises of safety through refuge within the school, information outside the school, and allyship from educators.

I realized that while this protective turn toward sanctuary in response to a dramatic shift in federal immigration policy was significant, it did not fully capture what I witnessed as an observer in the school. Protective sanctuary rooted in legal precedent and privacy policy was only one part of a robust school culture in which bodily safety, social well-being, mental health, legal support, trusting relationships, and humanizing approaches to learning were deeply rooted in school structures and educator ideologies. What I saw was an embodiment of the Voces de la Frontera poster, a warm welcome and a protective embrace. The following chapter illustrates the potential of protective sanctuary in a school setting through the story told to me by Milagros and her teachers.

2

Coming to a New Country and a New School

Sanctuary from the First Day

THE SUN BEGAN ITS DEPARTURE, as well. The boy watched it through its trajectory for some time, until it was hidden behind the white houses surrounding the plaza. He recalled that when the sun had risen that morning, he was on another continent, still a shepherd with sixty sheep, and looking forward to meeting with a girl. That morning he had known everything that was going to happen to him as he walked through the familiar fields. But now, as the sun began to set, he was in a different country, a stranger in a strange land, where he couldn't even speak the language. He was no longer a shepherd, and he had nothing, not even the money to return and start everything over.

—An excerpt from *The Alchemist* by Paulo Coelho[1]

I first heard this excerpt from *The Alchemist* read out loud by the twelfth-grade English teacher at International High School (IHS). Diego, a young teacher with a love of gaming and slam poetry, slowly and dramatically read the story of a boy who travels across borders to pursue his personal legend from a lectern at the front of the classroom. Diego chose this book, knowing that it would resonate with students at IHS who had each made their own difficult journey across borders.

I thought about the boy in this book starting his day in one country full of knowledge and ending it in a new country knowing nothing when I walked Milagros from school to the coffee shop where we had lunch during our interview. Milagros and I had been sitting side by side, working on an essay that she needed to complete. We had only discussed her classwork for a few weeks, but when I asked if I could interview her, she eagerly agreed.

As we walked and talked in Spanish, I began to record and asked Milagros to tell me about how she came to the school. She began her story with a tale of her migration journey. When we met, Milagros had just turned twenty-one and was in her final year of school. She is a tiny woman with long black hair, high cheekbones, and rough olive skin who journeyed to the United States through the southern border with Mexico when she was sixteen.

Milagros was soft-spoken and looked down when she talked to me, often squinting at the floor. When we sat across from each other at the café, and she looked me directly in the eyes for the first time, I remember thinking how her eyes made her look far older than her twenty-one years. As she began to tell her story, I realized she had lived in an adult world for much of her young life.

Milagros is originally from a rural Guatemalan town close to the border of Mexico. She left school in the fourth grade to take care of her younger brothers and earn money for her family. By the time she was sixteen, Milagros and her family had saved enough money to pay a trafficker, sometimes called a "coyote," to help her migrate north, eventually floating across the *Rio Bravo* into Texas. The trafficker promised Milagros's parents that she would take a bus across Mexico and that they would make sure she got safely across the border. But that was a lie. Milagros spent the better part of a month in the back of pickup trucks and inside airless crevasses of tractor trailers with only a handheld fan for ventilation. After a perilous journey across Mexico in the deadly summer heat, Milagros crossed the river that divides Texas and Mexico. However, while she was midriver, border patrol agents spotted the group that she was with and pursued them in trucks and helicopters. To escape, she ran into the sugar cane stalks that lined the river and waited.

Milagros hid among the stalks for over a day until blistering mosquito bites on her face made it hard to see. She decided she had to move, but trapped between the river and the border fence, she was unsure where to go. She began to walk along the fence when she spotted an opening the "size of two cars" and walked into Texas. Exhausted, she fell into a deep sleep in a cemetery next to a church. She was awakened by Border Patrol agents who were there to apprehend her.

The agents took Milagros to a place that migrants call *la hielera*, the icebox, one of many detention centers for unaccompanied minors that are known for uncomfortably cold temperatures.[2] They sent her to the medical center, believing that the festering mosquito bites covering her body were signs of a skin disease. Milagros had been missing for so long at this point that her traffickers had told her parents that she was dead. Her parents believed that she had suffered the same terrible fate as her older cousin who also disappeared while crossing the border just months before. When she finally was able to call home, her family was so relieved. Eventually, the Office of Refugee Resettlement contacted Milagros's uncle in New York, and she was released into his custody.

Migration from Central America to the United States is not a new phenomenon. Central Americans have long journeyed north to escape violence and poverty and to seek safety, security, and economic opportunity in the United States. One may wonder what compelled Milagros to make the dangerous journey in which migrants are often robbed, kidnapped for ransom, and murdered. It is a journey that is particularly dangerous for women. Milagros traveled a path in which most women are raped. Some estimate that eight out of ten Central American women who migrate north will experience sexual violence, often multiple times.[3]

Had Milagros been from Mexico, or been just a few years older, her migration story may have ended with her apprehension and deportation at the border. Because she was a minor from a noncontiguous country, the Border Patrol agents who found her in the desert turned her over to the Health and Human Services Department rather than Immigrations and Customs Enforcement (ICE). This agency was to determine if Milagros was a victim of human trafficking and if it was safe for her to return to her home country. Milagros was protected by the William Wilberforce Trafficking Victims Protection Reauthorization Act of 2008, which slowed down the deportation of children to avoid returning them to dangerous or abusive situations in their home countries. In 2008, the year that Congress passed the law, the system was designed to manage the cases of around seven thousand children each year, which is the average number of unaccompanied minors apprehended at the border each year.[4]

The summer that Milagros crossed the border, the number of unaccompanied minors from Central America skyrocketed from 3,933 in 2011 to 10,146 in 2012.[5] The unexpected increase in cases overwhelmed the Health and Human Services Department. With cases backlogged, children were released to friends and family members nationwide while they waited months, and sometimes years, for their day in court. Milagros was flown from Texas to New York City to reunite with an uncle, her closest family member in the United States. It was her first time on an airplane. Her future in the United States was still uncertain, but as a condition of her release, she was required to enroll in school. At age seventeen, Milagros became a ninth grader at IHS in New York City without speaking English and with only a fourth-grade education in Spanish.

In the beginning, Milagros was very shy, and teachers had to coax her to speak, even in Spanish. When she did finally begin to talk, she recounted heartbreaking stories of her migration. But her traumatic experience did not end at the border. Her uncle, her only family in the United States, began to abuse her, and she could no longer live with him. Educators at IHS recognized that Milagros needed far more than academic learning. They connected Milagros to a lawyer, found her a safe place to live, and helped her enroll in a program for battered women. The eleventh-grade math teacher took her shopping for winter boots when it snowed, a twelfth-grade science teacher gave her a wardrobe of winter clothes from her own closet, and all the teachers in the school donated to a fund to help Milagros survive the transition. The school social worker created a schedule that allowed her to stay in school and work as a part-time dishwasher at a café in Manhattan, a job that her math teacher helped her find.

These actions made it possible for Milagros to escape an abusive home life and stay in school. Throughout all this, she studied diligently, learning English and trying to bridge the gap between her elementary school education in Guatemala and what she was expected to learn as a high school student in the United States. Educators at IHS understood that Milagros could not learn if she did not feel safe at home, went to bed hungry, or did not have the clothes needed to survive a New York City winter. Providing schooling for Milagros required addressing her physical safety, social-emotional needs, and legal issues before they could expect her to learn.

Unlike programs that focus on reductive, utilitarian values such as academic test scores and grade point averages, IHS addresses the specific barriers faced by students who are immigrants to the United States. This is a founding principle of the school that has grown out of a grassroots group of connected schools that have been operating in New York City since 1985.[6] The school model and pedagogical approach originated in an innovative small school in New York City in 1985. Since then, fourteen additional schools following a similar approach have opened across New York City. Schools and academies have also opened in California, Maryland, Minnesota, Virginia, New York State, and Washington, DC. Researchers have identified IHS's sister schools in this network as "sites of possibility" for immigrant students because of their history of innovative, humanizing, and holistic practices for immigrant youth.[7] IHS is now part of a national network of thirty-one public schools and academies serving only immigrant teenagers new to the United States.

One of these schools' cultural cornerstones is hiring teachers who can relate to their students. At IHS, thirty teachers, two assistant principals, one principal, two guidance counselors, a social worker, a family coordinator, a college counselor, a technology support specialist, a literacy coach, and a community liaison work with around four hundred students to generate a school culture in which trusting relationships with students are critical and cultural knowledge is valued. Of the thirteen support staff members, eleven are fluent or bilingual in English and Spanish or English and Chinese. The principal, whose parents were immigrants, understands Spanish and speaks Italian and Portuguese. The assistant principal was a Peace Corps volunteer in Croatia and speaks some Russian. Two-thirds of teachers can converse in at least one other language besides English. Half of the teachers speak another language fluently or are bilingual or multilingual. In addition to English, teachers speak Chinese, Spanish, Korean, Tagalog, French, and Nepalese.

One of the teachers that Milagros grew close to was Luz, who came to the United States from Colombia with her mother when she was sixteen. She is from a small city near the Pacific Coast but lived for a short time in Bogotá before coming to New York. Moving from one city to another and then to a new country took a toll on Luz. She did not understand why she and her family had to uproot their lives to come to a place as cold as New York City. She arrived in the middle of winter and did not own a coat. In December of 2000, Luz began classes at the first school in the network of which IHS is a part.

With little knowledge of the school system, immigrant families often rely on word of mouth or the recommendation of the Office of Enrollment and middle-school teachers to determine where to send their children to school. Luz's mother found this school for recently arrived immigrants by talking to a friend of a cousin. On her first day of school, Luz remembers being ushered into a room and sitting at a hexagonal table with students who spoke many languages. They spoke English together, but Luz could not understand a single word. It was like a light came on when the girl beside her turned and said, *vamos a hacer un presentación. Tu tienes que leer esto,* handing her an index card. She felt relieved that someone spoke Spanish and terrified that her new translator had just informed her that she had to stand up in front of the class and present with the group in a few minutes. What she was supposed to say was written in English on the index card. A few minutes later, she stood in front of the room, reading in English.

Luz, now a teacher at IHS, can relate to Milagros's experiences because these have also been a part of her experiences. Luz started high school in the middle of her tenth-grade year. She remembers it in a haze. "The first year, it was okay; I was just going with the flow. I passed my classes, but I didn't really understand much. The second year, junior year, that is when I took the English Regents. But I had no idea that I was supposed to take a test. I failed it three of four times," she told me. The struggle to learn a new language and culture, plus the pressure of taking tests and writing papers, became overwhelming during her senior year. Her mom was also struggling to make ends meet in New York City, working long hours and never having enough money. "I was struggling with a lot of issues that many teenagers may never encounter in life. A couple times, I was not going to school—and then came back and was trying to catch up." Luz recalls that whenever she stopped coming to school, her teachers and friends would find her and convince her to return.

Luz made friends easily; she is tall and thin with voluptuous curly hair. She has an abundance of energy and a warm but serious personality. As the new girl, she enjoyed her newfound popularity. "I was not really a shy person, so it was easy to make friends." By the end of her senior year, Luz was thriving, passing her classes and the state exams. She had also created a portfolio of her academic work, of which she was exceedingly proud. She presented this work to a panel of teachers—a prerequisite for graduation. At the end of her presentation, one teacher asked, "So what are you going to do next?" Luz remembers going blank; she had no idea what she wanted to do. "I am not sure if it was lack of focus or goals or just because I was a teenager living day by day, but maybe it was also that my teachers did not sit down with me and tell me, 'You got to do this.' I don't really know." She replied that she would go into the Army. Her teachers pushed back against that decision; they thought she needed to attend college. They invited her to stay a fifth year at the school and created a position for her to work as an intern in the office to help the principal and mentor other students. The school paid for her to take college classes at a nearby community college.

This fifth year in high school changed Luz's life trajectory. Because of that experience, Luz decided to attend college, study education, and eventually become a math teacher at IHS. She explained, "I was able to build such a strong relationship with many teachers there and I still see them. Without them and my mom, I would not be here right now. It might sound cliché, but I seriously was not thinking of college." Luz's teachers helped her apply and enroll in college, drove her to her new student orientation, and helped her decorate her dorm room.

> I had not even visited the college before, but the guidance counselor graduated from that college, so she told me that it is a great college. So, we applied there, and I got accepted to the Education Opportunity Program, an opportunity program for minorities. Because my mom and I were kind of poor too, [my teachers] bought me a bunch of things for my dorm room, like a blanket, pajamas, a little basket for the laundry. Then, two of the teachers brought me to orientation. That was the first

> week that I was ever away from my family. It was the longest week, and I was so scared! [My teachers] taught me how to take the bus back to the city. So I did all of that alone, and that first week was liberating. I was just like—I can do this! This is so exciting!

In her fifth year of high school, Luz discovered that she loved math and enjoyed helping other students understand math. She studied math education in college, returned to IHS for her student teaching, and was offered a job before she graduated. She was still in touch with the teachers who had helped her attend college, but now she was their colleague. In September 2018, after teaching at IHS for almost a decade, Luz became the co-assistant principal at IHS, where she shares an office with Zaria, another first-generation immigrant woman.

Like Lara, Luz's career began at IHS and its sister schools. The guidance of her teachers, an extra year in high school, the support to go to college, and the teaching job they offered her when she finished college made her feel valued and welcomed. Before taking the job at IHS, Luz completed her student teaching requirements at an affluent public middle school that served mostly wealthy, white children. "I just felt like they didn't need me," Luz explained. Instead, she felt that she could be both empathetic to her immigrant students' needs while also maintaining high expectations for academics and behavior. She understood that students at IHS needed her to do more than teach math—they needed her to fill multiple academic and social-emotional roles, and she was prepared to do that.

PROTECTIVE SANCTUARY AS A PREREQUISITE FOR INNOVATION

In chapter 1, I argue that what currently exists in most cities and schools with sanctuary resolutions are protective sanctuary measures that emerged due to an acute threat from the federal government. Protective sanctuary up until now has primarily been understood through legal frameworks. In this chapter, I tell the story of Milagros and Luz to illustrate how protective sanctuary can be cultivated in the culture and essence of a school. IHS and its sister schools are designed to protect students from systems and structures that demoralize and disenfranchise them.

Barriers to education for immigrant youth often begin before they enter a classroom. In 1982, the Supreme Court ruled in *Plyler v. Doe* that all children are entitled to a public education regardless of citizenship or immigration status, making it illegal for schools to refuse to enroll undocumented students. Still, that law does not stop schools from creating intentional and unintentional barriers to prevent students like Milagros from enrolling. High schools are scrutinized if their graduation rates and test scores drop and often avoid the risk of enrolling older students when they do not speak English, have few, if any, high school credits, and cannot produce school transcripts. Principals, who face increased accountability pressure based on test scores, sometimes discourage students who do not speak English from enrolling in their schools or pressure them to transfer out if they are at risk of not graduating.[8] While the practice is illegal, it is common for schools to turn away immigrant students when they attempt to register and discharge them before earning a diploma.[9]

Research consistently shows that recently arrived immigrant teenagers who do not speak English are less likely to graduate from high school. The adjusted cohort graduation rate for English learners varies significantly by state, ranging from 46 percent in Louisiana to 88 percent in Indiana, compared to 87 percent for all public high school students.[10] There are currently 46.3 million immigrants living in the United States and more than 11 million are undocumented.[11] A quarter of children in American public schools have at least one foreign-born parent.[12] More than one million children are undocumented and more than four million children who are US citizens have an undocumented parent.[13] Schools have responded to this large and growing population with a diversity of backgrounds and needs by branding migrant, immigrant, refugee, and asylum-seeking students as "English learners" and creating newcomer programs designed to test, drill, and return newly arrived immigrant students to English language learner (ELL) classes or the general population of students as quickly as possible. Unfortunately, this hyper-focus on teaching English quickly has failed to increase graduation rates and has diminished immigrant students' widely variant educational needs to their ability to speak English.

Instead of turning students away, creating barriers to enrollment, or focusing only on quickly teaching them English for a test or returning them to the general population of students, IHS is focused on safety, care, and belonging. Belonging at school affects a child's well-being, identity development, and agency. Researchers have determined that immigrants who feel they belong in a country or community experience significant psychological and social benefits.[14] This is particularly true for undocumented children who are coming of age in a new country.[15] The importance of belonging is so well established that it was written into law in *Plyler v. Doe* in which the majority of the Supreme Court wrote that depriving undocumented students of an education "takes an inestimable toll on the social, economic, intellectual, and psychological well-being of the individual, and poses an obstacle to individual achievement."[16] This is a legal right that has been increasingly under attack in the years following the first Trump presidency and will likely face legal challenges during the second Trump term.[17]

Schools are often the first point of contact that immigrant families have with public institutions in the United States, particularly those who are undocumented and undetected. While all children in the United States have a constitutional right to attend public schools, older teenagers like Milagros are often turned away. At IHS, they are received with open arms, and their safety and well-being are the schools' first priority. Where other schools rush to assess a newly arrived student's English proficiency, educators at IHS worried about Milagros's legal status, abusive home life, food insecurity, loneliness, and lack of winter clothes.

The school provided a protective sanctuary for Milagros by helping her move into a safe living situation, securing legal representation for her asylum case, and taking her shopping for winter boots and a coat. This interpretation of protection goes beyond the legal responsibilities of sanctuary schooling but is still focused on acute challenges that must be addressed before a young person can be responsibly expected to learn and prioritize schoolwork.

Similarly, Luz's teachers intervened in her educational trajectory to ensure that she stayed in school and to buy her more time to decide about college. The guidance of her teachers, an extra year in high school, the support to go to college, and the teaching job they offered her when she finished college made her feel valued and welcomed.

When taken together, Milagros and Luz's stories can be understood as a deeply rooted culture of protective sanctuary within the network of schools. Because of practices that buffered Luz from dropping out or joining the military, Luz was able to break into a middle-class profession dominated by white women. As an immigrant teacher of color and former "English learner," Luz is now able to be a role model for Milagros and use her own lived experience to connect with other students with similar backgrounds. While research supports diversifying the teaching force, efforts to recruit more teachers like Luz and ensure that they remain in the profession have made very little impact.[18]

Milagros graduated from IHS after seven years at the age of twenty-two and now has a high school diploma and permanent residency in the United States. She was able to bring her brothers to the country and recently got married. Luz attended the wedding. I believe that both women would have lived very different lives had it not been for the buffers their schools and teachers provided against difficult-to-navigate immigration enforcement policies and social and educational policies that prevent immigrant students from full participation in schools, the labor market, and higher education.

Sanctuary schools should think more expansively about how best to protect their students. Protective sanctuary must go beyond noncompliance with immigration officials. Identifying the structures that can harm students and enacting policies and practices at the school level to act as barriers for immigrant students can have enormous impacts. This requires educators, school leaders, social workers, and mental health professionals working in schools to put immigrant students' needs ahead of testing, compliance, accountability, and learning English.

This is easier said than done, but I believe that reorienting values that center students' needs beyond the classroom is a requisite of sanctuary schooling and a prerequisite to understanding sanctuary as innovation. Part II of this book looks deeper at the structures, symbols, and innovative practices that demonstrate the potential of sanctuary schools in the United States.

II

Sanctuary as Innovation

3

Designing a Sanctuary School

Innovation in the Schoolscape

SANTIAGO LOOKED OUT INTO THE *horizon and saw, just as he did days before, a hawk flying in the air. An image flashed before him, and this time it wasn't of an impending war, but a school. "I don't understand," the boy said to the Alchemist. "Why are the hawks showing me a school? What is that place?" The alchemist looked at the boy and smiled. "It's called," he began, "International High School. A very special place where students from all over the world are searching, just like you, for their personal legends. Take a closer look and you'll see a hallway stretching with immense possibilities as these young individuals all carve a pathway to success. See the many hours spent on bettering themselves: reviewing for tests, revising projects, performing plays, fundraising for good causes, and through it all, leaning on each other for support, because the old saying is true: when you really want something, all the universe conspires in helping you to achieve it."*

The opening vignette for this chapter, written by Diego for International High School's graduation ceremony, beautifully illustrates how the physical and social environment of International High School (IHS) is much more than a backdrop for education; it is a landscape rich with potential and shared experiences. Just as Santiago in *The Alchemist* sees a new land as a place of discovery and aspiration, IHS is portrayed as a sanctuary where students from diverse backgrounds converge, each on their journey to uncover their personal legends. The description of students engaging in various activities—studying, revising projects, performing, and supporting each other—paints a vivid picture of the dynamic and supportive ecosystem within the school. This landscape of the school is not merely about physical structures but also about the intangible and vibrant interactions and collective pursuit of success that define the culture of belonging and mutual support at IHS. Through this narrative, Diego encapsulates the essence of IHS as a place where the universe conspires to help students achieve their dreams. This chapter illustrates how the seemingly ordinary aspects of the school environment should be recognized as the foundation for innovation, providing sanctuary for the children who need it most.

While educational researchers often study interactions between students and teachers and their perceptions of each other, we spend less time exploring classroom setups, hallway decorations, and interactions outside the classroom. Recently, scholars have been paying more attention to school spatiality, the built environment, and the overall climate, reflecting the complexity of school environments beyond previous research approaches.[1] The term "schoolscape" has been used to describe the interplay between the physical and social environment for teaching and learning.[2] The metaphor of the schoolscape encourages us to consider how we perceive a landscape. First, we survey the horizon to identify the type of place we are in—whether it is vast, lush, mountainous, urban, or rural. Then, we closely examine the environment's components, including flora, fauna, infrastructure, and the relationship between the land and its living inhabitants.

In this chapter, I use "schoolscape" to describe the physical and intangible aspects of the landscape at IHS, including the school's size and location, entrance, schoolyard, and classroom layout, as well as the nonphysical, including school actors' orientations toward concepts like trust, time, culture, collaboration, and care. I explore how school stakeholders cooperate within the school's ecosystem and how they convey the school's stated mission and design. I asked students and teachers to recall their first impressions of the school, describe its atmosphere, and help me understand the shared norms and values at IHS. This chapter illustrates how the unique schoolscape fosters a culture of belonging at IHS.

"IHS, WHERE I BELONG": STEPPING INTO INTERNATIONAL HIGH SCHOOL

The first day I visited International High School, I took the Q train from Brooklyn to Manhattan. The subway stop is in the center of a bustling main street with a public library, produce stands, law offices, hair salons, and restaurants. Next to a shiny new Starbucks, street vendors sell dragon fruit alongside beach towels. When I climbed down the green metal stairs and navigated through the busy streets for the first time, I quickly realized that IHS is in a borderland between urban and suburban, commercial and residential. In the morning, the sounds of school children laughing, parents giving ultimatums in many different languages, and street vendors selling hearty pupusas to get construction workers through a long morning fill the air. The neighborhood is an immigrant enclave in New York City.

The streets get less congested as people fan out to the schools, churches, temples, restaurants, and businesses in the area. Day laborers make their way to a gas station just a few blocks away. Most mornings, men crowd the corners of a busy avenue just blocks from a massive police precinct. Across from the gas station is JFK High School, a large comprehensive

New York City public high school serving fewer than two thousand students. The massive campus sits on five acres of gently rolling hills.

International High School, unlike the prominent JFK High School, is small and tucked away on the third floor of a building it shares with a middle school. The middle school's name is prominently displayed in large letters on the front of the building, while the sign for IHS is much subtler and requires a closer look to spot. Surrounding the school is a bright red fence adorned with life-sized plastic children, including a girl in a cumbia skirt and another in a sari. These figures are the first indications of the school's values that greet students, visitors, and passersby.

The front entrance of the school is tucked away behind a cement courtyard. This courtyard, bordered on one side by a small patch of grass and several red picnic tables, is a popular spot where students gather in the morning. The front door, like the fence and the picnic tables, is bright red. Upon entering, visitors encounter a security desk in an echoing foyer. On my first visit, I greeted the guards warmly, showed my identification, signed in, and affixed a bright yellow "visitor" sticker to my shirt.

The security counter blocks the entrance to a spacious corridor adorned with flags from around the world hanging from the ceiling. Unlike many other urban schools, there are no metal detectors or bag scanners here. On hot days, the doors on either side of the security desk are propped open to create a cross breeze through the foyer. The back door opens onto a beautifully designed yard used by teachers and students throughout the day. When I began my study in 2016, it was a parking lot, but the leadership team at IHS secured a one-million-dollar grant from The Trust for Public Land to transform it into a multipurpose outdoor space. In August 2017, the city broke ground on a schoolyard designed with input from students, staff, and the community. Completed in 2018, the yard now features a state-of-the-art playground, trees, and green infrastructure elements like porous pavement and synthetic turf.[3]

In the foyer, vibrant murals cover the walls. The largest mural features a portrait of Lady Liberty's face set against a bright pink sunset in

New York's harbor. Flanking this central piece are smaller murals depicting scenes from Chinese New Year celebrations, complete with dragons emerging from the ocean and men and women playing drums. The Statue of Liberty symbolizes the welcoming of immigrants to the United States, while the murals of Chinese traditions represent the heritage of over half of the school's student body.

Students in the middle school below IHS are easily identifiable by their uniforms. When the final bell rings, they flood the halls in green, blue, and red polo shirts, moving through the entryway and out the bright red doors. The foyer quickly shifts from peaceful to chaotic and claustrophobic as students stream out of the gym or into the cafeteria. In the morning, the building smells of bleach; at lunch, it smells of chicken nuggets; and by the end of the day, it carries the scent of growing, hormonal teenage bodies.

IHS students stand out because they are older and do not wear uniforms. By senior year, many adopt the urban style of New York City, wearing gray and black hoodies, graphic t-shirts, and distressed jeans. They have learned to dress fashionably by American standards. One senior girl, for instance, has a monetized YouTube channel where she posts makeup tutorials on achieving Rihanna's eyes and Kardashian contours. Newer IHS students are noticeable for different reasons. They often wear tight tops, embellished button-up shirts, or jeans with elaborate embroidery on the back pockets, making it easy to identify recent arrivals.

After climbing two stories of stairwells, visitors encounter an oversized painting declaring "IHS, Where I Belong" in baby blue cursive. The same message is written in smaller letters in Spanish, Mandarin, Korean, Arabic, Japanese, Urdu, Russian, and other languages. On the other side of the stairwell, the school's twelve community principles are listed in multiple languages, reminding students that values like collaboration, peace, justice, love, diversity, and holism are cherished here.

Directly in front of the stairwell doors is the main office and the principal's office. A folding table with breakfast or lunch boxes is often set up outside the main office, and the principal's door is usually wide open. One of the first things that captured my attention when I visited the school for the first time was the colorful mural titled "Our Roots." The imagery in the painting celebrates the cultures, journeys, dreams, and aspirations of the immigrant students at IHS. This mural became the cover of this book and the story of how it was designed and painted collaboratively with Brooklyn-based artist Angel Garcia, with teachers and students, exemplifies the innovative schoolscape at IHS.

"OUR ROOTS": SYMBOLS OF BELONGING FOR IMMIGRANT STUDENTS IN THE SCHOOLSCAPE

In 2014, fourteen student artists collaborated to create a vibrant mural at IHS, with the support of three teachers and funding from a nonprofit organization in New York City called Groundswell NYC. Angel, a professional muralist, provided guidance and expertise throughout the project. The mural is divided into three main sections: The Celebration of Various Cultures, The Struggles of the Immigrant Journey, and The Dreams of Immigrant Youth.

The mural's symbolism is richly detailed. On the far left, the Tree of Life incorporates symbols from various religions and patterns from different regions worldwide. Adjacent to this, the puppeteer figure represents the exploitation by more powerful nations and the adverse conditions that force people from their homelands. The central, monumental eye in the mural serves as a gateway to the hopes and dreams of immigrants. This eye, which features patterns from many regions and the United States flag at its center, symbolizes the quest for truth and enlightenment and highlights the beauty of the diverse cultures within the school community.

To the right of the eye, the two figures holding nets illustrate the social, political, and economic challenges that immigrants face on their journey to the United States. The final panel envisions a hopeful future for students, suggesting that through social justice and education, immigrants can achieve success and a better life.

This mural not only depicts the migration journey to the United States, but also represents the lived experiences of the students at IHS. It stands as a significant symbol of belonging for students entering the school. Surrounding the central imagery, students can find references to their past, such as a landscape from China and a bubble featuring the Yemeni flag's crescent moon and star. They can also see representations of their future, including graduation and life in the United States.

The mural exemplifies IHS's commitment to redefining traditional academic hierarchies. Teachers select student artwork that celebrates home cultures, showcase work at various levels and in multiple languages, and publicly display formative versions of student work to highlight progress. This approach provides tangible evidence of students' growth and celebrates their achievements, even when the work is still evolving.

Subtle symbols of belonging, such as the mural and displayed student work, support the more explicit signs of solidarity within the school. Belonging is rooted in trust and safety, which are crucial for students' feelings about themselves and their learning environment. Educators at IHS understand that students must trust their teachers' sincerity and commitment before they can fully engage in their education. This need for trust and safety is particularly pronounced for immigrant students who navigate a polarized society, build new identities, and face anti-immigrant rhetoric and policies.

Overt symbols of belonging include the "Sanctuary Cities Now" poster mentioned earlier and the "Know Your Rights" bulletin board near the main office. This board provides crucial information about interactions with Immigration Enforcement and Customs (ICE) agents, summarized on brightly colored flyers posted throughout the school, including in bathrooms. These flyers assert, "Everyone has certain basic rights, no matter who is president," reinforcing the message of rights and belonging for students.

IHS, and other schools in the Internationals Network, visually stand out from other schools I have worked in or visited. Observing the wall displays helped me understand the school's core values and culture. The meanings that humans assign to symbols orient them to their social worlds.[4] What educators choose to paint on their walls and staple to their bulletin boards are symbols of what a school community values and who the school is for. In a typical school, you might expect to see trophy cases celebrating sports victories and bulletin boards filled with honor roll lists, perfect attendance accolades, and exemplary student work. In these settings, high-achieving students are honored and celebrated. Students who do not see their trophies in the cases, their pictures on the wall, or their work being celebrated often feel invisible in school, as if they do not belong. It is common for immigrant students to feel unimportant, insignificant, and invisible in public schools.[5] This social isolation within a school can prevent students from thriving in the classroom.[6] Students' opportunities to learn can be even more constrained in regions of the country where xenophobic and anti-immigrant rhetoric is high.[7]

My initial experience at IHS mirrored that of many students—both thrilling and daunting. Through conversations, particularly with Gonzalo, a student in his sixth year at IHS, I came to appreciate how the school environment fosters a sense of safety, belonging, and empowerment, illustrating the profound influence of the schoolscape on school culture.

"JUST *ONE* HALLWAY FOR HIGH SCHOOL?": A SMALL SCHOOL WHERE IT IS IMPOSSIBLE TO BE INVISIBLE

Gonzalo's mother left the Dominican Republic when he was eight. She came to the United States with a plan to bring him and his siblings as soon as possible. By the time he was eleven, she had secured his immigration papers and he moved to New York City. During the three years that she was away, Gonzalo lived with his father but had little supervision at home. He started drinking when he was eight years old. "I used to be at clubs, and they used to be like, 'oh you try this.' At eight years old, I saw a lot of things, guns, knives, people fighting, people dying. . . . I used to go out a lot . . . I used to get home late, nine or ten, as a little kid." He was both nervous and excited to move to the United States and be back with his mother, but he faced new challenges on his first day of school as a sixth grader in a large, urban middle school. He told me about his first day in the lunchroom:

> My first day I sit down at a table for lunch. I was looking down, not eating anything, not knowing nobody. And this one kid spoke to me. And I didn't speak English so I was like, I don't understand what you are trying to say to me. Then he just got up and pushed me. And then the Dominican kids got up and were like, oh, are you Dominican. I was like, yeah. They were like, oh they don't like us. They don't like you because you are Dominican. And I was like, what?! They were like, just come join us. I was like, ok. I went to sit with them.

In middle school, Gonzalo quickly learned that he had to hang out with other Dominicans for protection. He compensated for his lack of English by getting into fights when he was confronted. He explained that in middle school, "I was new, no English, so the first thing you learn is the bad words. And as I learned them and as people say them at me—I used to get mad. I couldn't answer back perfectly, but I did it physically."

Like Gonzalo, about half of the four hundred students at IHS come to the United States and are socialized into middle schools that are ill-equipped to handle newcomers' many needs. Gonzalo was put into intensive English as a New Language (ENL) classes but learned little English. His scores on the New York State English as a Second Language Achievement Test (NYSESLAT) barely budged over three years. He thinks this is because he felt unsafe and unmotivated in school, a phenomenon well documented by educational researchers.[8] Because of these test scores and because he had only been in the country for fewer than four years, he was eligible to attend IHS.[9] Faced with entering high school, Gonzalo was ready to take the same approach he took in middle school.

On Gonzalo's first day of high school, he accidentally showed up at JFK High School, the large school a mile away from IHS. He recognized the large school as something out of a movie and, after walking the last mile to his actual new high school, remembers being shocked that IHS was so much smaller than his middle school. He expressed his dismay in an interview, saying:

> I was like *this* is it? (motioning to the hallway)—what is this? Just *one* hallway for high school? And my middle school was like four or five floors! And when I got over here it was like one floor. What kind of weird high school is this? High school just one floor? And then they were like "yes" and I was like "okay, okay" and then they showed me around to class and the students was just sitting down, *like paying attention*. In my middle school people would just sit on the desks. You do this (crossing his arms), you do that (slouching in chair giving me the side eye). Headphones on, hoodie on, hat on, guys with jackets, everything, sagging, and all of that.

IHS's single hallway includes eighteen classrooms, a front office, a principal's office, an assistant principal's office, a counseling center, a college access center, a food pantry, a teacher's lounge, and restrooms. The classrooms include one science lab, one digital media center, and an art room. Clustered around the front office and principal's office near the doors where students enter the school are the ninth- and tenth-grade classrooms. Team Empower has two classrooms to the left of the front office. One classroom is shared by the science and math teachers; the other is shared by the English and social studies teachers. To the right of the front office and principal's office are four other ninth- and tenth-grade classrooms for teams Evolution/Revolution and Innovations. The bulletin board outside the art room, across from the main office, displays a rotating exhibit of culturally relevant student-created work displayed throughout the year. Projects include mask-making, story-telling murals, and self-portraits. Further down the hall are the assistant principal's office, the college counseling office, and the eleventh-grade classrooms. The twelfth-grade classrooms are at the far end of the hallway.

Instead of desks, students sit around hexagonal tables formed from two isosceles trapezoidal tables with their longest sides pushed together. Instead of rows of desks facing a teacher at the front of the room, students at IHS face each other. The shape of the tables is purposeful and has been replicated in every Internationals Network school in the city to encourage students to talk to one another and work collaboratively. Projects in the ninth and tenth grades are almost always collaborative, and classrooms are filled with the sounds of students and teachers talking in multiple languages. Gonzalo recalled watching students in the classroom during his first day at IHS:

> I was like what is this? Who are these people? Why are people just sitting and just staring at the teacher? And I was like wow. And then I got to class I put my hoodie on, because that was my nature—it was what I was I used to. So, I went to class and the teacher was like, "take your hoodie off." I was like, "oh I'm not taking my hoodie off." You know, being disrespectful to teachers and everything. And Bryan talked to me and he was "oh this is not a school where people fight, this is a school where people just get along from different races" and I was like, after he spoke to me, I kind of understood it more. Like, what should I do, how should I behave, and then I never looked for troubles and everything. People were just nice to me.

Bryan remembered these interactions as multiple conversations over the course of the year. He would invite Gonzalo to his office, or take a walk with him, and talk to him about how much his teachers cared for him, to help him develop strategies for expressing his feelings, or tools for resolving conflicts with friends. Bryan remembers Gonzalo becoming a happier child during his ninth-grade year. He began to tell jokes and smile often. By the time I met Gonzalo, he almost always had a smile on his face.

On Gonzalo's first day, he was assigned to a team of five teachers and a small cohort of about twenty students with whom he spent the entirety of the school day for a full two years. Ninth- and tenth-grade students at IHS follow a course of study that is unusual for US high school students. There are five interdisciplinary grade-level teams. Three teams are for ninth and tenth graders, one is for eleventh graders, and one is for twelfth graders. Each team is further divided into classes of 20–25 students of various academic aptitudes, home languages, English ability, gender, and personality. These heterogeneous cohorts attend every class together for the entire year. This cohort model is common in typical elementary schools but is atypical for middle or high school students. The use of heterogeneous grouping and a cohort class structure are core components of IHS's design. Educators at IHS believe that this approach to teaching and learning helps students quickly build relationships with their peers and teachers and increases their sense of belonging and feeling of safety at school. As a result, students can more easily focus on learning. Lara, the principal at IHS, explained that, like Gonzalo, many ninth-grade students have been taught to fear school environments where they feel unsafe or excluded:

> People immediately think, "Oh, it's great, they were in junior high" or whatever. But you have to re-acculturate them. There is a lot of work that needs to be done because the middle schools are not so great . . . there are a lot of really rough schools around here. A lot of our kids are treated really poorly in those schools and they either hate school because of it, or they develop a wall basically, or like a protection against these outside forces.

Each year, approximately one hundred new ninth-grade students enroll at IHS for a total enrollment of around four hundred students each year. Students come from forty-seven different countries and speak around thirty languages. Depending on the year, more than half of students attend some middle school in the United States before coming to IHS. The other 30 to 50 percent of students enroll in school for the first time as high school students at IHS. Most have had pre-migration educational experiences where they learned they are not valued students because of their race, class, or social strata. Lara explained:

> Sometimes they've come from places where only the most highly achieving students are given opportunities. They're kind of down on school. They haven't always had positive experiences. I think some of the first work that we do is getting them to feel like school is meaningful, that they belong here, that school is *for them,* that it's not just for those other kids that do well. By doing that, I think it opens doors, it opens opportunities for them that they never thought could be available to them.

Gonzalo said that he began to enjoy school for the first time in his life in the ninth grade because "at least he felt safe."

Educators at IHS know that students must feel seen, respected, and cared for before they can learn. Some students, like Gonzalo, learn that they must fight to be safe in school. Other students come to IHS days or weeks after arriving in NYC for the first time. Students new to the United States come from a variety of educational models, and are adapting to a new language, culture, and school norms.

In most other US schools, even those designed for newcomers, students who do not speak English are immediately placed into a regimented ENL program. Because traditional ENL programs are so focused on teaching English quickly, immigrant students who are learning English often have fewer opportunities to take elective courses like music, art, and athletics, and are less likely to be encouraged to take advanced classes.[10] They rotate from teacher to teacher, and from class to class, often falling further and further behind their peers. This approach has led to a high dropout rate of students who have an English learning classification going into high school in NYC and across the country.[11]

Ninth graders at IHS are warmly embraced. Their teachers are attuned to their personal histories, family dynamics, friend groups, and personalities. The counselors and social workers dedicate significant time to learning about the lived experiences of the newest students. The curriculum, from science and math to art, allows students to tap into their preparation experiences and share the knowledge they bring with them to the United States. By prioritizing safety, wellness, trust, and care over English learning in this crucial year, students are able to relax into learning and find joy in coming to school. Parts of the physical schoolscape, including the small size of the school, what is on the walls, and the set-up of the classroom tables, align with the approach, making it impossible for students to disappear. When ninth-grade students change classrooms, they walk across the hall or to the next door with the same twenty students throughout the day. Seeing the same five teachers every day creates a safety bubble for students. Those five teachers, who either share classrooms or are in neighboring classrooms to the rest of the team, meet each day in a shared planning period and often eat lunch together to talk about their students' individual social, emotional, and academic needs.

"MY FRIENDS, THEY REALLY HELPED": CREATING SPACE AND TIME FOR RISK TAKING, MEANINGFUL RELATIONSHIPS, AND LEADERSHIP

Educators at IHS strive to make students feel seen, included, and valuable in the community from their very first day of school. For example, on Xiansheng's first day of ninth grade in the United States, he was asked to participate in a simulation of a meeting of the United Nations with his new ninth- and tenth-grade classmates. Xiansheng began school in May and his classmates were ready to present the research they had been working on for months. The classroom tables had been moved into a tight circle with three students sitting behind each table facing inward. Each group of students had a different country flag placed in front of them and a homemade model of a microphone. The Delegation Leader for each country sat between the researcher and the media coordinator. The Chairperson and Secretary General facilitated the debate from the table in the front of the classroom. These leadership roles were all held by tenth-grade students.

In a typical classroom, Xiansheng may have been excluded from the project. He was unprepared to fully participate, and the school year was almost over. But at IHS, it is not uncommon for students to arrive at different times throughout the year. Nevertheless, from their very first day, students are encouraged to participate in all class discussions and presentations.

Xiansheng was appointed to the delegation from Egypt. His classmates dressed up for this special day. The boy next to him was in a suit and tie. The girl in the same delegation was in a black dress and heels for the occasion. Xiansheng, in jeans and a t-shirt, slumped back in his chair, his face fluctuating between an uncomfortable grin and grimace. He nervously scanned the room looking a little scared and confused, staring at whoever was speaking but without understanding what was being said.

When the simulation ended, Ms. Gail, a ninth-grade English teacher and polyglot originally from Guyana, asked the students to reflect on the experience. Each student said something as the discussion moved around the circle. Some students offered tacit suggestions like, "everyone needs to talk more" while others offered well-developed feedback for how students could better prepare for the simulation by doing more in-depth research. When it came to Xiansheng's turn, he looked back and forth in a panic. Then, the tenth-grade Delegation Leader next to him leaned over and whispered the instructions in his ear in Mandarin. She and Ms. Gail had strategically sat Xiansheng next to her in anticipation of this moment. He shrugged. She told him just to try. All the students were looking at him but were not impatient. They waited, silently. He sat frozen for what may have seemed to an outsider like an uncomfortably long time, yet no one in the room was uncomfortable. The students and teacher know that slowing things down and being patient is a first step toward helping new students feel seen and heard. The silence is meditative. We all watched as Xiansheng's impromptu translator coaxed him to talk, comforting him by telling him he could say whatever he wanted and that she would translate for him. Finally, he spoke. He said only a few words, but he spoke, and she translated. It did not matter what he said, what surprised me was how the room erupted into congratulatory applause. Xiansheng got a few slaps on his back because he had just completed a rite of passage for ninth graders—speaking in front of the entire class for the first time.

Like Xiansheng and Gonzalo, most ninth-grade students rely on their tenth-grade peers for translation throughout the year. In rare cases, there may not be another person in the class who speaks the same language as a new student, so teachers and students use gesture and translation applications on their smartphones to communicate. Cilene, a twelfth grader from Colombia, recalled:

> I had a lot of help. My friends, they really helped a lot in the process because when I was in ninth grade they were in tenth grade. They knew English already so in the beginning what I used to do was just to ask them how do you say this, and they would just throw a dictionary at me and be like "look for it and if it is not there I'll tell you." They helped me a lot because that pushed me. I didn't notice that my English got better, I really didn't notice. Something I like to do is go back to my old essays and read them and then I realize they make no sense. I didn't realize when people used to tell me oh, your English got so much better. I didn't see it.

Tenth graders at IHS stay with the same interdisciplinary team of teachers and in the same class as most of their peers in their ninth-grade class. Teachers on each of the three ninth- and tenth-grade teams have developed a two-year curriculum that follows the same standards and practices and the same skills using different projects and assessments. Having students "loop" with the same teachers in a stable cohort is a critical innovation in IHS's social schoolscape and where I began to see how teachers transitioned from protecting their students by helping them feel safe to empowering their students to take risks, experiment with leadership, and see value in the linguistic and cultural diversity they bring to the school community.[12]

In tenth grade, Gonzalo was delighted when asked to take on leadership roles that he may have not experienced in a typical school setting. At IHS, all tenth-grade students are expected to be teachers, translators, and leaders in the school community. They are held to higher academic expectations than ninth graders and are encouraged to act as cultural and academic guides for incoming ninth-grade students. Students take this role very seriously. They think of it as an act of reciprocity. They have all been the kid who does not speak English. Gonzalo remembers the first time that he was asked to translate, not for a peer, but for a teacher. He smiled broadly as he recalled:

> The first time I translated it was for somebody who was new and came into the office and then a teacher came, I don't remember who it was, and she didn't speak Spanish. And I translated for them and the teacher said at the end, after I finished translating, that I just made that lady happy and then she just—she gave me a smile when she left.

When he was asked to translate, Gonzalo felt that he had an important job and a valuable skill worth sharing. Every student interviewed for this study talked about how they were translated for in the ninth grade and how they translated for peers and teachers in the tenth grade and beyond. Each of them acknowledged how empowering it was to see their own progress, support their peers, and possess knowledge valued by their teacher and school community. Sometimes referred to as language brokering, this practice raised students' awareness about their multilingual identities and valued place in the school community.[13]

Language translation may seem like an insignificant practice to institutionalize, but when a teacher asks a student to translate, they indicate that the student's knowledge of more than one language is valuable and appreciated. It may even be a skill that their teacher does not have. Tenth graders are propelled forward in their academic and social development because they are responsible for their newer peers. Teachers recognize that all learning, including language learning, is inexorably linked to a student's social, emotional, and physical well-being. This is why English acquisition and learning academic subjects is not the singular focus in ninth and tenth grade. Instead, the school focuses first on helping students develop a sense of belonging in the country and in the school while slowly increasing academic and language expectations. The focus in the ninth grade is almost exclusively on social emotional support and socialization into the culture of the school and the culture of schooling in the United States. It is also a diagnostic year in which teachers and school leaders learn about a student's home country schooling experience, migration history, home life, and out-of-school needs like health care and legal aid.

Tenth graders practice the same standards and skills for a second year with more emphasis on academic performance. For example, in a social studies class, students might learn how to gather evidence from a test to write a persuasive argument. This learning goal will be taught both in the ninth and tenth grades. However, the content changes from year to year. In ninth grade, students might develop an argumentative essay related to revolutions around the world and then in tenth grade, advance the same skills to develop an essay on the civil rights movement.

The physical elements of the schoolscape, such as the school's small size and the use of tables instead of desks, along with social structuring strategies like cohorts and looping in ninth and tenth grades, enable the intangible aspects of the school culture—peer and teacher relationships—to flourish. These social and structural innovations provide the time and space for students to build connections with each other, for teachers to collaborate closely, and for all stakeholders to develop deep, trusting relationships. These foundational relationships, grounded in trust and care, are critical in facilitating smoother transitions to the upper grades and supporting the innovations introduced in those years.

"NOW I'M 18 AND I JUST THINK THINGS FROM A DIFFERENT POINT OF VIEW": BUYING STUDENTS PRECIOUS TIME IN NURTURING SPACES

In a normal year, approximately seven out of ten twelfth-grade students at IHS will graduate, and two will return for a fifth year (or more) of high school. Four of the seven who graduate will go to college. One out of ten will leave the school for any number of reasons. A few will drop out, often to go to work; some transfer to accelerated high school programs or GED programs, and some go back to their home country. This is in dramatic contrast to most New York City schools, where only four out of ten students with backgrounds like IHS students will graduate, and even fewer will go to college.[14] While the literature on the impacts of grade retention is unclear, and at times contradictory, educators and families often agree that not graduating on time in high school can be a stigmatizing experience that can negatively impact a student's self-esteem.[15] At IHS, however, educators work to destigmatize fifth- or sixth-year students, extending the reach of sanctuary for as long as possible. They recognize that their students do not all begin at the same place academically, so they cannot be expected to all finish in the same amount of time.

Each year, the counselors at IHS purposefully plan to instill in senior students who are unlikely to graduate at the end of the year the idea that extra time in high school is a wonderful opportunity to continue to learn and grow, rather than a failure to graduate "on time." Current fifth- and sixth-year seniors are invited to an annual meeting with other students who might be in the same position in the following year. This meeting is designed to counter the social stigma of not graduating within four years and alleviate the pressures that they might feel to drop out and get a job. Along with teachers and the counseling team, the students who took longer than four years to graduate are encouraged to talk about what they have accomplished by staying in school for another year or more. Gonzalo recalled his meeting with the assistant principal, Bryan, about coming back for a fifth year:

> My mom told me to stay in school and teachers like Bryan told me to come back and try to finish because he knew—he saw it in me—he said, "Oh I see it in you, I know you can finish, you're just being lazy"—I kind of listened to him because I knew he was telling the truth that I was just being lazy, I know I could have finished.

If students return for a fifth year, the counseling team designs schedules that allow them to work or take on other adult responsibilities and still attend classes. When asked about being a fifth-year senior, Gonzalo responded:

> It's not a good thing to be honest, but it's good to see your old school, good to see your old friends. And I came back and I saw all my teachers and everything. I got a good welcome. I didn't feel like I was not welcome in the school. I didn't feel like coming back. I told myself, I'm not going back. Then I was like, let me just go and get my high school diploma and not give up. Not yet.

Lara believes that students like Gonzalo simply need support for more time:

> [They] need another year, not just for language development, but just in terms of knowing how to tackle tasks, get things done, and organize themselves. We see tremendous growth in some of our fifth-year students. It's actually quite shocking how some kids just are doing nothing their senior year and then all of sudden in their fifth year they turn into this new person. They grow up a little bit.

The school's graduation rate reflects this ideology. Their six-year graduation rate is consistently ten to twelve percentage points higher than their four-year graduation rate. In June 2018, IHS's four-year graduation rate was 71 percent, while the six-year graduation rate was 81 percent. When asked about his fifth year in high school, Gonzalo said:

> My mom used to tell me "just get your high school diploma so you can get a good job" and I was like I won't even need that. But now, now as I got older, now I'm 18 I just think things from a different point of view. I just see what things are like—I should get my high school diploma and start working and go to college.

I often sat with fifth- and sixth-year students in the assistant principal's office to help them finish papers and study for exams. This is how I met and developed relationships with Milagros and Gonzalo. The office space features a large round table and a couch where students can hang out or work. Unlike many AP offices, which are often set up as disciplinary spaces, this office serves as a coworking space where adults and students come to together. I used the space similarly; after observing a class, I would come to what was then Bryan's office to write my field notes. Now, Luz and Gail, both former teachers at the school, share the office as co-APs, while Bryan has moved to the principal's office.

When I visit the school these days, my first and last stop is at this office because it is where I have built the closest relationships, learned the most about the school's culture, and observed how staff navigate conflicts, support individual students, and innovate solutions to ongoing challenges. It was in the AP's office that I came to understand how educators at IHS create space and time for the students who struggle the most.

The role of the high school assistant principal, often understudied, is typically seen as that of a disciplinarian.[16] Many high schools have an assistant principal for each grade whose primary role is to enforce discipline and hand out punishments. However, IHS has transformed this role by creating a nurturing space where students who need more time to graduate can work and access support. This reimagining of the AP office as a nurturing co-working space is an innovative element of the schoolscape that helps keep students in school longer and ensures that they have every opportunity to graduate.

"EXPLORING THE GREATER WORLD": THE SCHOOLSCAPE'S UNCONDITIONAL WELCOME UNCONSTRAINED BY TIME

In *The Succeeders*, Andrea Flores discusses in the chapter titled "Your Story Is Your Ticket: Becoming a Moral Minority and Reproducing Exclusion," an exchange between Latinx students in a college access program who debate the keys to success in the United States. A twelfth-grade student asks, "Why do you think the rich stay rich, the poor stay poor, and the middle class stays middle?" Another student replies, "Because they know people." The senior then asserts that success is "not about what you know, but who you know" (p. 82).

Flores frames this interaction as an example of how nepotism and networking perpetuate the social hierarchy, a process that she identifies as social reproduction. She further analyzes this and other student discussions as reflections of "paradigmatic American moralizations about success," where youth are encouraged to value, internalize, and use notions of individual hard work, responsibility, and the pursuit of social mobility through education to navigate a system set up for them to fail (p. 103). Teachers at IHS recognize that their school is attempting to disrupt the status quo and, at the same time, their students will eventually have to navigate the society that currently exists. The internship program really emerged from this cognitive dissonance. While the schoolscape is structured to keep students in high school for as long as they need, and cocoon them in supportive services while they are there, they also wanted to give students time in high school to practice being in the world while having the time and space to make sense of it while still protected at IHS.

At IHS, I observed teachers wrestling with the challenge of providing a safe, supportive environment while also worrying about what will happen to students after graduation—in college and the "real world." This concern is common among educators in counterspaces that shield students from a harsh reality that their teachers fear they may enter unprepared.[17] The tension is especially evident in the eleventh grade, particularly in the internship program, when students start to leave the protective walls of the school and try out what they have learned in the larger world.

During the second semester of eleventh grade, IHS students spend four afternoons a week in a semester-long internship. Ideally, the internship is meant to help students who feel a sense of belonging at IHS to begin to feel that sense of belonging in the community and the United States. It helps students imagine their lives after high school and teaches them institutional knowledge about the US labor market that they, and their families, may not know. The internship pushes students into real-world situations in which they must practice the social, academic, cultural, and linguistic skills that they learned in ninth and tenth grade. Teachers attribute the considerable language and developmental gains that they see in the eleventh grade to these "real world" experiences. For example, Gonzalo did his internship at a school for the blind in Manhattan. Each day, he took the train alone into a part of the city that he had never visited. He was given more responsibilities in his internship than he had ever had in his life.

Two of the four eleventh-grade teachers told me that one of the reasons they were excited to work at IHS was because of the internship program. The history teacher told me:

> [The internship program is] what drew me to the school. When I first read about this, I was like, oh my god, this is amazing. How can we pull this off? To have kids get real-world experience at such a young age? When some college students can't get internships, you know? And for

> [the students] to get out there into the real world and learn all these new things, it is great. When I first interviewed with Lara, I said, I want to do this. This is me, this is my goal to help them not just in history but in life.

During the first semester of eleventh grade, students develop resumes and cover letters in class. Then, they apply and interview for internships with one of the hundreds of partner organizations that have taken interns from IHS in the past. Students pursue internships in schools, flower shops, hair salons, nonprofit organizations, legal clinics that advocate for undocumented students, law offices, video editing companies, childcare centers, and police precincts. Each internship site is approached and recruited by teachers and counselors at IHS, sometimes at students' request. One teacher explained the process to me:

> Every year, I always ask the students, hey, what are you interested in? And, if we don't have it, I'm going to go find it. So, I have found new internships for them because I want them to be interested in something. Somebody said "I want to intern at a hotel," so I went and got a hotel. This year somebody said police, so we set up a police [internship]. In one of my early years, a lot of students were interested in law, so I got to go out there and I found three different law internships. Every year is a little different, and [we] try to find what they are interested in.

Recruiting internships has become increasingly difficult in recent years because the number of undocumented students at IHS has increased considerably. Most schools, hospitals, and government offices will not host students who do not have a social security number. One teacher recalled a case in which an undocumented student wanted to work with the District Attorney but was unable to do so because of her documentation status. In response, her teacher, who was previously a lawyer, found her an internship in a private law office and then helped her find a summer internship at Legal Aid. Now, the student is enrolled in college and is studying pre-law.

Both teachers and students see the internship as a major growth experience for language development and in students' ability to navigate American workplace culture, vocabulary, and etiquette. It is where students also begin to develop their professional identity as they are prompted to think about their future. During the spring semester, students spend ten hours a week at their internship. According to an eleventh-grade teacher, "Internship is a time for the students really to get out of this building and go out on their own. It's a chance for them to start exploring the greater world." Students take English, social studies, math, and science once or twice a week, but the rest of the time is spent either at the internship or debriefing the internship experience in a seminar-style class and preparing the exhibit that they present to the entire school community when their internship culminates.

During the internship seminar, eleventh-grade teachers push the classroom tables together to create one long conference-like table that the students sit around. The seminar class of ten to fifteen students is kept small to encourage participation in discussion. In one of the first internship seminars of the semester, Eva, the eleventh-grade art teacher and internship coordinator, asked students to create a list of vocabulary or commonly used phrases specific to their internship. One student, who is interning in an elementary school theater classroom, says her new phrase "one-two-three eyes on me, actors ready!" Another student, who is interning at a flower shop, gets sent on "missions." He recalled, "they tell me, 'I have a mission for you to go get us coffee.'" The other students laugh at this story and commiserate about some of the menial tasks that they were asked to do in the first days of their internship, like running errands and making copies.

Later in the semester, students are encouraged to gather artifacts from their internship site to share with their classmates and engage in conversations with people at their internship sites by interviewing their supervisors. In class, they create a pamphlet in their native language describing the site and write a reflection on their experiences. Teachers or peers who speak the student's native language read and offer feedback. In many of these pamphlets and essays, students write about their personal growth and language development through the internship.

I met one student who wrote about how he was not given a badge to enter the building where he was interning. He was frustrated that each day he would have to wait in the lobby for twenty minutes or more for someone to come escort him to the office. In his essay, he wrote about how he addressed this problem by advocating for himself. He recalled:

> I decided to finally go talk to my mentors about how it wastes my time every single day. So, I did go and talked to them and gave them an idea of how it makes my life hard every day. Then, finally, they made me a temporary pass until I could get a real one. Now [with my official pass] I am allowed into the building easily. I think it was good thing to do to speak up for myself because after that day I felt comfortable and accepted there and most importantly I have more time to work. By doing it, it slightly gave me an idea about the real world and how people and our coworkers might not do certain things for you but you have to be standing up for yourself and ask for it if you think you deserve it and it's worth asking.

Learning to self-advocate is just another one of the many ways that students develop in their internship. Students are left largely on their own at their internship sites except for two field visits from the eleventh-grade teacher, who also sees them in their weekly internship seminar class. One of the visits is scheduled, and the other is a surprise. Students are also asked to turn in signed timesheets to the school. Most students need little monitoring. Others, who show up late or not at all in their first days of internship, are supervised more closely. Like other programs at IHS, the internship experience is highly individualized for each student.

I describe what students experience in the internship as a kind of revolving door. They leave the school for internship, but come back to check-in and debrief what they saw, learned, and experienced, which is not always positive. The door continues to revolve in different ways for students in their fourth year of high school and beyond. They see the students grade as a simple designation that says little about their preparedness for graduation.

The internship year is followed by at least one more year focused on preparing for college, passing two state-mandated exit exams, and completing performance-based assessment tasks. For some students, this last step takes two or more years to complete. While the eleventh grade emphasizes pushing students outside their comfort zones and encouraging them to take risks beyond school, the twelfth grade is centered on graduating and planning for life after high school, which both teachers and students understand to be an enormous transition.

Many IHS students are the first in their families to consider college, most will be the first to attend college in the United States, and depending on the year, 25 to 50 percent of the graduating class are navigating life after college without documentation. The older students get, the more pressure they feel to work and earn money to support their families here and abroad. The real world begins to encroach on the students and the sanctuary school.

Consequently, twelfth-grade teachers, mentors, counselors, and support staff often take on roles like those of middle-class parents, organizing college visits and helping students with college and scholarship applications. Students continue to leave the sanctuary school to work at McDonald's, to return to their home countries, and to work on construction sites and as Uber drivers. While they are gone, their teachers and friends keep tabs on them. If they are at risk of not graduating while away from IHS, they use all the tools at their disposal to encourage them to return. Students like Gonzalo may disappear for long stretches of time and then return months later to a school that will welcome them back and continue to believe in them as long as they can, and in most cases, until graduation. However, the revolving door does not end there. Alumni come back to work at the school, as do former parents and siblings, which I discuss in greater detail in chapter 4. What is key to note in the schoolscape is that the school is designed to welcome students and welcome them back unconditionally, without exception. Students are never treated as undesirable, a lost cause, or a wasted effort. Students do come back again and again throughout the year, before or after the funding deadline, in the middle of the term, at the end of the day on a Friday, and find a sanctuary school designed for them where they are welcomed back with open arms and a warm embrace.

For example on graduation day in June 2017, when Diego framed IHS as a place that conspires to make dreams achievable, I felt discouraged that Gonzalo was not there. It was the end of his fifth year of high school and I had hoped that he would be graduating. His teachers were frustrated too. I sat facing the row of seniors where Gonzalo would have been sitting had he finished this year. Scanning the faces of the seniors who I got to know well over the year, I noticed Gonzalo's cousin, Marc, sitting in the middle of the third row. Gonzalo and Marc, both fifth-year students, were often together walking the halls or hunched over laptops in the assistant principal's office when they were not in class. That is where I met both boys at the beginning of their fifth year of high school. Like Gonzalo, Marc was initially cold and distant when he was unsure if he could trust me, but he warmed up as we shared lunch during our interview. After our conversation, he and Gonzalo would always greet me in the hallways with a head nod and a shy smile. On graduation day, Marc sat tall with his chin up, bright-eyed and smiling, and totally engaged with the speakers. He was a proud, confident, soon-to-be high school graduate. I wanted that for Gonzalo, too.

I was unsure if I would see Gonzalo again. He did not respond to my text messages over the summer, and with the end of the academic year and my full-time data collection commitment, my visits to the school became less frequent. Nevertheless, I tried to visit a few times each month to check in, maintain relationships, and volunteer for projects when needed. For the first month of the 2017–2018 academic year, I did not see Gonzalo. Then, on a visit in late October, there he was, at a desk in the back of the classroom, backpack on, hunched over a laptop. We made eye contact, and he smiled broadly, as did I. He was back for another year!

We didn't have much time to talk that day, and I didn't want to distract him from his studies, but I told him, "I was worried you weren't coming back." He looked up and responded, "I don't give up. I never give up." When I saw Gonzalo in 2018, he had just a few graduation requirements left, the most daunting being the New York State Regents Common Core English Language Arts (Regents ELA) exam, which he had failed more than six times. He took the test one more time, earned his last few credits, finished his portfolio assessments, and graduated on a February afternoon a few months after I saw him. For Gonzalo to graduate, he needed five years and six months. I am confident that in a different school, this would not have been Gonzalo's story.

Rethinking time is a key innovation in IHS's schoolscape. This chapter has highlighted the importance of slowing things down to help students feel safe, empowered, and supported, both inside and outside of school. Providing students with more time to graduate is a critical part of this approach.

In education policy, how time should be spent in schools and when milestones should be met is hotly debated. Time is seen as a valuable currency. Reformers and policy makers understand that meaningful change takes time, but often, reforms must show results quickly or become extinct. Reforms can quickly become politically unpopular, too costly, or not sufficiently eye-catching. Teachers and school leaders are burdened by the often-unreasonable expectations that students at all grade levels learn more at a faster pace. While this frantic approach to education can hurt all students, it is most harmful to the students most often marginalized by bureaucratic systems.

To truly support students, creativity in using time and space is essential. Teachers and school leaders must examine the educational landscape and question existing rules. Are these rules truly serving students' needs? If the rules are followed as they are, is the best support provided for students? What are the potential consequences of not following them, both for educators and for students? And, can innovative ways be found to meet district policies while prioritizing the holistic needs of students? Addressing these questions can help create a school environment where students have the time and space that they need to succeed.

RETHINKING THE SCHOOLSCAPE: A NECESSARY INNOVATION FOR SANCTUARY SCHOOLS

IHS's schoolscape, much like a landscape, continues to morph, adapt, and evolve. A perfect example of this is my visit to IHS in June 2024, while I was working on this chapter, to meet Chuvak. Back in March, I was at home, scrolling through Instagram, when a picture of Chuvak in a starched white collar and blue tie, sitting in the principal's office chair, popped up on my feed. His little black eyes were barely visible through the fuzzy white fur that framed his face, and his little lips were pursed together, giving him the appearance of taking his job quite seriously. The Instagram post announced that IHS had enrolled in a comfort dog program through the Department of Education, allowing Chuvak to spend three days a week at the school.[18]

When I asked Lara and Bryan about the process, they both shared the same story. Bryan had adopted Chuvak as a puppy while he was still the assistant principal at IHS. He wanted to surprise his kids with the puppy and needed a place to hide Chuvak for a few days. On the last day before winter break in 2018, Bryan snuck Chuvak into the school. "We couldn't believe how people reacted," Lara told me. "We knew the students would be excited, but we had teachers crawling into his dog bed to snuggle with him," explained Bryan. After that day, Lara and Bryan hatched a plan to enroll in the comfort dog program and get Bryan's new puppy trained by the Good Dog Foundation.

Introducing a comfort dog into the school community is the latest innovation in IHS's schoolscape, but I am confident it will not be the last. The moment that immigrant students step into IHS, they see that their identities and experiences are acknowledged and valued. The decorations and displays throughout the school reflect this commitment to honoring students' home languages and cultures, both in obvious and subtle ways. Beyond the visuals, IHS's traditions and daily routines also celebrate where students come from. The schoolscape is thoughtfully designed to create a welcoming atmosphere, integrating both the physical space and the school's rituals to reinforce a culture of belonging. Everything from the posters on the walls to the school's routines sends a clear message of acceptance and support.

Educators at IHS understand that a supportive schoolscape is crucial for students' success. It is not just about making students feel good; it's about creating an environment where they can thrive academically and personally. Experts agree that for immigrant students to succeed academically, socially, and economically, they need to be in schools that are safe, engaging, and relevant to their experiences.[19] At IHS, educators know that students like Milagros and Gonzalo need to feel secure before they can fully focus on learning English and other subjects. They see the schoolscape as a foundation for being able to address their social, emotional, and academic needs.

4

Sanctuary Begins with People

Innovation in Leadership and Community

ON THE LAST DAY *of my undergraduate methods class, I told my professor that I felt hopeless about learning [how to use] cooperative methods [in my classroom]. . . . I said, "What's the point of us learning how to use cooperative learning and having a student-centered classroom when we may go into a school whose administration does not support this?" She responded, "[Y]ou [just] have to make sure that the students pass this test." I was really disheartened.*

[Then] my student teaching experience [was also] unpleasant, and I hated being in a large, comprehensive school. Despite its grade A rating, which supposedly meant it was a good school due to high test scores, I found the teachers there lacking. I had teachers, senior teachers tell me, "Everything you learn in college doesn't work, just throw it out."

My cooperating teacher would take someone else's lesson plans, give them to me, and insist, "You have to teach this." When I asked if I could create my own, he said, "No, you have to do this." It wasn't even his lesson.

There was no real collaboration; it was just direct instruction. I remember getting so frustrated at times [my cooperating teacher would] tell me my pacing was too slow. [Then] he would [take over the] lecture and face the board, writing furiously, leaving me standing there with students looking at me, waiting for me to do something. By the end of the period, he'd finish the handout and all the problems, then look at me and say, "Wow, look, I'm sweating. Look how much work we got done." And I thought, "We? Who is we?"

—Carolina, an eleventh-grade math teacher at IHS, describes her teacher-education experiences in college

Carolina is an exuberant, passionate, and much-loved teacher at International High School (IHS). As the daughter of Colombian and Cuban immigrants who grew up in Florida and New York City, she knew from college that she wanted to become a math teacher. However, the more she learned about the profession, the more disillusioned she became. She was troubled by the overwhelming focus on "the test," referring to the math Regents exam that nearly all high school students in New York State must pass to graduate. Carolina found it frustrating to study collaborative teaching methods in her textbooks, only to be told by both her professors and the senior teachers mentoring her during student teaching that she would likely never get to use those skills in the classroom.

When Carolina graduated from college and began her job search, she specifically sought positions where she wouldn't have to teach to a standardized test. This decision significantly limited her options, as fewer than forty high schools in New York City at the time had waivers allowing their students to use alternative assessment practices to earn a diploma. These schools, now some of the most well-known and sought-after in the city, were allowed to let students demonstrate their readiness to graduate through projects known as performance assessments. Each school had its own approach to these assessments, incorporating the types of cooperative and project-based learning methods that Carolina had studied as an undergraduate college student.[1]

I met Carolina during her fourth year at IHS and was immediately drawn to her classroom. Despite being one of the youngest and least experienced teachers at the school, she had already surpassed the critical early years when many educators leave the profession; nationally, most teachers leave within five years.[2] Carolina spoke enthusiastically about how much she had grown as a teacher since her student days and how much she still had to learn.

New teachers are often advised to "shut the door and teach," which suggests that they should leave behind the bureaucracy of education policy, ignore the jargon of ineffective professional development, and rely on their common sense to do what's best for their students—despite knowing they may never be treated as professionals. This was certainly my experience as a first-year high school science teacher; I could count on one hand the number of veteran teachers or principals who observed my teaching. Over my seven years in the classroom, I was observed maybe twenty times, each lasting between three and forty minutes. By my second year, I was a team leader and assigned numerous duties that ate into my planning time. My students never took state tests since I didn't teach a tested subject. School leaders cared very little about what I was teaching as long as my students were well-behaved. In contrast, my colleagues teaching tested subjects were observed so frequently that it was more like surveillance than an opportunity to improve their practice. What I observed at IHS was a flow of information and feedback that supported the development of teachers well into their careers.

When I asked Lara about teacher development at IHS, she referred to one of the five guiding principles of Internationals Network schools: "one learning model for all," meaning teacher development is approached in the same way as student, staff, and leadership development. Initially, I was skeptical. Like many educators, I had experienced the irony of attending professional development sessions where the instructor would tell us how to teach more effectively without using any of the methods for which they advocated. Conversely, I had also sat through teacher professional development sessions where the instructor used the *exact* same methods they would with students, which often felt patronizing and simplistic. Lara challenged me to imagine what it would mean if every teacher was valued at the school, not just those teaching tested subjects. What possibilities could unfold if teachers remained at the school year after year, deepening their expertise, reducing the need for constant hiring, allowing for more selective recruitment, and providing stronger support for new teachers? What if, as a leader, she made decisions in collaboration with teachers rather than acting as a top-down executive? What would it be like to work at a school staffed by educators who truly believed in what they were doing and how they were doing it?

I began to see these possibilities by learning more about Carolina's journey to IHS and her development as a teacher once she was hired. By tracing Carolina's professional trajectories and those of her colleagues and mentors, I observed what a commitment to teachers can mean over time for a school and a network. Carolina was hired for her potential as an educator but also because she was bilingual in Spanish and English, and because of how she talked about her Colombian, Cuban, and American heritage and her experience growing up as a child of immigrants. Carolina was chosen through a collaborative process that valued her potential and her background. Over the next few years, she benefited from mentorship and support, helping her shift from a traditional, efficiency-driven teaching model to one that embraced project-based learning and addressed content and literacy in the math classroom.

Building on the idea that innovative practices should extend to teachers, this chapter argues for sanctuary practices that nurture educators working with immigrant youth. It emphasizes the importance of collective hiring practices, considering teacher identity and lived experience in the process, focusing on teacher retention, distributing decision-making power to foster community, and employing community members with deep knowledge of the Internationals in schools and as a strategy for cultivating a network of schools with shared values. While effective individually, these practices become transformative when combined and allowed to evolve over time.

"ARE YOU WILLING TO TRY SOMETHING OUT OF YOUR COMFORT ZONE?": COLLECTIVE HIRING OF RISK-TAKING TEACHERS WITH DIVERSE BACKGROUNDS AND EXPERIENCES

Getting a job as a teacher at IHS today is not easy because it is rare for teachers to leave. This was not always the case. Hiring teachers when the school first opened was not easy. Lara, who was a founding teacher at the school, recalled that "in the beginning, we just needed teachers. Nobody wanted to come all the way out." For many years, the school leadership struggled to find teachers with the qualities they desired. After fully staffing the school, Lara discovered that there "were some people I needed to get rid of" because of their unwillingness to collaborate or inappropriate behavior toward students. However, as the school's culture became more established, teacher retention increased, and Lara was able to delegate the hiring process to the Personnel Committee and the team of teachers with whom new teachers would work.

Twelve years after the school was established, many teachers recalled the rigorous teacher-selection process they went through to get their jobs, including multiple interviews with several school actors, group interviews on Skype, and day-long interviews where they met with almost all the teachers in the school and taught demo lessons to students. Teachers recounted experiences of highly unsuccessful demo lessons in which everything went wrong. Many realized in the process that the school's leadership and the Personnel Committee focused more on a candidate's ability to collaborate and reflect on their practice than on delivering a flawless demo lesson. They sought a teaching orientation that could be nurtured and developed rather than expecting a fully formed pedagogue. Carolina remembered her interview similarly:

> My demo lesson was on volume, the popcorn thing. I don't know if you have seen it where you use [differently shaped] containers to figure out which one holds more popcorn. . . . It was very different from all the other demo lessons that I had done. The reason why I did that one was because I strongly believed that it is the kind of way teaching should look like, something where like I'm actually doing it with my hands. I'm feeling it, and I'm doing something, putting it inside something so I can visualize what [we are] measuring.

Lara, the principal, remembered this demo lesson, too, which she described as chaotic with popcorn flying all over the room:

> I think about when we hired Carolina four years ago. She tried something, I mean she was a new teacher, she didn't know what she was doing, and she tried this new lesson and it was fine. She did something with cylinders with popcorn and finding the volume or something. She had popcorn flying around . . . she tried all this crazy stuff. And afterwards . . . Carolina tore herself up about [her demo lesson] and then was like, what do you think? Can you tell me what you think? Did you think I should do it this way? I was like, okay, I love this person. She wants the feedback. She was automatically like (snaps fingers), well maybe next time I would do this and that differently.

In another demo lesson, Lara recalled a young teacher who did an experimental demo lesson but still got the job.

> I don't remember what the math concept was, but [the students] had to pump their hands across the table and time them and see how much more quickly they would do it each time . . . I can't remember. He totally didn't know what he was doing but he was trying something new. I was like, wow, that's cool. That's the thing is, are you willing to take a risk and try something out of your comfort zone?

The interview protocol includes asking participants to reflect on past teaching experiences and giving the applicant time to reflect on their demo lesson. Lara explained:

> We say, tell us about a project [or unit] you've done, what went well? What would change if you could do it differently? When they say, "Well I think it was pretty good. I wouldn't make any changes." I think, red flags, red flags! We're always like, really? Nothing? Then, when we have them do the demo, we do a reflection afterward. Two of us will sit with them and say, "Okay, what do you think? How did it go?"

Educators who were reflective risk-takers and who asked for feedback were more successful than those who were experienced and overconfident in the interview process. How teachers are hired at IHS reflects a deep commitment to continuous development and collective decision-making. Teachers are hired assuming they will be long-term members of a close-knit and collaborative community.

Deciding who to hire is influenced not only by a willingness to take risks but also by identity and lived experiences. Members of the Personnel Committee believe that teachers with an emotional connection to their work or shared experiences with their students are more likely to understand their students' perspectives, work diligently, and treat families with care. IHS's careful and competitive hiring process has allowed the school to cultivate and retain a staff of thirty racially, ethnically, linguistically, and culturally diverse teachers. In the United States, where white teachers make up 79 percent of the nation's public school teachers, this is both rare and a reflection of the school's culture.[3]

IHS's teachers come from diverse backgrounds, with about half identifying as people of color and half identifying as white. Almost all speak a second or third language with some level of fluency. Approximately two-thirds identify as immigrants or children of immigrants. They vary in age and experience and are traditionally trained in colleges of education and through alternative certification pathways. Most teachers stay at IHS for their entire career. Since I started visiting the school in 2016, six teachers, a counselor, a social worker, and a literacy coach have left the school. Four retired, one moved out of the city, one went to graduate school, one changed careers, and the social worker took a promotion to the district level where she could help coach social workers in other Internationals and Affinity schools. Everyone agreed that the one teacher who left to take another teaching job was not a good fit for the school. There have been a few other teachers who have come and gone in the last eight years, but the teachers that stay year after year share four common traits: openness to collaboration, reflective practice, deep personal connections or commitments to immigrant communities, and deep knowledge of and fidelity to the Internationals Network model.[4]

Because so much time is spent on teacher development at IHS, the Personnel Committee is more focused on the potential of candidates than on who they are as teachers when they are hired. This means that they sometimes take risks on teachers like Carolina, who are young and inexperienced but eager to learn. Or on Ben and James, two white, monolingual teachers who worked together in a strict charter school network before applying for jobs at IHS. Or Micha, a soft-spoken polyglot who worked in media research before becoming a teacher.

Almost a third of teachers at IHS immigrated to New York and learned English as teenagers or adults, like Prasna, a ninth- and tenth-grade science teacher from Nepal. Prasna learned English as a teenager and was worried about entering the job market after college because she did not feel confident about writing a cover letter in English. Her advisor encouraged her to apply to IHS so that she could help students who had a similar immigration experience as she did. She sees herself as a lifelong English learner but thinks this makes her a better teacher. For example, she mentioned how she could anticipate how the word "table" can be confusing for students learning science because they might be thinking of a table, the furniture you eat off of.

She also shared specific examples of how learning English later in life and teaching students in the same position influences how she thinks about how best to incorporate literacy into science content. At the beginning of the school year, she focuses on teaching descriptive adjectives, which are good vocabulary words and essential for being a good scientist.

> My first week is about adjectives when I first start my lesson. For example, hard, soft, mushy, smoky, cloudy—these are things we use when doing qualitative and quantitative observations. Then, they'll have to write a sentence in science using the adjectives. I give them this list of words that they can use—descriptive language. . . . I think it works because I don't want students to just say it's good, you know, or it's bad. I want them to be able to describe it. Descriptive language is so important in science. The first few ice breakers would be looking at something, touching it, and describing it, so station activities are all based on measurements and descriptions.

She also discussed how she has used her background to model vulnerability and curiosity when learning a new language in the classroom. When she writes on the board, and she is unsure if words are spelled correctly, she talks to students about her process:

> When I write vocabulary on the board . . . I make mistakes; I look at it and tell my students, "I'm not sure. Let me figure this one out." I point it out because I think our students particularly need that—to know it's okay if the spelling is wrong, if you have the meaning. But then I like them to understand that if you're not sure [you should] go and check. Don't assume it's right. . . . I leave those [misspelled] words most of the time. I say, "Okay, we'll come back to that word. I'll go double-check [the spelling] and then write it down [correctly]."

Prasna's approach challenges the idea that teachers must be all-knowing and project authority, and as a result her students feel more comfortable making mistakes in her class. Almost a third of teachers at IHS speak English with an accent.[5] At IHS, the Personnel Committee believes that representation in how one speaks English is as important as having a racially and ethnically diverse staff. They understand that a teacher who speaks English with an accent likely speaks other languages, has experiences in other countries, and can be a good professional model for students. This is atypical. Accent discrimination is still pervasive around the world. While illegal in the United States, it can be difficult to prove and is common in the hiring and treatment of educators in K–12 schools, colleges, and universities.[6] At IHS, it is treated as an asset.

Another third of teachers who work at the school are children of immigrants, including Lara. Some of these teachers also identify as white and speak English with an American accent, but grew up translating for their parents and seeing the consequences of language and accent discrimination. Lara recalled watching her Portuguese father and Italian mother struggle to learn English and be treated badly because of how they spoke English. She remembers how many of her cousins experienced mistreatment in schools because of their immigrant backgrounds. These experiences influenced her decision to work at Internationals Network schools:

> I was really drawn to Internationals because I come from a family of immigrants, I was the first to go to college . . . my dad didn't go to high school. Education was important to them, but they had to work. . . . I think about my own mom and how when she immigrated, she was from this tiny little town in Italy, tiny, tiny, like five hundred people. But she ended up in Ardmore, Pennsylvania, right outside of Philadelphia. . . . When she came, she was like six months away from graduating. This was in the mid-sixties, and she had to go back to ninth grade, and she was like twenty-something when she graduated high school. She didn't want to go back to ninth grade, but she did it.

The teachers at IHS who do not identify as immigrants or children of immigrants have had experiences that help them relate to their immigrant students. Several teachers married into immigrant families and felt drawn to IHS because of those experiences. Others have traveled extensively and learned new languages, further enriching their understanding of their students' challenges.[7] For example, the assistant principal, Bryan, was a Peace Corps volunteer and struggled to learn Ukrainian. These commonalities among new hires show that IHS has a nuanced commitment to diversity in which lived experience is balanced with a willingness to be uncomfortable, whether in a new country or in interview demo lessons.

Once the Personnel Committee hires a new teacher, the school has established systems and structures to ensure the new teacher is successful. The school makes time for mentorship, collaboration, relationship building, and collective decision-making, which has resulted in a school staff that enjoys each other and returns to teach year after year despite the many challenges they face with their immigrant students. It also allows community members to begin to understand deeply why specific school practices exist and how innovative approaches used in the Internationals Network schools have evolved over time.

"WE ACTUALLY LIKE EACH OTHER": BUILDING A COLLECTIVE OF TEACHERS WHO SUPPORT EACH OTHER AND STAY

Carolina wanted to teach differently once she was hired at IHS but was unsure where to start. She quickly realized that she had no idea how to create a project that could lead to a performance assessment.

> When I was first starting, I was starting from scratch, creating my own curriculum from scratch, my own projects from scratch, everything from scratch, and I'm the only geometry teacher here. From scratch. I had a textbook, and I had research that I was doing while I was trying to figure out how to teach. I was dying.

Although teachers at IHS have incredible autonomy in what they teach, they are expected to develop high-quality projects that are designed well enough for students to earn the highest possible grade on the standardized rubrics used across Internationals Network schools. Relearning how to teach this way can take years to do well and even longer to master. For example, Micha, a second-career teacher who loved learning new languages was still struggling to teach well after several years at the school. He needed help with organization and classroom management. Lara had Micha work with the literacy coach for lesson planning and another teacher for classroom management, she switched him to another team, observed him often, and met with him one on one to talk about how to improve his practice. Unfortunately, even after several years, Micha still struggled. Lara recalled:

> He was often late to class. He struggled to organize his classroom. His classes were frequently chaotic. He would get so into working with one kid that the other kids would throw things at each other. I was in the classroom, and he wouldn't even notice. Or I would walk in; he wouldn't notice. I remember one time he came in with a microphone, one of those Madonna microphones, and he used it in the classroom because some kids wouldn't listen to him. I said, and I never do this, but I said, you can't do that. I was like, no. Period.

Lara denied his tenure for years but recognized his commitment to becoming a good teacher. In his fifth year, he began to succeed in his classroom and now is one of the most veteran teachers at the school. He takes great care with project planning and will embark on learning a new language if a new student enrolls and no one else at the school speaks their language. He is a true asset to the school, but like Gonzalo, he was on a different timeline for development.

Like Micha, Carolina struggled to design math projects that taught content well. "My students always end up liking me because of the social-emotional aspect; they feel connected to me [because I speak Spanish], but I noticed that content-wise, they don't feel comfortable." To learn how to teach math content in the form of a project, Carolina visited other math classrooms regularly to observe other teaching styles. "I really admire my colleagues. I feel like they are doing such an amazing job, and it motivates me . . . they can build strong relationships with their students *and* teach content in a meaningful way."

When Carolina wanted to observe her colleagues' teaching, or when Micha felt overwhelmed by student behavior, Lara would find substitute teachers to cover their classes for a day so they could step away from the day-to-day pressures of teaching and think about their longer-term goals. For example, when Carolina was trying to finish her master's thesis and plan a final student project for the year, she felt overwhelmed. Lara brought in substitute teachers for both Carolina and a more veteran teacher so that they could spend a day planning the project together. Lara also called me to ask if I could help Carolina with her master's thesis because it was a qualitative study of the school's assessment practices. With these supports in place, Carolina was able to develop a high-quality project, finish a master's thesis that helped her better understand her own work in the classroom, and graduate with a degree that would ensure a pay raise through the district. Then, when Carolina graduated from her master's program, Lara and the teachers threw her a surprise graduation party.

This type of support is what Lara means when she talks about "one learning model for all." Just like Gonzalo was buffered from unrealistic expectations, given time to develop, cared for beyond the classroom, and celebrated for his successes, teachers like Carolina and Micha are given time to develop their craft and are nurtured in the school community. Carolina and her colleagues continue to benefit from support structures four and five years into their careers. While some might argue that this extended support is inefficient and that teachers should master their craft more quickly, data shows that we expect too much of teachers too quickly, leading to burnout and disenchantment with the profession. Over

40 percent of new teachers leave the profession within their first five years, and fewer college students are studying education.[8] The financial impact of this turnover is significant, as is the impact on student achievement.[9] At IHS, Lara's long-term investment in mentoring new teachers has paid off, resulting in a notably low turnover rate. In the year this study took place, only two teachers left the school, both of whom had been there for over five years and neither of whom transferred to other schools.

Research suggests that when schools improve the organizational contexts in which teachers work, teachers are more likely to stay, and student achievement on standardized tests improves more rapidly.[10] School leadership is particularly influential in whether teachers remain at their schools. Additionally, studies have shown that when new teachers receive longer induction periods and careful mentorship in supportive school environments, they are more likely to stay in both the school and the teaching profession.[11]

The organizational context that makes collaboration, support, and mentorship possible for teachers requires the careful engineering of school leaders so that the master schedule, school layout, and decision-making processes reflect the same commitment to the teachers as the school makes to students. Lara strongly believes that asking teachers to work together without giving them the time to do so is a recipe for failure. Teachers typically have two planning periods every day. One for themselves and one for a team meeting, either with their interdisciplinary team to discuss student progress and design interdisciplinary projects or with their content teams to plan and align the curriculum. Creating a master schedule that complies with requirements for student instructional time and the teacher union's contract hour requirements is a complicated game of Tetris for a school leader. Trying to build in daily collaborative planning time is almost impossible. Lara and the rest of the leadership team spend weeks on the schedule over the summer.

Another aspect of the supportive environment is proximity. The classrooms of teachers on the same team are also located close to one another, and there are often two teachers sharing a classroom. These classroom blocks also become social areas for teachers. Almost daily, teachers on the same interdisciplinary team sit at a classroom table and eat lunch together. The teachers' lounge was almost always empty except for teachers using the bathroom or making copies. One teacher joked, "I know it is surprising, but we actually like each other." When I would join these team lunches, the teachers talked about their weekend plans, their children, and their students. It was informal and relaxing. Lunch is short, and the teachers are always eager to get back to work, but these lunches serve a social purpose and are important for teachers who work together so closely to have time to get to know one another. When teams are not working well together, Lara has conversations with the team and all the individual teachers to see what shifts can be made. Together, they decide what shifts should be made.

Collective decision-making does not stop with hiring and staffing decisions. Committees make most of the decisions in the school. Lara does not make decisions alone. Over the course of this study, I watched her navigate tricky personal differences and sensitive staffing decisions. There were moments in which I wondered why she didn't just make a decision quickly and put an end to the matter. She was steadfast in her approach. While many schools have committees with a particular focus, under Lara's leadership, they had legitimate power to determine the professional development teachers needed, how best to engage families, what grading policy to adopt, how to use the budget, and much more.

The committees at IHS include a Professional Development Committee that selects a theme for the year and plans monthly professional developments around that theme. An Attendance Committee works with chronically absent and late students and their families to help them get to school. The Personnel Committee reviews applications from potential new teachers when teaching positions become available. The largest and most influential committee at IHS is the Coordinating Council, composed of five team leaders, representatives from each discipline area, a member of the counseling department, the literacy coach, committee chairs, and sometimes students. This council makes the most important and often controversial school policy and practice decisions. However, decisions are not made in a single meeting.

Typically, a council member introduces an issue for discussion. The group then deliberates and formulates a plan to gather feedback. Council members have a week to consult with their colleagues and bring the feedback to the next meeting. Over the week, different groups within the school discuss the topic, bringing new questions and concerns back to the council. If there are strong but differing opinions across the school, Lara initiates a listening campaign, meeting with various stakeholders to understand their concerns in more detail and help them consider alternative perspectives.

The decision-making process is thorough and transparent. In addition to the feedback loop, meeting minutes are recorded in a shared Google document accessible to all teachers. Decisions often take several weeks to finalize because decisions are finalized when there is consensus and not by majority rules voting. While this approach may not be the most efficient, the school staff believes it ensures that all ideas are considered and the final decision is one that everyone understands and can support. Lara argues that when people feel like they have been included in the decision-making process, "even if it doesn't go their way, usually they'll support it."

Mentorship, team cohesiveness, and collective decision-making is the professional backbone of IHS's school culture. Teachers believe that the many support structures result in low teacher turnover at the school—they have all been working together for a long time and are content with their jobs. They also believe that their participation and input decision-making across the school helps them work effectively as a team. These efforts have allowed for a teacher corps at IHS with significantly more experience and more continuity than is typical in high-need urban districts in New York City and across the country.

LARA'S LEADERSHIP: GROWING UP IN INTERNATIONALS NETWORK SCHOOLS AND LEADING THEM INTO THE FUTURE

In January 2018, a professor at New York University invited Lara to speak to her graduate students about educational leadership. Lara began by describing the school and the challenges that she faced as a high school principal to the class. Then, during the question-and-answer session, a student asked her to give an example of when she had to make an "unpopular executive decision." Lara responded, "I try not to make any executive decisions without people feeling like they've at least shared their thoughts on it." The student looked skeptical and pushed back on her answer, in disbelief that she'd be a school leader and not make executive decisions that were sometimes unpopular.

Lara began to explain how decisions are made at the school through committees, but the student still looked unconvinced. The professor interjected, "I think the school survey is quite revealing—and it's pretty phenomenal." She held up a few sheets of paper that contained the school's public survey data released each year by the Department of Education and read from the report:

> What percentage of teachers think that the principal communicates a clear vision for the school? One hundred percent of the teachers say that she does. What percentage of the teachers say that the curriculum instruction and learning materials are well coordinated across different grade levels? One hundred percent of the teachers agree with that. What percentage of the parents felt that the principal worked to create a sense of community in the school? Ninety-seven percent of the parents agreed with that. And what percentage of the teachers say that they trust the principal? One hundred percent of the teachers say they trust the principal.

The class, full of early and mid-career educators, fell silent. "Wow. . ." someone murmured at the back.

Lara quickly redirected the conversation away from herself by cutting into the conversation, "I think that's because of the work the teachers do too. I mean they're part of the vision, they're part of the work with families. I mean I can't possibly work with all the families. . ."

The report that the professor read from was the School Quality Snapshots released by the Department of Education about IHS during the 2016–2017 school year. On the survey used to gather data for the snapshots, Lara's staff overwhelmingly reported that she "inspires school community" and creates an environment where "relationships between administrators, educators, students, and families are based on trust and respect."

I did not interview Lara until I had spent over four months in the school. When we finally sat down for an interview, I quickly realized why, during interviews with teachers, the topic of Lara's leadership often emerged unprompted. Teachers recalled times when she helped them through a difficult time in their personal lives, taught them to be better teachers, helped them integrate into the school and find mentors, celebrated their accomplishments inside the classroom and out, found funding for their projects, school clubs, and trips, and made them trust that their concerns mattered. Students in the school also talked about Lara's warmth and literal open-door policy. Her door was almost always open, and anyone could stop in to say hello. Lara was easily accessible to the students, her faculty and staff, parents, the community, and to me.

I interviewed Lara three times in the first year of this study and continue to meet with her about once a month to discuss educational research, policy, and practice. Lara and I have become good friends in the decade since I first stepped foot in IHS. She knows more about New York City schools than anyone I have ever met and seems never to forget a name or face. I text her for advice on navigating the schools for my children and advise her on her doctoral program, which she started a few years after this study. I am endlessly intrigued by how she thinks about leadership as a community-engaged, collective practice.

What stood out to me about watching her explain her style to graduate students was how hard it was for the students to imagine, particularly for those who had worked in schools for much of their careers. Lara tried to explain her collaborative and inclusive approach to decision-making but found it challenging. Traditional leadership often emphasizes top-down decisions, which are straightforward to explain because they are common. Most people have experienced a boss, parent, or mentor subscribing to this approach. Lara's emphasis on the teachers and their collaboration with families for the school's success shows her humility. Her approach contrasts with more conventional, hierarchical leadership models and underscores her commitment to a democratic, community-oriented leadership style.

Lara's own journey as an educator, principal, district leader, and now nonprofit executive director is explanatory when trying to understand her mindset. Lara began her teaching career at LaGuardia International High School as a student teacher in 1995. In 1996, she was hired as a humanities teacher at Brooklyn International High School (BIHS), a collaborative environment where she worked for eight years. If the Internationals Network were a family, BIHS would be the mother school to IHS. As a teacher at BIHS, Lara learned that all staff members, including newer teachers like her, were expected to contribute their input during meetings. Lara appreciated the consensus-driven style of her principal, which ensured that everyone understood and supported decisions or voiced their beliefs.

Lara and two other colleagues from BIHS became founding teachers at IHS in 2004. She and her colleagues spent a year planning the school before it was opened. IHS, modeled after BIHS, grew into a full, four-year high school, with its first class graduating in 2008. During IHS's first year, Lara taught full-time while preparing to become the assistant principal as the school expanded. She was the full-time assistant principal for four and a half years before becoming the principal of IHS in 2011.

Lara surprised everyone when she left her post as principal in 2019 to become a deputy superintendent for the district. She agonized over the decision for weeks after the job was offered to her. She didn't really want to leave the school but felt she could make positive changes in the district and support other principals. What finally convinced her to take the job was a call with a district employee who explained why her school was doing poorly compared to other schools with similar numbers of Asian and Latinx students. She responded by explaining that racial/ethnic comparisons were misleading since all her students were new to learning English and the country. The bureaucrat shrugged and said, "This is just the way it is." Lara raged about this interaction afterward, knowing things could change and how to get them changed.

Lara guided the schools in the Department of Education's Affinity District, which includes the fifteen New York City–based International High Schools from 2019 to 2023.[12] These were difficult years because of the COVID-19 pandemic. Some of the hardest-hit places in the world were the immigrant communities in New York City.

By this point in her career, Lara was familiar with how significant events like a terrorist attack, the election of an anti-immigrant president, or a global pandemic could strain a school's culture. For example, on September 11, 2001, she was working at Brooklyn International High School, which had a large Muslim student population and was located just across the East River from the Twin Towers. In the aftermath, she and her colleagues ensured their students' safety by walking them home and later worked to address the anti-Muslim sentiments their students faced daily.

By the time the COVID-19 crisis hit, Lara was no longer the principal of IHS, but the closing of the school was chaotic. Public schools in the city stayed open longer than private schools and universities, putting teachers and students at great risk of getting sick. In late March 2020, the school's beloved technology specialist, an immigrant from Colombia, remained to ensure all students had a laptop before being sent home. Tragically, he was later hospitalized and passed away after several months on a respirator. In addition to this heartbreaking loss in the community, emergency online learning presented unique challenges for English learners, and many of IHS's collaborative practices were difficult to adapt to a virtual environment. Teachers went as far as delivering food to students on bikes and accompanying students to the morgue to identify family members. When the district allowed schools to choose between returning to in-person instruction or remaining online, the IHS staff were divided. Some felt it was essential for students to have a physical place to go, while others believed it was too dangerous. The resulting social fractures were painful and sometimes seemed impossible to overcome.

In 2011, Lara could not have predicted what the school would face in 2020, but she was deeply committed to the school's future leadership. Bryan, a standout team leader, caught her attention. His passion for the school, deep investment in the students, and the respect that he commanded from his peers made him an obvious candidate for future leadership. Lara noted that Bryan intuitively understood the school's unique model, quickly embracing the student-centered approach and enjoying the challenge of pushing students' thinking through projects. As Lara looked to the future, she recognized that Bryan's strengths extended beyond his teaching. He was an effective teacher and had a talent for mentoring other teachers, making him a respected leader within the school. His ability to think beyond his own classroom and consider the broader impact of decisions on the entire school gave Lara confidence in his leadership potential. When she became the principal of IHS in 2011, Bryan was chosen to succeed her as assistant principal.

Lara saw similar qualities in Luz. She noticed that Luz also had a knack for understanding the broader implications of school decisions and was able to propose thoughtful solutions. Lara began encouraging Luz to consider moving into an administrative role, recognizing her potential to take on more leadership responsibilities. "I'm pushing her to go into an admin program," Lara explained. She had been planting the seed early on, just as her own principal had done for her, subtly suggesting that Luz would make a great administrator one day. When Luz had a baby, Lara saw it as the perfect opportunity to nudge her further in that direction.

She explained to her that, although an assistant principal position would still involve a lot of work, it offered more flexibility compared to the constant demands of classroom teaching. Lara knew that Luz might be ready for this change, especially given the challenges of balancing the classroom with her new role as a mother. She also saw that Bryan and Luz had different styles, personalities, and strengths. She believed that Luz would be the best option for AP if Bryan became the principal after her.

Lara shared this succession plan with me in May 2016, three years before she left the school. Upon her departure, Bryan stepped in as principal, with Luz assuming the role of assistant principal. A year later, Gail, the humanities teacher known for leading the Model UN exercise, joined Luz as a co-assistant principal. Ensuring strong leadership for the future was a key part of Lara's legacy and essential to the school's continued success. She attributes the school's ability to maintain high graduation and teacher retention rates during the COVID-19 crisis to the leadership of Bryan, Rosmery, and Gail—three individuals who fully embrace Lara's commitment to honoring and respecting the multifaceted lives of teachers.

In 2023, Lara became the Executive Director of the Internationals Network of Public Schools. Having started her career as a student teacher at an International High School, she now oversees the future of these schools. Her experiences of professionally growing up within Internationals have shaped her strong belief that the best way to ensure the school's continued success is by hiring people with a "deep knowledge" of the schools and the Internationals model.

I focus on Lara's story because it is inspiring but also because, in many ways, it is typical within the Internationals Network. There are currently seventeen Internationals Network high schools in New York City, and each one is like a branch of a family tree. The newest schools were founded by faculty who had previously taught at the oldest schools. For example, the founding team of the International High School for Health Sciences were teachers from International High School. The principal at Lafayette

IHS was a founding teacher at Prospect Heights IHS and worked at Union Square IHS. And the principal at Clairmont IHS is in the planning year to open a new school in Queens in 2025. These are only a few of countless examples of knowledge sharing across the network. Each school has an origin story that starts with knowledge sharing and often with founding members who have worked in or attended other schools. This appreciation of deep knowledge does not stop with staff members; it also extends to alumnae and family members.

"THEY MADE ME UNDERSTAND I WASN'T A USELESS STUDENT": VALUING THE DEEP KNOWLEDGE OF PARENTS AND ALUMNAE

At IHS, teachers and leaders recognize that deep knowledge does not just come from teaching at one of the schools; it can come from sending your child to the school or having been a student there. I witnessed this firsthand at IHS with former students like Manchu and the mother of a graduate of IHS, Lupe.

Manchu was born in rural Fujian, China, to parents who did not have the opportunity to finish middle school. His father eventually moved to the United States while his mother remained in China. When Manchu arrived in the United States in 2005, he faced significant challenges, especially in middle school, where he felt neglected and lost in the system.

Reflecting on his middle school experience, Manchu admitted, "All my three years of middle school, I have no idea what I have done. I learned nothing . . . for some reason, they still granted me the certificate to graduate. I have no idea how I earned that." The indifference of his middle school teachers left a lasting impact. He recalled, "I thought I was unattended by the teachers; they never cared for me. They didn't really ask how's your day today or stuff like that." This lack of support led to a pattern of truancy, where he would arrive at school hours late with no consequences. "My parents didn't even know," he shared, noting that the school never bothered to inform them of his absenteeism.

Things changed dramatically when Manchu started at IHS in the ninth grade. "When I first came to the ninth grade in this school, I still didn't understand a word in English. That's how bad I was in middle school," he said. However, IHS was a turning point for him. Unlike his middle school, the teachers at IHS noticed him, cared about his progress, and took active steps to support him. He vividly remembers a pivotal moment when his teachers intervened. "One day, they sat down with me. . . . That was the very first time I thought, these teachers actually care about me. They want to spend time sitting down with me and explaining the importance of education and the point of coming to [school in] the United States." This meeting had a profound effect on him, making him realize that he wasn't a "useless student," as he had been made to feel in China and in middle school.

After graduating from IHS in 2011, Manchu went on to Queensborough Community College, where he excelled, graduating with a 4.0 GPA. He then transferred to Queens College, where he completed his bachelor's degree in political science. Even though he wasn't a natural test-taker—struggling with standardized tests like the Regents and later the GRE—he persevered, knowing that his journey was about more than just scores.

Upon completing his studies at Queens College, Manchu returned to IHS, this time as a staff member. He started working in the college counseling office, helping seniors apply for college and financial aid.

> I like the job that I'm doing. It's a meaningful job. . . . I hope I can make a difference in some of the student's lives, and that's really what's important to me. . . . For me, it's a way to give back to the community. If there wasn't this high school, I wouldn't be who I am today, for sure. Several years ago, I had no interest in going to class. If it had not been for this high school . . . I probably would have dropped out.

Manchu's journey from a struggling middle school student to a successful college graduate and dedicated counselor is a testament to the power of supportive, caring educators and the transformative environment of IHS. But like Lara, Manchu's story is not rare. Manchu knows several former students who, like him, have returned to work in International High Schools because of the life-changing impact these schools had on them. "There are quite a few students who graduated from the international system and come back to work, not necessarily in this high school, but in international schools," he noted.

Alums are also recruited back to the schools because of their lived experiences and the deep knowledge of the schools that they gained by being students at International High Schools. Across the network, former students are now parent coordinators, security guards, paraprofessionals, social workers, Upward Bound advisors, substitute teachers, teachers, counselors, social workers, assistant principals, and even one principal. Hiring former students in these positions adds another level of community trust and appreciation.[13] It is an innovation in understanding the potential and reach of sanctuary as a practice in welcoming, welcoming back, and thinking about representation expansively.

In addition to hiring former students, many schools hire parents, mostly mothers like Lupe. Hiring mothers from the school community brings a unique and invaluable perspective to the school environment, fostering a sense of familiarity and care that deeply resonates with students. Lupe, a dedicated school aid and mother of a former IHS student, recalls her journey:

> *Yo vine a este país en el 2004. A los 10 meses de estar aquí, fui y traje mi hijo conmigo. . . . Cuando terminó Junior High, lo inscribí en esta escuela. . . . El no quería estar aquí porque no había equipo de béisbol, pero yo tenía miedo, yo decía esa escuela es muy grande para ti.*
>
> I came to this country in 2004. Ten months after being here, I went back and brought my son with me. . . . When he finished Junior High,

> I enrolled him in this school. . . . He didn't want to be here because there was no baseball team, but I was afraid, I said that [other] school is too big for you.

This decision ensured her son's safety and comfort and paved the way for her involvement in the school, where she eventually began working.

The impact of having a mother like Lupe on staff extends beyond her formal job duties. As someone who was already an active member of the parent association, she had a strong connection to the school even before she started working there. Lupe helped create a nurturing environment that extended beyond academics.

> *Ellos me dicen, "Miss, es cierto que [tu hijo] estudió aquí?" Y yo digo, sí, y donde está él? El está grande ya? A veces me visita y yo les digo, mira, ese es mi hijo.*
>
> They ask me, "Miss, is it true that [your son] studied here?" And I say, yes, and [they ask] where is he now? Is he grown? Sometimes he visits, and I tell them, look, that's my son. [showing them a picture]

Students look up to Lupe as a mother figure. Some even call her mom or mami. Her presence offers students a sense of continuity and belonging, as they know she is there to support them just as she did for her own son. This familial atmosphere, created by hiring parents like Lupe, is another example of what types of experiences and knowledge the school values.

RETHINKING EXPERIENCE, REPRESENTATION, AND KNOWLEDGE: COMMUNITY BUILDING AS AN INNOVATION IN SANCTUARY SCHOOLS

There is an ongoing debate in the United States about how to build a more diverse and resilient teaching force, particularly in urban schools serving traditionally marginalized youth. Teacher educators generally agree that teachers should be culturally aware and responsive to the needs of increasingly diverse student populations. They argue that non-white teachers can be better role models for students and increase student achievement.[14] Some argue that white, middle-class teachers, who make up the majority of the teaching force, may not fully grasp the challenges faced by traditionally marginalized youth who often experience racism, classism, xenophobia, and monolingual ideologies inside and outside of school.[15] Others suggest teacher preparation programs should focus on recruiting more racially diverse candidates while simultaneously equipping all teachers to address issues of race, ethnicity, and institutionalized racism in developmentally appropriate ways. Ideally, these teachers would incorporate culturally relevant teaching practices and confront their implicit biases through reflective practice.

Others argue that a higher quality and more diverse teaching force depends on initiatives like stronger unions, higher salaries, incentives to retain teachers in low-income areas, and more selective teacher preparation programs.[16] The debate over what makes a good teacher has been intensified by the emergence of alternative certification programs like Teach for America, Teaching Fellows, and NYC Men Teach, which have become popular routes to teacher certification and often prepare recent college graduates to begin teaching in under-resourced schools, sometimes in as few as eight weeks.

This chapter illustrates what a sanctuary school can do for graduates of teacher preparation programs when they are radically welcomed into the school environment. The stories of Carolina, Prasna, Lara, and Micha, among many others, show what happens when educators think expansively about extending the sanctuary practices of care, belonging, activism, and community beyond their immigrant students. When schools apply the same practices to their staff, educators flourish and, in turn, students succeed. While unconventional in many public schools, the labor practices shown in this chapter embody one of the five guiding principles of Internationals Network schools—"one learning model for all." Educators at IHS are diverse in many ways, yet they understand that their work does not exist in isolation; their identity and teaching approach are interconnected with those of their colleagues and students. Collective hiring practices that honor diverse experiences and identities, focusing on teacher retention and shared decision-making, are vital in fostering school environments where educators feel deeply invested in their roles and connected to their students. Hiring parents and former students and supporting their advancement into leadership positions strengthens the school culture and ensures an expansive community with a deep understanding of the sanctuary school's history and a shared vision for the future.

5

Advocacy and Coalition Building

Innovation to Support Sanctuary Practice

THANK YOU TO THE *whole Internationals team for supporting and planning this [National Leadership Retreat]. This retreat is probably the oldest structure we have at the Network, and truly the most powerful. This retreat started thirty years ago, even before the organization existed. It started with three principals going to dinner each month to talk about their practice and to learn from each other. And through that connection, teachers began to learn from each other, too. It's where some of our key practices began to develop; portfolios, collaborative learning, projects, performance assessments, internships, and the list goes on.*

These leaders chose to meet and learn together because what they were doing was something different and they knew that they needed each other in a system that didn't understand them or their work. They needed each other to learn from, support, and act as advocates together.

There is always power in numbers, especially in dealing with large, often opaque bureaucracy. The leaders began to think bigger and realized that developing an organization would enable them to grow this successful model and continue to create structures that allow educators to learn from each other, provide support to each other, and advocate together. That was when the leadership retreat started as we know it.

And the first retreats, where there were only maybe fifteen people around the table, was when the leaders developed the HELLO model as we know it.[1] *We codified what was working in our schools. And since then, we have been able to use this time to come together to continue to grow and share our practices to innovate and more fully develop this model and our newest leaders.*

From the beginning, our school leaders are people who have helped to shape the work of our organization, to grow as a leadership network. That is all of you! I am so thankful that you are all here for each other and to help shape our organization in its next chapter.

In her first address as the new Executive Director of the Internationals Network of Public Schools, Lara captured the essence of a grassroots movement that began nearly four decades ago. Speaking at the 2023 National Leadership Retreat, just eight weeks into her tenure, she reflected on the origins of the network—a story about three principals meeting over dinner, discussing their challenges, and finding strength in each other's company. When asked about the Network's origin story, Claire Sylvan, the first Executive Director of the Internationals Network, remembered more formal monthly gatherings of like-minded educators and activists. She explained:

> In the 1990s, as the second and third International High Schools were opening, the school leaders began meeting regularly—monthly gatherings that were more formal than the informal dinners held later on. I know this because I led those meetings. Back then, the network was known as the International Schools Partnership, or possibly

> International Partnership Schools—though the name is a bit fuzzy now, as many of those who were involved are now retired. We simply referred to it as "the Partnership." This initiative was initially funded by combining two major sources.[2]
>
> Over time, funding dried up, and only dinner among the principals was supported. However, during the period when funding was available, we created multiple structures that fostered relationships that persisted even after the money ran out. These structures included cross-school visitations, cross-school funded faculty projects, retreats among the three schools to co-design the performance assessment system, and full-day professional development sessions for teachers.
>
> When we eventually secured funding to open new schools and rebuild the formal network, it was during one of these dinners that the principals made the decision to move forward and asked me to take on the project—which is now the Internationals Network for Public Schools.

While Lara, who was a student teacher during this time, remembers the lore of the dinners, and Claire, who was at the gatherings, remembers the battle for funding and legitimacy in partnership with other radical educators and activists, it is clear that these gatherings were the seedbed for what would become a powerful collective of educators committed to information sharing, strategizing, and advocacy across schools who shared a clear instructional design and vision. These practices did not just evolve in isolation; they were forged in shared experience, where these leaders knew that only by working together could they navigate a system that often failed to understand or support their work with immigrant youth.

The retreat, now the network's oldest and most impactful tradition, grew from those initial meetings. What began with a handful of dedicated educators around a dinner table evolved into a national movement—one that continues to thrive on shared principles of mutual learning, support, and advocacy. As Lara highlighted, this tradition of collaboration and coalition-building is the backbone of the Internationals Network. It is a tradition that has helped codify the Internationals' successful educational models and empowered educators to challenge systemic barriers and advocate for their students.

The history of the Internationals Network is rooted in sustained advocacy, coalition-building, and a deep commitment to policies that meet the needs of immigrant and migrant students. Since the founding of the first International High School in 1985, the network has grown to thirty-one schools serving students from 119 countries, consistently prioritizing equity and holistic student development. Leaders within the network have been instrumental in driving policy changes at both the state and district levels, contributing to initiatives like the Seal of Biliteracy and advocating for more flexible graduation timelines for English learners.

This chapter explores how high-level advocacy efforts around assessment directly impacted the daily lives of teachers and students at International High School (IHS) during this study. The chapter begins by discussing the coalition-building strategies employed by Internationals Network leaders to secure a waiver from New York State, allowing the use of Performance Assessments in place of traditional exit exams. It then explores how this decade-long effort led to significant changes in what and how teachers at IHS were able to teach.

STATE EXAMS AND THE FIGHT FOR PERFORMANCE ASSESSMENT, 1995–2015

The Regents exams have been a cornerstone of the New York State education system since 1865. Between 1865 and 1995, the tests evolved into comprehensive exams given in a variety of subjects but did not significantly impact a student's ability to graduate. However, in 1995, the Board of Regents began mandating a set of standards and corresponding exit exams in seven subjects that all students had to pass to graduate.

Innovative educators and advocates for marginalized students began to protest this decision almost immediately. Claire, who was a teacher at that time, recalled, "It was a disaster for kids in special education and the English learners. The EL graduate rate was at 28 percent at one point." At the same time, teachers from the first International High School opened two new schools: Manhattan International High School in 1993 and Brooklyn International High School in 1994. Leaders at these three schools, along with other educators across the city, recognized the need for a different approach to the testing policies that were marginalizing nontraditional students and punishing teachers who worked with them.

A group of educators, including Deborah Meier, a New York City principal, Steve Phillips, superintendent of the alternative superintendency in New York City, Eric Nadlestern, principal of International High School, and Ann Cook, along with others began advocating for an alternative assessment option. Their efforts resulted in a waiver being granted to twenty-one schools in 1995, allowing them to use performance assessments instead of standardized tests. This decision was made by Thomas Sobol, the state commissioner of education, who was focused on reducing bureaucracy and supporting schools in urban areas. Sobol was interested in learning more about how performance assessments were being used at innovative schools and saw the potential to expand these practices.

The principals of the two new International High Schools, who had been meeting regularly with Eric to discuss their shared challenges, decided to form a network partnership to develop a performance-based assessment system, among other innovations across schools. Unfortunately, little data was collected on performance assessment during this time by the state, and Sobol resigned in frustration when Governor George Pataki was elected. Sobol's successor, Commissioner Richard Mills, shifted accountability policies back to a focus on standardization and testing. In 1999, Mills revoked the waiver after a panel that he appointed argued that tests were the only valid and appropriate form of assessment. The next five years were marked by intense legal battles and advocacy from educators, students, parents, and education experts.[3] Because of their work, the waiver was eventually reinstated and extended in 2004.

It took nearly another decade to expand the waiver to additional schools.[4] In 2013, International High School, along with the other schools in the Internationals Network that were not included in the original waiver, were granted a waiver.[5] This allowed IHS to replace several standardized tests with performance assessments, often referred to as PBATs at IHS (pronounced "P-bats," an acronym for performance-based assessment tasks), to evaluate students' readiness for graduation.

Today, IHS is one of around fifty schools in New York State, the majority of which are in NYC, where students complete a combination of standardized exams and PBATs instead of the five Regents exams that most students in New York State are required to pass to graduate.[6] During this study, IHS was in its third year of using PBATs and was still in the process of transitioning from a project-based curriculum that still had to prepare students for tests to one centered around project-based learning and graduation-level performance assessments, particularly in the upper grades.

As of 2024, IHS students must still pass the math and English Language Arts Regents exams to graduate. They also complete six performance assessments, including a native language project, a personal statement, a literary essay, a research paper, an original science experiment, and a math model. Each PBAT is designed to help students develop content knowledge and writing, reading, speaking, and research skills. The personal statement often serves as a draft of their college essay, helping students articulate their immigration stories. The native language project, typically completed in the earlier grades, allows students to draw on their multilingual backgrounds to showcase their home language and culture.[7] Each PBAT becomes part of a student's graduation portfolio. The following sections explain how.

SHARING AND LEARNING THROUGH THE NETWORK: THE PORTFOLIO COMMITTEE, 2015–2017

During the partnership years, from 1995 to 1998, there was a monthly meeting, which at first included only principals. Later, assistant principals and teacher leaders were invited as well. When the Internationals Network was formed in 2003, they continued these monthly meetings between principals and eventually started a professional development committee with representatives from each school and monthly principal mentor meetings.

In 2016, I saw how the networkwide meetings were used to strategize and share information by observing the Portfolio Committee. The committee was in its second year of meetings when I began attending. Over the course of two academic years, thirty-four teacher representatives from all fifteen schools met once a month to begin creating a guide for schools on how to transition from testing to performance assessment.

The Portfolio Committee operated collaboratively, with members from different schools sharing and discussing their practices to create unified guidelines. Each meeting was dedicated to a different topic, and representatives from each school would discuss how to balance a unified teaching model with the flexibility for individual schools to adapt practices to their specific contexts.[8]

The Portfolio Committee began with the question, "What is a Performance Assessment, and how do we explain this to parents, teachers, and other community members?" The group agreed to define portfolio assessment as a method of evaluating students that involves collecting and reviewing a range of their work throughout their high school career rather than relying on a single test. The committee agreed that performance assessment aligns with the principle of experiential learning, where students engage in hands-on projects and real-world tasks. As a group, they read research that suggests portfolio assessments have several advantages over standardized tests because they are inclusive and accommodate all students, including English Language Learners (ELLs). The research they cite in the guide argues that, unlike traditional tests that measure knowledge through isolated questions, portfolio assessments allow students to showcase their learning through various types of work, such as essays, research papers, and lab reports.[9]

Each month, the group would debate the common requirements and systems for portfolios and how each school might adapt the specifics to fit their context. In the process of drafting chapters, such as record keeping and rating, they examined and compared protocols, physical and digital record-keeping methods, and grading systems across various schools. In one of the meetings that I observed, they were focused on understanding how portfolio grades could be recorded and communicated, particularly in relation to transcripts and how colleges interpret these records. For example, they included a section on communicating the significance of portfolio projects to colleges and the Department of Education. The group also considered the role of grading and norming, debating the merits of holistic versus departmental grading, and discussed strategies like video norming to standardize assessments across the network. Their approach reflected a balance of sharing established practices from the schools that had been using performance assessment for over a decade, addressing concerns about how portfolios are perceived externally, and refining internal processes to support accurate and fair student evaluations.

The final guide took two full academic years to write because the committee engaged in consensus building and information sharing across fifteen schools to ensure that it was definitive, institutionalizing portfolio assessments as an essential aspect of Internationals Network schools. The final document details the types of student projects each school must do according to the agreement with New York State and suggests practices for their design and execution. There is a chapter on mentoring that emphasizes the role of adults in guiding and supporting students through their portfolio development, and a chapter on panel presentations explaining how students present their work to panels, and the expectations for these presentations. The chapter on rating covers the criteria and rubrics used to evaluate student work and ensure fair assessments. The guide also covers how revision, accommodations, and record-keeping should focus on iterative improvement for diverse learners and should be documented to comply with the waiver agreement. Finally, the guide ends with a chapter on building a portfolio culture.

As the guide was being developed, school leaders were simultaneously sending teams of teachers to visit other schools to observe portfolio processes in a practice they called "intervisitation."[10] Over the course of four years, I was able to participate in intervisitations, focus group interviews, and observation of mentoring at two other International High Schools. One was an original waiver school and the other was transitioning to a performance assessment school on the same timeline at IHS. I was able to see both the challenges of the transition and the possibilities of the future by observing schools using the same guiding principles and philosophies on learning and assessment, but with an almost ten-year gap in figuring out how to transition away from testing mentalities; design projects that helped students develop writing, research, and presentation skills; figure out the logistics of mentoring; and communicate the evaluation process to stakeholders. As the guide was being developed, teachers at IHS were innovating in real time to adapt to a new assessment policy opportunity while also remaining beholden to the English Language Arts Regents exam that was often a major barrier to graduation for many of their students.

"YOU CAN'T FAKE A PBAT": TRANSITIONING FROM A TESTING SCHOOL TO A PBAT SCHOOL, 2015–CURRENT

"Teaching to the test" never really happened at IHS, even before the waiver.[11] "We had already been doing the work, doing the project-based learning. The waiver just let us focus more on making that work better," Lara explained. Before receiving the waiver, teachers in other content areas felt conflicted about how to use instructional time. Lauren, the social studies teacher who was teaching about the election, remembers:

> When I came here, the students were taking Regents—so they had to pass Global, US, ELA, one Math Regents—I guess Algebra—and the Biology. I remember when I first got here—the original rule for [English learners] was a 55 was okay for graduation requirements. But they were phasing that out by—I guess—making it more rigorous. I came in as that phasing out was about to happen. So, the first year they were allowed four 55s but had to have one 65. Then it went to three 55s, and two 65s. Until it came to the year that they would have to have 65 or better on every Regents exam—just like every other student in New York City—and that is the way it was for the past five or six years.

As accountability expectations changed in ways that she believed were harmful to students, she felt more pressure to prepare them for the test even though it went against the philosophy of the school. Lara explained how challenging it was to push teachers to use projects while also being beholden to high-stakes exit exams.

> There was always the pressure of the Regents . . . we never felt that we had to do every single thing on the Regents, but I think the way that we attacked them before was that we felt like we could do these big topics and bring in some of the student experiences to those topics and the kids would still do fine on the Regents, and that was fine.

Teachers would want to design projects on the immigrant experience but would have to incorporate topics that "didn't quite fit," for example, asking students to memorize facts about Ellis Island instead of focusing on more contemporary routes to the United States that are not covered in the exam but are more relevant to students' lived experiences.

With the waiver, teachers began to reevaluate what they were teaching and why. When prompted to describe the process of adapting instruction to meet the performance assessment waiver, Lauren explained:

> I have definitely cut back on content. I think my struggle as a history teacher is that they are going to college, they are not native to this country, and I worry that they are at a disadvantage not knowing what the Great Depression was about. But now with the PBAT are they going in more prepared? Knowing what a thesis is? What arguments are? How to cite their sources? How to write a bibliography? Yes. And do they need to know that in college? Definitely. I am just trying to find that balance in my teaching.

The process of preparing students for a performance assessment, particularly among teachers who were accustomed to test-based accountability, was difficult; even three years into the process, Lara explained, some teachers were "still kind of holding on to some of those big topics that we don't really have to hold on to anymore."

The work of becoming a performance assessment school and developing a culture around those practices is ongoing and challenging. Teachers at IHS believe the transition from the use of Regents exams to performance assessments created time and space for them to develop a more culturally and linguistically responsive project-based curriculum to meet their students' emergent linguistic and academic needs. It takes time and experience to design and implement projects that teach students to develop original arguments and write clearly. Teachers seek feedback from their peers to strengthen their projects before beginning them with students and intermittently throughout the process. Lara describes the work as a process of conversations across grades:

> I think [collaboration] is making our [PBATs] stronger . . . better aligned. I think it's a vertical conversation that just has to happen now. Right, it's like—well what are you doing for the PBATs? What are we doing?

> How does what I do build off what you're doing? And, what kind of scaffolds are you providing in ninth and tenth grade that we have to pull on in eleventh grade? All of those conversations are happening now, so I think it really helps to just bring people together and then think about how we're all working towards these goals together.

Even with the waiver, students still have to pass the English Language Arts (ELA) Regents exam, but because students take far fewer tests now that the school has the waiver, teachers are more relaxed about the ELA test. Teachers assume that most of their students will fail the test several times. Still, they let students sit for the exam up to three times a year anyway to get a benchmark score and begin an appeal process that could ultimately end in the student graduating with a lower score. If students fail the test but achieve a grade of 50, they can appeal, take the test two more times, and eventually still graduate if their teachers show they have passed their English class and taken advantage of other supports, like a test prep elective.[12]

Educators see the ELA test as part of a system to be gamed rather than a tool for improving instruction. They strategize about how different scores can help their students navigate life after high school. Lara explained:

> We try to get them 70 on the math and 75 on the English. For some of them, I'm thrilled that they're getting a 65. But [the college counselor] does a lot of the college transition stuff. So, I think she's really been pushing to get the kids to get the 75.

Students who are able to earn a 75 or higher on the ELA or math exams do not have to take remedial classes at the City University of New York (CUNY) campuses and can begin earning college credits more quickly. This is the goal of some students while simply earning a high enough test score to graduate is the motivation of other students and their teachers.

The teachers at IHS have embraced spending more time on the performance assessment process and less time dedicated to testing preparation. They perceive the performance assessment as a more rigorous assessment of student skills and knowledge and better preparation for college and career than standardized tests. One teacher explained it in this way:

> You can't fake a PBAT.... With [standardized tests] you can get lucky... guess on a few questions... and squeak by. I have trained kids to take the state history test who speak no English. You can't give a kid a script for a PBAT.

Students echo this sentiment and report that the PBATs allow them to study a topic deeply. As a result, they become more confident in writing, speaking publicly, and defending arguments in English. One student explained:

> The PBAT is better. In the PBAT you have to present what you learned in school, in class. With the exit exam, they are going to ask you a question about something you never learned about. With the PBAT you got a chance.

A well-designed project sets clear expectations for students. Guided by rubrics, teachers at IHS work with discipline teams to develop these projects before sharing them with other teachers in the school or the students. This allows teachers to incorporate peer feedback before beginning a project with students.

Students experience the Regents exam as a guessing game and the PBAT as a more rigorous and equitable process. One fifth-year senior, who did not graduate on time due to incomplete PBATs, still describes the PBATs as "easy, because we do them in class," compared to the Regents exam, which is, according to one student:

> A bunch of stuff we have never seen before. On the test, you have to sometimes guess. The teachers do test prep and stuff... but that does not guarantee that if you go to that class you are going to pass.

When I asked if showing up for a PBAT guarantees a passing score, she explained that it did not.

> Last time I presented I didn't pass the math PBAT because I did it all on the computer. They asked me, "now do it on your own without the computer." I got to the graphing part and got lost. So, I failed the presentation part. I had to present again to show that I knew how to do the calculations.

Needing to make revisions on a performance assessment does not feel punitive or confusing to students like failing the Regents exam might. Instead, they see it as an indicator of their mastery of a topic at a particular moment in time and know that they can rewrite and represent the project until they are able to meet the expectations outlined in the rubrics.

"SHOULD I START OVER AND DO SOMETHING DIFFERENT?": IMPROVING INSTRUCTION AND CREATING OPPORTUNITIES TO SPEAK

In contrast to the process of administering standardized tests, designing performance assessments fosters reflection about curricular choices. Teachers believed that the waiver allowed them to improve projects they have taught in the past to make them more rigorous and relevant for students. One English teacher explained how she has become more reflective about her project design. Creating a performance assessment project forces her to ask herself, "Is this project that I've been doing [for years] worthwhile? Is it something that's actually helping students [learn what they need to learn] or can I enhance it? Or should I start over and do something different?"

Diego, the English teacher who had taught *The Alchemist* several times before the waiver, decided that his theme for the 2016–2017 school year would be Journeys. He began the year by teaching a unit about travel poems, including Robert Frost's *The Road Not Taken*. He followed the teaching of *The Alchemist* with a unit on *The Little Prince* because each of these texts was related to the year's theme.

The biggest change that he made since the waiver was incorporating literature circles. In previous years, Diego had required students to write a literary essay after reading the text. After the waiver, however, he knew that the students would need to understand the text more deeply to develop their own thesis and analyze the text in writing and orally as part of their performance assessment. Previously, his goal was to help students pass the state's English Language Arts exam; now, his students must pass the exam and write and defend an original thesis in an analysis of *The Alchemist* and one other text they had read in class. He explained:

> I am thinking about how can I get them to do better with literary analysis. I have been working a lot, personally, for the last few years, on creating literature circles. I really like that activity for students because they get to engage in the reading. It is not just giving them comprehension questions to answer—they are reading and discovering certain things within these roles. I have a literary seeker—and their job is to find literary elements. I have a word searcher—they are focused on vocabulary words with their team. The passage picker focuses on important passages . . . and they all had an opportunity and a chance to do each role at least once. Now, with [performance assessment], I think, ok, we [have figured out] literature circles, but how can I get them to build evidence? I am still working on it. I think I am getting close to getting it where I want it to be.

I observed Diego's class for several weeks while the text was being taught and attended a class discussion in which students engaged in an evidence-based discussion and debated about key aspects of the text. I talked with several students as they drafted their literary essays who were able to analyze Santiago's experiences more deeply through the lens of their own migration journey. When I asked one student about the project, she responded:

> I think the main idea of the book was that through your journey, you meet many people that teach you new experiences. And your final goal is just as important as all the lessons that you learn through people. All the experiences that you learn, I think it's really important. Santiago was going through something, so he was basically trusting the process and enjoying the journey, which leads to improvement in himself and growth.

In addition to acknowledging students' shared experiences related to migration, Diego scaffolded his instruction to meet the needs of students at different levels of language acquisition and literacy by providing copies of *The Alchemist* in English, Spanish, and Mandarin. He also had the book in graphic novel form in several languages.

Over several weeks, the class read the book aloud in English, pausing to take notes and complete their literature circle roles. Students then generated questions and gathered evidence from the text to prepare for a Socratic Seminar. On the day of the seminar, students were divided into two groups: half sat in an inner circle, while the other half sat in an outer circle. Each student in the inner circle had to ask and answer questions posed by their peers, using evidence from the text to support their arguments. Meanwhile, students in the outer circle observed a peer in the inner circle. They filled out a sheet that tallied how many times the inner student spoke and provided space to note what the student did well and what they could improve on.

I observed the seminar over several days and across different classes. The twelfth-grade students used sentence starters I had seen introduced in the ninth- and tenth-grade classrooms, like "I'd like to add to what you said. . ." or, "The evidence I've seen suggests something different because. . ." Students spoke in confident English, occasionally mispronouncing words or attempting to translate expressions from their home languages.

In one exchange, a Bangladeshi student tried to explain what she learned from the book. Her initial attempt was mumbled, prompting a classmate to ask, "What?" and another to say, "Can you repeat the first part?" Instead of becoming insecure or shy, she took a deep breath and tried again, saying loudly, "If you are dealing with a bad day or a bad time... it could be a better day tomorrow." She scrunched her face in frustration, sensing it was not exactly what she wanted to convey. Another student chimed in, "There is a saying about it being a bad day, not a bad life," and another offered, "There is a saying about something like a rainbow . . . you can't have a rainbow without rain." The class erupted in excited cheers about their collective breakthrough in textual analysis.

Teachers felt that the waiver allowed them more time to help students develop confidence in speaking, oral communication, and presentation skills. Group projects after the waiver were more likely to culminate in both a final piece of written work and some form of presentation, like the Socratic Seminar in Diego's class. In these low-risk speaking opportunities, students are reminded of phrases that help them agree or disagree with their peers, interject, ask for clarification, or redirect a conversation.

Students are also taught about a process for engaging in academic conversations when they are prompted by a teacher to, for example, provide a page number and location of the evidence from a text they are using to strengthen an argument. Even in my conversations with groups of students, far from the eyes of teachers, I noticed students using these phrases to engage one another in a conversation. For example, in a student focus group comparing the experience of performance assessments to that of the Regents exam, one began to talk about his preference for performance assessment. A second student added, "Can I go on from where he left off?" The student then explained his perspective further before another student used a similar transition to continue the conversation.

I found how they were speaking with one another as compelling as their comparisons of the test versus the performance assessment. One teacher joked that in the ninth and tenth grades, teaching this style of communication and speaking engagement is like "watching paint dry . . . but it works." The teacher went on to explain:

> I used to be like, how are they ever going to learn this stuff if we don't teach them English first. In my first few years, I really pushed to teach them more grammar, but after six years of watching the process [of content-language integration], I am a believer. They actually do learn the content and the language at the same time. It seems slower, but it is actually faster in the end.

Teachers' approaches to teaching English through content-language integration rather than through drills and memorization are evident in the scaffolding strategies used in every classroom, including Physical Education. "We are all literacy teachers," one P.E. teacher told me. This looks like delivering short, simple instructions multiple times and projecting instructions on the whiteboard to give students visual clues. Students with more advanced English skills are asked to translate instructions for other students. It involves teaching students how to annotate texts, use dictionaries and translation apps, structure essays one sentence at a time, and edit draft after draft in suggestion mode on Google docs.

"BECAUSE OF WHAT'S GOING ON WITH OUR STUDENTS, I HAVE TO FOCUS ON TEACHING RACISM": TEACHING AUTHENTIC CONTENT AND COMBATING ANTI-IMMIGRANT NARRATIVES

The waiver also allowed teachers the freedom to adapt projects in real time to address the lived experiences of their students. In 2017, one of the ninth- and tenth-grade teams had a number of their students either deported or appealing active deportation orders in court. As a result, this team decided that along with increasing social-emotional and mental health support to all students, they would also adjust their curriculum to help students better understand and articulate what they were experiencing as immigrants in the United States at this juncture in time. For example, Micah, the social studies teacher who received lots of support as a new teacher, abandoned his planned project on revolutions and redesigned the project to focus on the intersection of racism and xenophobia. He explained:

> As a social studies educator, I try to pull a lot of stuff from current events [to design a] curriculum that meets the needs of the students. . . . For example, generally, I would teach revolutions at this time of the year, but I thought that because of what's going on with our students, I have to focus on teaching racism.

Micah elaborated on the project he designed to help students develop vocabulary for describing their experiences:

> [Students] have talked about how they feel angry and scared and feel that immigrants are unwelcome in this country. We talk a lot about how immigrants are being treated and the reality that we live under an administration that is racist and says racist things and creates racist policies. . . . [In the project,] students are examining, analyzing, and internalizing acts of discrimination, prejudice, racism and acts of tolerance, acceptance, and equity. They've been using pictures to analyze them. I found pictures of segregation, sexism, welcoming immigrants, Islamophobia, and white supremacy, like Richard Spencer's quotes and what he believes.[13] Then students look at them and they decide, what is it? An act of discrimination or an act of tolerance?

Through analyzing these photographs, students are building their own vocabulary lists. The teacher explained that they are learning about a spectrum, with acts of discrimination on one end and acts of acceptance on the other. Students created two sets of words to describe what they see: one list includes terms like prejudice, discrimination, racism, bigotry, and oppression, while the other features words like ally, protect, resilience, activist, and outreach. In the next stage of the project, Micah plans to shift the conversation to "immigration through the lens of xenophobia":

> I'm going to be going over the five major myths that people have about immigrants. One of them is that it's easy to enter the United States. Another one is that immigrants are all dangerous rapists and murderers. You know where that came from. Another one is immigrants don't want to learn English. Another one is that immigrants don't pay taxes and are a plague on the economy. So, having these prejudices and then using stereotypes to label all immigrants exacerbates xenophobia. That is like the inner understanding of this. Then, students can understand that it's based on myths and false stories.

The project culminated in students creating their own public service announcement about discrimination related to one of the topics they studied in depth. Micah believes that equipping students with the new vocabulary and data they've learned allows them to confront myths in a powerful and empowering way, an experience that wouldn't be as impactful if he were simply preparing them for a test. He also thinks this knowledge could help students stand up for themselves when faced with prejudice based on immigration myths.

In our interview, Micah highlighted that he designed the project to resonate with his students' lived experiences as immigrants in the United States. His focus on addressing the xenophobic rhetoric that students encounter in the news and on social media has not only deepened their understanding of the US political system but also increased their sense of agency. They learned to identify and confront specific issues like institutionalized racism, which directly affect them as immigrants. As with all his projects, he ensured that students would read, write, speak, conduct research, and develop original arguments throughout the process. These are essential skills that will prepare them for their final performance assessment in social studies—an argumentative essay—in the eleventh and twelfth grade.

"SEEING A DIFFERENT SIDE OF STUDENTS": FOSTERING SELF-EXPRESSION AND CONFIDENCE IN CULMINATING PRESENTATION

All performance assessments at IHS culminate in an oral presentation to a panel of three or more adults, as well as often including peers. I have observed over one hundred PBAT presentations at IHS and other Internationals Network schools. I still return to IHS nearly every year in January and June during what is known as "Regent's weeks" across New York City high schools. While most students take exams for days on end, while others who have passed all their Regents exams stay home, IHS students and others in performance assessment schools come to school to work on completing or presenting their final projects. The Internationals Network's efforts reclaimed weeks previously dedicated to test preparation and reduced the excessive time spent on standardized testing, giving schools more opportunities to focus on meaningful teaching and learning.

Like the other PBAT presentations I had observed throughout the year, Patricia's presentation followed the same format. The panels usually begin with the student making a formal introduction, thanking the panelists for attending, and summarizing his or her presentation. After that overview, the student is asked to leave the room so that the panelists can discuss the papers in question. Panelists are given the papers before the panel and often come with questions already generated. The student is invited back into the room and is usually given ten minutes to present the work and ten minutes to answer panelist questions. Teachers and visitors often compare the panels to an oral defense one might do to defend a thesis or dissertation.

Patricia introduced herself by reading from index cards in her shaking hands. Her mouth had gone dry from nervousness and sounded sticky when she spoke. Before she began her presentation, Lara asked her to leave the room. The three of us began to discuss Patricia's essays using a rubric to guide our conversation. We each read the essay before the panel began and filled out our own rubrics. Even before Patricia presented, we had an idea of what grade she would earn in the end based on her writing. In her literary essay, Patricia wrote about the theme of hope in the texts *The Circuit* by Francisco Jimenez and *The Boy Without a Flag* by Abraham Rodriguez. In her eight-page essay, she compared and contrasted the stories of two characters who, like Patricia, were coming of age in immigrant families in the United States. Her essay drew on evidence from these texts to explore issues of learning a new language and developing an American identity.

The panelists evaluate each student's PBAT essay and oral presentation using a rubric that was developed and standardized by teachers and leaders from Internationals Network schools. There are rubrics for four mandatory content areas (English, social studies, science, math), a native language project, and a personal statement that are used across schools and have identical formats. Teachers at Network schools have also developed rubrics in engineering, art, and other content areas that may not be offered at all schools. They often present these rubrics and their corresponding projects at the annual network professional development to share what they have done with other educators. Each rubric spans four possible scores: three passing scores (*outstanding, good,* and *competent*), and one failing score (*needs revision*). Each content area rubric addresses multiple "bands" or performance standards. For example, in the math rubric, the seven bands include: a) problem solving and planning, b) reasoning process, c) fluency, d) connections, e) representations, f) communication, and g) presentation.

On the rubric, each of these bands is linked to a Common Core State Standard. Students earn a "competent" by providing a "limited explanation of how the evidence presented supports each argument" or an "outstanding" by having "thoroughly explained and analyzed the connection between all evidence and arguments being made." The rubrics are written using language designed to encourage students to engage in higher-order thinking. For example, students are asked to explore the "implications" or significance of their project and to make connections between what they learn in school and what is happening in the larger community, country, and world.

The adults involved in the evaluation include teachers, administrators, counselors, social workers, and outside evaluators, like me. The three of us on Patricia's panel discussed her thesis, essay organization, use of evidence and analysis, the connections she made between the two texts, her language use, and writing conventions. In some bands, she earned a score of outstanding, but in others, her analytic and writing skills only reflected a score of competent. We developed questions to ask her about the bands in which her writing was weaker. For twenty minutes, we considered the merit of Patricia's essay. Does it have a strong thesis? Is it well organized? Does she use "varied and convincing evidence that thoroughly supports" her argument? Are the connections she makes between the two texts "insightful"? We generated a list of questions to ask Patricia when she was back in the room.

The last band on the rubric is for the presentation. This band requires students to clearly communicate an understanding of the paper's arguments. It also rewards students for developing new ideas or presenting relevant evidence, arguments, and analyses that may not have appeared in the paper. A practiced presentation could move Patricia's grade up or down slightly in any of the bands. Teachers at IHS assert that the oral component of the PBAT presentation is as important as the writing part because the "speaking modality" of language learning is often neglected in traditional classrooms, particularly for English learners. In interviews, teachers recalled stories of students who were outstanding writers but who would fall apart in presentations and others who struggled to articulate their ideas in writing but performed well in the presentations. Teachers believed that watching their students present helped them to better understand their students' strengths and weaknesses in both content and language acquisition.

I did not know Patricia well before this PBAT panel. She rarely spoke in class and was very shy. However, she surprised her teachers and me in February when she played a leading role in the school's rendition of *A Midsummer Night's Dream*. As Hermia, she boldly professed her love of Lysander and wailed loudly when he abandoned her for Helena, generating shrieks of shock, laughter, and appreciation from the audience. Her English teacher turned to me in the middle of the play, in delighted surprise, saying that this was a side of Patricia no one had seen in her three years at the school. We were not sure what side of Patricia we would see today in her first oral defense of her work.

After discussing her literary essay and personal statement and generating a list of questions for Patricia, we invited her back into the room. Lara directed her to take fifteen minutes to talk about her literary essay. Using index cards, Patricia systematically discussed her thesis, summarized the texts, and outlined the evidence she selected to support the arguments in her paper. As the minutes ticked by, her hands began to steady, and her voice became more confident. The shy Patricia was replaced by a confident Hermia—she knew she was performing. After her presentation, Patricia engaged in a conversation with us about the texts and her assessment of them, sharing:

> I connect my story [with the boy in *The Circuit*] because, as I said before, I also crossed the border and I know that feeling when you are behind the river and then you say oh, that's America, and that's how I'm going to get my dreams to come true. Even though I was scared about crossing that river, my hope was more powerful than my fears.

Patricia's transformation during her presentation—from a nervous student to a confident speaker—illustrates the powerful impact of meaningful assessments that connect with students' lived experiences. By linking her personal story to the themes in *The Circuit*, Patricia not only showed her understanding of the text but also highlighted the value of PBATs in fostering self-expression and confidence. This moment reflects how advocacy and policy efforts influence educational practices at IHS and how, in turn, these practices shape policy. At the school level, educators, leaders, and staff determine what students need and interpret how those needs align with policy. While advocacy opens the door for improved and more appropriate educational practices, it alone does not create them. This ongoing process of learning, advocating, and influencing policy creates the conditions that allow students to engage deeply with their learning and make meaningful connections to their own lives.

RETHINKING POLITICS, ADVOCACY, AND COALITION BUILDING: EXPANDING SANCTUARY INNOVATIONS TO POLICY WORK AND SYSTEMS CHANGE

Over the last twenty years, a coalition of educators, leaders, and grassroots advocates from the Internationals Network of Public Schools has partnered with other educators involved in the small and progressive schools movement, as well as organizations like Advocates for Children, New York Association for Bilingual Education, the New York Immigration Coalition Ed Collaborative and Diploma Coalition, Make the Road New York, the City University of New York Initiative on Immigration and Education, the National Newcomer Network, and the Bill and Melinda Gates Foundation, along with numerous other advocacy groups, nonprofits, and foundations. This extensive collaboration has created the conditions for innovative teaching and meaningful learning at IHS, New York State network schools, consortium schools, and other public schools across the country, enhancing what teachers can teach and how students can learn. These efforts have given teachers the freedom to craft meaningful and authentic learning experiences for immigrant students learning English and adjusting to life in the United States. By grounding education in the lived experiences of these students, teachers have successfully kept them engaged and invested in their learning and empowered them to speak back to harmful, inaccurate, and racist anti-immigrant narratives. Classroom innovations, bolstered by a broader social justice movement, underscore the power of advocacy and coalition building to challenge misinformed education policies at the state and local level and combat anti-immigrant narratives in the classroom.

Lara and her staff at Internationals, many of whom are now lifelong friends, retired principals who have come back to work for the network, are still very much involved in ongoing policy and advocacy efforts at local, state, and national levels, and they have made substantial gains in their efforts to create space for more inclusive and supportive educational environments. For example, due in part to the work of Internationals Network staff and other progressive advocacy groups, New York State announced in 2021 that it was in the planning phase of an initiative called the "Performance-Based Learning and Assessment Networks (PLAN) program" to explore the conditions and supports that schools and educators need to shift their instructional practices and build statewide systems of assessment that draw upon multiple measures. The advisors to the plan include the current Superintendent of Affinity Schools, of which Internationals and the Consortium are a part, the former Executive Director of the Internationals Network, and a social studies teacher from Claremont International High School.

Then, in June 2024, after a meeting of the New York State Board of Regents, the most powerful group in setting state education policy, the New York State Education Department (NYSED) announced a new vision for transforming graduation requirements in November 2024. The new initiative, as outlined by NYSED, includes allowing students to demonstrate mastery through various methods, such as work-based learning experiences, dual credit programs, and approved assessments like performance assessments.[14] Their recommendation to remove specific diploma assessment requirements, such as the Regents exams, echoes the Internationals Network's long-standing advocacy for more flexible and equitable graduation criteria.[15]

The advocacy and coalition-building efforts of the Internationals Network, which started with educators sharing information across schools and advocating for better systems as a collective, have expanded the concept of sanctuary by engaging in policy initiatives to ensure that students in their network schools are provided with every opportunity to learn and thrive. They also see it as their responsibility to influence local, state, and national policymaking, aiming to extend innovative sanctuary practices to as many immigrant students as possible through systemic change. The history of policy changes around assessment in New York reflects the principles of innovative sanctuary and radical welcoming, as educators and advocates recognized, responded to, and addressed the state's failures to adequately and equitably meet the needs of their immigrant students and school communities. By advocating for system-wide changes, they have ensured that the next generation of immigrant students, especially those from marginalized backgrounds, will be more fairly evaluated on their knowledge as they work toward earning a high school diploma. The intersection of advocacy, coalition building, and innovation has not only reshaped educational practices in individual schools but also affirmed the vital role of schools as political spaces. These spaces, committed to progressive, well-researched practices of care, belonging, protection, innovation, and empowerment, can transform how we think about the potential of schools to be innovative sanctuaries for immigrant youth.

Part II of this book has explored the innovative ways in which sanctuary practices at IHS and within the Internationals Network have evolved to create transformative educational spaces for immigrant students and educators. Through the development of a supportive schoolscape, the intentional fostering of an interconnected and diverse school community, and the expansion of sanctuary through advocacy and systemic change, these chapters demonstrate how sanctuary is not a static concept but a dynamic force driving educational innovation. The conclusion of this book will focus on what mindset shifts are needed in schools throughout the country to foster practices of radical welcome and sanctuary that can continue to inspire and shape a future in which immigrant students can go to schools that holistically support their rights to an education, celebrate their knowledge, and empower them to take on life in the United States, regardless of the political moment.

Conclusion

Radical Actions and Mindset Shifts to Transform Schools into Sanctuaries

THROUGH THE STORIES of educators, students, parents, graduates, and leaders, this book has illustrated how a radically different school has created a radically different educational space for immigrant students, even in times of division and divisiveness. Taken as a whole, this book asks you, the reader, to imagine new ways of providing sanctuary to all vulnerable children and youth. The conceptualization of sanctuary as dynamic and expansive, rather than static policy, lays the groundwork for key mindset shifts around the possibility of sanctuary in reshaping the educational experiences of immigrant youth. This chapter lays out four key mindset shifts that educators must make to create true sanctuary for immigrant students. Following these mindset shifts are sections detailing the actions and policies that flow from a new way of thinking. The intent of this chapter is to ground these mindset shifts not in the head but in the hands. As the arms of the Voces de la Frontera poster embraced immigrant students in welcome, so too must they do the work of sanctuary.

RADICAL MINDSET SHIFTS: A CLEAR VISION FOR SANCTUARY SCHOOLS THAT INNOVATE BEYOND PROTECTION TO EMPOWER IMMIGRANT YOUTH

This book began in a tumultuous time for immigrant communities and the schools that served them. The first Trump administration was particularly cruel to immigrant families seeking asylum at the border and particularly racist and Islamophobic in its creation of policy. However, immigrant communities have been riding the waves of immigration politics for hundreds of years in a defined pattern of torment followed by a bit of calm. Immigrant communities bear the burden of geopolitics, nativist fear-mongering, and political chess in ways that are, at best, unfair and racist, and at worst, terrifying and deadly.[1] This book is going to the printer as the second Trump administration takes office. While the first Trump administration hacked away at immigration law in chaotic and often illegal ways that were eventually overturned in court, the second Trump transition team appears to be much more organized. Project 2025 outlines a policy agenda that represents a troubling regression from fundamental human rights, particularly for children.[2] Tom Homan has suggested that he will move to detain and deport mixed-status families and Steven Miller plans to pursue the "denaturalization" of naturalized citizens. Moreover, the plan to rescind all "ICE memoranda identifying 'sensitive zones' where ICE personnel are prohibited from operating" is particularly alarming for schools.[3] In other words, the intent to terrorize immigrant communities and the schools that serve them once again is clear.

One of the things I find most heartbreaking about the election polling and results is that so many voters think they are in favor of mass deportation but have very little knowledge about what that means or the impact it will have on entire communities. Most people born in the United States know very little about how people migrate to their country and have an almost mythological understanding of the history of immigration policy and its social and economic impact on future generations in the United

States. Popular narratives of grandparents arriving in America with a little pocket change and pulling themselves up by the bootstraps do not acknowledge how migration has only been recently criminalized. It also ignores how quickly new immigrants actually learn English, become financially independent, avoid contact with the criminal justice system, and contribute greatly to the economy and public schools.[4]

Those of us who study immigration are frustrated by the untruthful storytelling, on the one hand, and the theatrics on the other, making the process of coming to the United States using legal avenues impossible in a single lifetime and criminalizing those desperate enough to leave home and cross borders without authorization. The reality is that the US government has failed immigrants by not passing comprehensive immigration reform, by ignoring how immigrants contribute to society through labor, taxes, innovation, and population increases, and by putting immigrant communities in precarious situations. By using devastating exclusion tactics, fear, and punishment, the US government, politicians, and policy makers have pushed immigrant communities to the edges of society by treating them as scapegoats or ignoring their needs altogether.

Schools should not *have* to be sanctuaries for immigrant youth, but they *must* be as long as the failures of states continue to put recently arrived young people in increasingly perilous situations. Heba Gowayed writes:

> Through resettlement and asylum, [refugees and asylum seekers] come face to face with national systems shaped by inequalities foreign to them that determine their access to resources as they rebuild their lives and imagine their futures. Their experiences reveal that these destination countries, while offering legal solutions to displacement, do not guarantee bright futures—they can deny newcomers' potential by failing to recognize their abilities and invest in the tools they need to prosper.[5]

It is true that schools alone cannot pass comprehensive immigration reform or rewrite immigration policy, and "there are no easy remedies for persistent educational inequalities; these inequalities are interwoven with the injustices of our society."[6] However, they can be places of innovation, imagination, and justice.

Public debates about educational justice for immigrant youth often focus too narrowly on economic productivity and achievement as measures of successful schools. For immigrant teenagers who are learning English, this means being relegated to dysfunctional and ineffective English immersion programs, where even well-meaning educators who care deeply for their students do not feel like they have the time, resources, capacity, and background knowledge to get to know their immigrant students and their stories.[7] Others don't care to know because of indifference or lack of curiosity.[8]

Educators at International High School (IHS) and the Internationals Network of Public Schools, in contrast, are imagining, innovating, and teaching others what they have learned about how to provide sanctuary to immigrant youth through protective and empowering school structures, systems, and practices that they have been developing for decades. In my previous work, and in collaboration with others, I have described how educators at IHS protect and empower their students as resistant, responsive, and justice-oriented.[9] I have framed the school as a subaltern *counterpublic* and highlighted how IHS and its sister schools create a sense of belonging for students, cultivate community partnerships, give teachers great freedom and autonomy, and work to reform accountability policies and practices.[10] What I have only recently recognized is how extraordinarily radical the ideas expressed by these educators and captured in this book really are.

At a recent event where Lara was a speaker, an audience member stood up at the end and said, "All of these things you are talking about seem really obvious." While I agree that some practices highlighted in this book might not seem groundbreaking, their radical nature lies not in novelty but in their implementation and sustainability. These ideas—though logical and often considered best practices—are still rarely enacted in mainstream education. Those that are enacted are often done piecemeal and declared a waste of time shortly thereafter, replaced with the newest trend in reform. But when these radical ideas—welcoming new students from the first day, making sure their every need is met before expecting them to learn, learning their entire story and aspirations, building a schoolscape in which students are seen, heard, and celebrated, investing time in teacher development and treating them like true professionals, and engaging in advocacy and policymaking at the local, state, and federal level—are put together and allowed to marinate over time, protected from the urgent meddling of ambitious neoliberal reformers, something truly radical emerges: a sanctuary school in which immigrant students are protected and empowered no matter who is president, throughout pandemics, and in all sociopolitical contexts.

This conclusion introduces four radical mindset shifts essential for fostering sanctuary schooling. First, it examines the need to recognize the flaws in the social contract and the failures of state and district policies, urging educators to critically challenge the systems that shape schooling. It then explores the importance of fully knowing students beyond data points or test scores by embracing their full identities, backgrounds, and ways of knowing the world. It also emphasizes the shift from prioritizing short-term outcomes to valuing stability and long-term well-being in students' lives. Finally, it calls for a reevaluation of students' roles within the school community, encouraging schools to reconsider how they measure student success and honor their contributions. Together, these shifts set the stage for reimagining sanctuary schooling as both an act of protection and a path toward systemic change.

MINDSET SHIFT I: RECOGNIZE FLAWS IN THE SOCIAL CONTRACT AND FAILURES OF THE STATE

The last time there was meaningful immigration reform in the United States was in 1986 when the Immigration Reform and Control Act of 1986 was passed to criminalize working as an undocumented person. It also provided a pathway to citizenship for almost three million people. Since then, immigration reform efforts in Congress have failed in 2001, 2005, 2007, 2013, and 2023.[11] There are currently over eleven million undocumented immigrants in the United States, many of whom have been here for a lifetime and have children who are US citizens.[12] Immigrating to the United States through legal avenues is virtually impossible for most people, and the process of changing status takes years.[13] There are clear benefits for those who come to the United States to work and build a life. Immigrants contribute significantly to society and the economy. They are keeping schools open where numbers have been dropping and are crucial to industries from agriculture to technology and innovation.[14] Despite the overwhelming evidence that the United States needs immigrants to sustain its democracy, economy, and society, immigrant communities are scapegoated and publicly denounced in racist and vulgar ways. Since 2015, hate crimes have increased by more than 80 percent and increased more during election years.[15] Many victims of hate crimes have immigrant origins or ancestry. Of the forty-four million immigrants in the United States, a full third live below the poverty line.[16] Put simply, the United States has failed its immigrant communities.

School policies determined at the state level have compounded the social precarity of immigrant communities by failing to take into consideration pathways to graduation for English learners. Despite a legal obligation to ensure recently arrived immigrant English learners can effectively participate in the educational programs offered by a school district, the guidance districts receive are not specific enough. So, while all high schools have programs for English Learners that check the legal boxes of compliance with federal mandates, they do not uphold a social contract and responsibility to treat newcomers with the same attention and care they do their US-born peers.

The flaws in schools' social contract with immigrant communities are evident throughout the nation. In high schools nationwide, 69 percent of students learning English, many of whom are immigrants, graduate compared with 84 percent of all students. Currently, English learners in high school are often forced into remedial classes that are not credit-bearing and have limited access to complex content, advanced course-work, and enrichment.[17] There is no common method for classifying English learners or requirements for exiting a program across states, and the data gathered on English learners is not disaggregated, so it remains challenging to get a clear picture of which English learner students are at the highest risk of not graduating.[18] Newcomers, in particular, are asked to learn English at an impossibly fast pace in order to meet graduation requirements and are at risk of aging out of the public school system before being given adequate time and instruction. Schools are often penalized if students do not graduate within four years and are not recognized when students graduate within five or six years, which dis-incentivizes school leaders from enrolling recently arrived immigrant students.[19]

Finally, the only legislative win for immigrant students since 1986, Obama's executive action to grant Deferred Action for Childhood Arrivals (DACA), no longer serves high school or college-aged students, and the teachers who are DACA recipients are constantly in precarious positions as the executive action faces a barrage of legal challenges.[20] While DACA's fate is unclear, advocates anticipate that the second Trump administration will only increase the uncertainty and precarity of remaining DACA recipients. Put simply, the United States has failed its immigrant youth and, if the second Trump administration keeps their campaign promises, children and youth will become a target of immigration enforcement in the years to come that could put them in great danger.

A Teachers' Work Is Inherently Political

Because of the failures of the state and flaws in the social contract, the first and most important mindset shift that teachers and school leaders must make is that their work is inherently political. Educators must acknowledge that there is no neutrality in public education, and silence is an endorsement of hateful, racist, and anti-immigrant rhetoric. From segregated classrooms serving privileged white students to sanctuary schools serving large numbers of immigrant, undocumented, and other racialized and traditionally marginalized students, teachers must see their work as oriented toward justice for all children and acknowledge how the state and society have strategically disadvantaged immigrant communities in a multitude of ways.

School leaders often believe it is their responsibility to comply with policies put in place by the local, state, and national governments. Lara and her colleagues at IHS and the Internationals Network believe that it is their job to act in the best interest of their students. These two perspectives on leadership are not always incongruent, but for students learning English in US high schools, "too few state politics take into consideration how the pathway to graduation may look different" for recently arrived immigrant English learners.[21]

The advocacy and coalition-building efforts of the Internationals Network reflect the broader, systemic application of sanctuary principles. By engaging in policy-level initiatives, the Network attempts to influence the adoption of policy that is congruent with the needs of their students. Their work highlights the responsibility of educators and leaders aiming to extend sanctuary practices to a wider population of immigrant students to influence local, state, and national policymaking.

Balancing the need to offer intellectual sanctuary for immigrant students requires teachers and school leaders to buffer with local, state, and federal regulations. Navigating and challenging multiple systems that do not prioritize the needs of immigrant students requires educators to circumvent compliance in service of their students. IHS takes advantage of its policy wins, like a waiver from the state for exit exams, by creating a pro-immigrant curriculum and instruction tailored to the specific needs of its students. The school also employs appropriate assessment practices and actively counters state assessment policies that they view as inequitable. Through the coordinated use of project-based learning, content language integration, and performance-based assessment tasks (PBATs), IHS provides opportunities for meaningful learning rooted in student experiences and identity development.

For educators, finding time to engage in the deep study of the failures of the state and moving away from a compliance-first mindset can be challenging and a little scary. The structures in schools that relegate English learners to the margins are often invisible or taken for granted as typical, normal, or rooted in tradition. Pushing back against existing systems that have been normalized requires knowledge and persistence. Prioritizing students over compliance can be dangerous, particularly in states that do not have strong union protections. And even in states with strong unions, those unions are in place to protect teachers first and put student needs second. Becoming aware of the structural and systematic injustices that immigrant students face is an important mindset shift. Taking action to resist and reorient those structures requires actions and policy changes.

Actions and Policies That Recognize Flaws in the Social Contract and Failures of the State

Policies at the Federal Level

While corrective actions and policies may be difficult to enact during the second Trump administration and the Department of Education will likely cease to exist as we know it today, there remains a need to remind elected officials to continue to advocate for immigrant communities. Some federal actions that could support schools serving immigrant youth include:

- **Comprehensive Immigration Reform:** A path to citizenship for the eleven million undocumented people in the United States is only possible through congressional action. Following the mindset shift that teaching is inherently political, educators can organize to lobby for systemic change at the federal level. Legislation could provide a pathway to citizenship for unauthorized children in the country.[22]

- **Guidance from the US Department of Education:** Immigration to the United States is the highest it has been since 1910 and by 2050, immigrants will account for 82 percent of the nation's population growth.[23] It is imperative that the US Department of Education provide specific guidance on how to better serve English learners and how to do a better job of receiving, recognizing, and welcoming newcomers.

Policies at the State Level

- **Disaggregate English Learner Data:** At the state level, disaggregating English learner data allows researchers to better understand the challenges faced by long-term English learners, English learners receiving special education services, and how time in the United States and age of arrival impact students' opportunities in high school. Furthermore, doing so also allows states and local districts to reevaluate the ways in which they use data to create appropriate comparison groups that measure school impact by disaggregating English learner's data and using a newcomer designation. The California Department of Education began disaggregating this data in 2022.[24]
- **Standardized Testing:** While policies standardizing learning objectives and achievement measures at the state level intend to equalize education, disparities persist. Despite the varying quality of high school education across the country, earning a diploma remains a critical gateway to higher education and the labor market. The need for more equitable and appropriate assessments for immigrant students is clear. In particular, English exit exams, like the ELA Regents in New York, pose a significant barrier for many recently arrived immigrant youth. Graduation rates soared for high school English learners in New York in 2020 when exit exams were canceled due to COVID-19.[25] Too often, students who have completed every other requirement for graduation are prevented from graduating because

of an overreliance on English exit exams causing more harm than good. This recommendation is actually not radical at all; it simply highlights a trend away from these harmful exams. While twenty-seven states used exit exams at the height of No Child Left Behind, only six continue using tests to determine graduation eligibility. In November 2024, New York's Board of Regents voted to eliminate Regents exams as a graduation requirement beginning in the 2027–2028 school year. Similarly, voters in Massachusetts passed a ballot measure to lift the standardized MCAS graduation requirement.[26]

- **Resist Nativist State Graduation Policies:** While most states are phasing out content exams as a requirement for graduation, other states including Arizona, Arkansas, Idaho, Kentucky, North Dakota, Tennessee, Wisconsin, New Hampshire, and Oklahoma now require high school students to pass a civics test modeled on the one hundred questions that USCIS officers can ask permanent residents who want to become naturalized citizens.[27] A dozen states have made filling out a FAFSA a requirement for graduation. These initiatives can harm or humiliate new and undocumented immigrants.[28] Florida educators have been at the forefront of resistance to discriminatory laws and efforts to censor teachers and university professors, arguing that they violate the "First and Fourteenth Amendments by imposing viewpoint-based restrictions on educators (including professors, lecturers, and student teaching assistants) and students that are vague and discriminatory."[29]
- **Establish State Exceptions for Credentials, Work Permits, and Employment Visas:** Progressive states should look for creative solutions for establishing credentialing protocols, work permitting systems, or policies for sponsoring employment visas so undocumented people can work. The Undocumented Students Led Network in California and the UCLA School of Law's Center for Immigration and Law & Policy believe there are ways that states and certain state entities can legally employ undocumented workers.[30] New York State

has considered state work authorization for asylum seekers.[31] Finally, the CUNY Initiative on Immigration and Education and UndocuEdu suggests that opening pathways for credentialing and employment is particularly important for potential educators to help address the national shortage of multilingual teachers.[32]

Policies at the City and District Levels

- **Use "Sanctuary" and Publicly Support Undocumented and Mixed-Status Families:** The term "sanctuary" carries powerful symbolic weight, signaling a commitment to stand against systemic oppression and to create spaces of safety and belonging. By adopting this language, schools align with a larger movement advocating for immigrant rights and justice, amplifying solidarity and resistance. These policies combat discrimination through anti-harassment training, restorative justice practices, and equitable access to education while creating supportive spaces, forging community partnerships, and educating students about their rights. By emphasizing sanctuary as both a symbolic stance and a set of actionable commitments, schools affirm their role as transformative institutions that uphold the dignity and humanity of all students. Oakland Unified School District provides the strongest example I have found, stating "we are a sanctuary district," and "we will do everything possible to ensure students and families are safe at school regardless of immigration status."[33]
- **Adopt Sanctuary Resolutions:** Schools should adopt comprehensive policies to establish themselves as sanctuaries (schools also use "safe haven" or "safe zone" in places where using sanctuary may be unsafe) that protect students and families regardless of immigration status. These policies should include prohibiting staff from assisting in federal immigration enforcement, refusing voluntary information-sharing with immigration agents, and safeguarding the privacy of student records. Additional measures should include creating

spaces and partnerships with organizations to support immigrant and undocumented students, educating students about their rights, and training staff on protocols for handling immigration-related inquiries. The ACLU of Southern California and Immigrants Rising provide guidance and models for protective "safe zone" school board policy.[34]

- **Establish Policies Restricting School Access by Non-Local Law Enforcement:** School districts should adopt a clear and consistent protocol to address requests from non-local law enforcement agencies, including Immigration and Customs Enforcement (ICE), to enter school premises, access students, or obtain student records. Non-local law enforcement, defined as agencies outside the jurisdiction of local authorities, should only be permitted on school grounds when explicitly required by law. To ensure compliance with the rule of law and the protection of student rights, schools must honor valid judicial warrants, court orders, and subpoenas, but the validity of such documents should always be confirmed by legal counsel before any action is taken. Staff should be trained on these protocols, which include notifying legal counsel immediately, requiring proper documentation, and denying access until legal review is complete. "New York City Public Schools Immigration Guidance for Principals on Non-Local Law Enforcement Actions at NYC DOE Schools, Including Immigration" is a good example.[35]

Individual Actions

Individual educators who want to address the failures of the state and flaws in the social contract can take meaningful action by learning about the rights of their immigrant students, networking with other educators nationally, and organizing locally. Reading this book is a start. The extensive notes in this book provide suggestions for readings where readers can go more into depth on topics of interest. Moving to a student-first mindset and moving away from compliance as a guide can be more challenging than becoming educated about the challenges that immigrant students face.

- **Know Your Rights and Help Students Know Theirs:** Start by educating yourself about students' rights if Immigration and Customs Enforcement (ICE) comes to school, using resources from organizations like Mobilization for Justice.[36] Share tools such as the Red Cards from the Immigrant Legal Resource Center (ILRC), which help individuals assert their rights during encounters with ICE.[37] Promote family preparedness by distributing childcare safety plans that assist mixed-status families in planning for who will care for their children if deportation occurs. Partner with legal advocacy organizations like Kids in Need of Defense (KIND), which provides representation for unaccompanied minors and asylum seekers. Finally, collaborate with professional organizations like the National Education Association (NEA) and the American Federation of Teachers (AFT), which offer tools to help educators transform schools into safe zones and ensure students know their rights. By taking these steps, educators can become powerful advocates, addressing systemic injustices and fostering a culture of belonging and safety for immigrant students and families.
- **Visit Schools and Network:** One way to learn more about what resistance to failures of the state looks like is by visiting schools and networking with educators who have made the mindset shift as well. Teachers and leaders can organize intervisitations to learn about what other schools are doing. They can also invite researchers into their schools to help them identify practices that systematically disadvantage immigrant newcomers. Lara reminds me often that "people don't get it unless they see it" and that revolutionary ideas are best nurtured in hubs where like-minded people can share ideas and build coalitions. As the Internationals Network expands to new areas of the country, they look for places where there is more than

one school or more than one principal who understands their vision and why they are different from other English Learner and Newcomer programs.

- **Become an Organizer:** Becoming a radical educator or leader in isolation can be lonely and ineffective. In a recent article, Jenna Queenan and collaborators chronicle the history of the New York Collective of Radical Educators (NYCORE), which was founded in 2001 around nine main points of unity, including addressing racism and economic inequality in the school system, opposing punitive disciplinary measures, and offering guidance on new school funding policy.[38] Reading about how to organize collectively to make radical changes in local politics and policies can help those new to movements think strategically about how to set priorities and engage in the messy and somewhat mysterious act of advocacy. I have found Dean Spade's book *Mutual Aid* helpful in understanding the challenges of organizing like-minded people around a shared radical goal to disrupt systems and structures of oppression. The New York Immigration Coalition (NYIC) is a good example of a policy and advocacy organization that formed in 1987 to unite the demands of smaller advocacy groups interested in the rights of immigrants. Today, they represent over two hundred immigrant and refugee rights groups throughout New York and have topic-specific coalitions, like the Education Collaborative. The Refugee and Immigrant Center for Education and Legal Services (RAICES) in Texas and the Central American Resource Centers (CARECEN) in California, Washington, DC, and New York are two other organizations that grew out of the sanctuary movement and continue to do local advocacy work for immigrant communities. Groups like the UndocuBlack Network (UBN), Detention Watch Network (DWN), and National Newcomer Network (NNN) are examples of national networks that engage in local, grassroots organizing to empower and protect immigrant communities. Finally, there are thousands of local groups across the country that are addressing local needs and politics. Find them in your community by looking on social media, visiting public spaces like the library or community gardens, and talking with colleagues and neighbors.

- **Connect in Your Community:** Using the hashtag #mutualaid, you can find many hyperlocal, issue-focused, or neighborhood-based groups of volunteers working collectively to address flaws in the social contract and failures of the state by providing food, clothing, housing, and other services to the most vulnerable members of society and the most likely to face discrimination in the specific location. For example, I volunteer with a mutual aid group called "Floyd Bennett Field Neighbors." We are volunteers from South Brooklyn and Rockaway Queens who organized around supporting families living at the migrant tent shelter New York City erected at Floyd Bennett Field. When the city began dropping families off in shorts and flip-flops at the tents in the middle of winter, we used social media to organize mass distributions of warm clothes. When the city enacted a policy to evict families from shelters every sixty days, we ran a campaign to supply every family with a suitcase. We are one of thousands of mutual aid groups that have proliferated in NYC and across the country since the start of the COVID-19 pandemic. Groups like this can pool community resources and respond to real needs quickly.

MINDSET SHIFT II: CENTER KNOWING AND CARING FOR STUDENTS

Helen Thorpe, in her book *The Newcomers*, wrote about Mr. Williams, a teacher who was "doing his best to teach all the students that the world kept sending him." She writes:

> One way I [was helpful] was by sharing the stories of students I got to know. Mr. Williams knew nothing about Lisbeth's odyssey until I told

> him. . . . Nor did he know about Saul's harrowing journey in the packed truck, nor that Jakeleen and Mariam had lived through the civil war in Syria. He and Miss Pauline know that Solomon and Methusella came from the DRC, but not that they had lived in a particularly violence-prone province.[39]

Thorpe credits her ability to get to know the students in a way that their teachers did not or could not to her ability to hire interpreters and spend time building trusting relationships with students as she learned their stories. Mr. Williams was of the same mindset as many of the teachers I encounter in traditional schools serving large numbers of newcomers. They believe it is their duty to help students start their new life here by learning English, passing tests, and getting a diploma rather than to learn about who their students were before coming to the United States or how they got here. Educators who want to provide sanctuary to students must shift their mindset from one focused on the future to one focused on holistic knowing of the whole child's past, present, family, and hopes for the future.

Enrique Sepúlveda III calls educators who care to know and take the time to learn "border educators" and describe their process as one of *conocimiento* and *accompañamiento* (knowing and accompaniment). Teachers at the sanctuary school recognize that, in some ways, sharing an immigration story can be transactional when trying to navigate structures and systems in the United States, whether it is applying for asylum or applying to college.[40] Border educators do not apply pressure to tell the story but help students intentionally reveal the parts of the story they want to tell when they want to tell them.[41]

Sanctuary begins with *knowing*. Educators, social workers, counselors, and other school staff members must know where their students come from, why they have come, and what they experienced in their journey. It is not their right to know. Rather, they are responsible for creating conditions in which students trust that their experiences will be validated and their knowledge respected if they share. Educators at sanctuary schools understand that these stories may explain challenges but are also experiences in which young people learn about the world. Educators in sanctuary schools listen to their students' stories and engage in deep study to learn more about systemic barriers affecting immigrant students, recognizing migration as a fully human experience, and believing immigrant students are knowledgeable in their own right.

Milagros' story illustrates the power of *conocimiento* and *accompañamiento* at IHS. As I was writing the final pages of this book, I met Luz and Milagros for dinner in Brooklyn. Since Milagros graduated from IHS, she has earned an associate's degree in social work, fallen in love, and will soon be a new mom. She has helped many family members access the same resources the school found for her to help them migrate and reunite in the United States. She currently works at the organization that provided her housing when she first left her uncle's house, helping other women leave abusers and rebuild their lives. In other words, she has thrived and helped others in their journeys. She believes that the school put her on the path to where she is today because her teachers took the time to know her fully and accompany her to safety.

Creating an environment in which Milagros felt safe asking for help, letting her teachers know her story, plotting her escape from danger, and holding her close until she began to thrive is the foundation of protection. Teachers at IHS listen to the experiences of their students, ensuring their basic needs, such as food, clothing, and safety, are met, providing a stable foundation for students to focus on their education. The school is prepared to act swiftly when urgent needs arise, such as a health crisis, revelations of abuse, or immediate legal issues. The ability to respond to these pressing situations ensures that students receive timely support, maintaining their well-being and stability.

A sanctuary school has a plan for emergencies, knowing their students will have crises they will need to help solve. Knowing they have a responsibility to care for students through these challenges means that the school can mobilize resources quickly, addressing both planned and unforeseen challenges to provide immediate support to students. While the school may not be able to provide physical sanctuary beyond the school day, ensuring students have safe shelter to go home to after the school day ends is integral to the school's protective approach to care. The sanctuary school will help to find safe housing for students experiencing homelessness or unstable living conditions, ensuring they have a secure place to live before they expect them to learn.

Actions and Policies That Center Knowing and Caring for Students

Policies at the Federal Level

The landmark Supreme Court case *Plyler v. Doe* (1982) established that states cannot deny free public education to children based on their immigration status, thereby asserting that all children, regardless of their legal status or the legal status of their parents, have the right to attend public schools. The decision was grounded in the Equal Protection Clause of the Fourteenth Amendment, which prohibits states from denying any person within their jurisdiction the equal protection of the law. Since 1982, *Plyler v. Doe* has played a crucial role in ensuring that immigration status does not impede access to education. However, it has not ensured an inclusive and equitable educational environment for all students, particularly recently arrived immigrant youth. One unfortunate and unintended consequence of the *Plyler v. Doe* ruling was in how schools adopted a de facto "Don't Ask, Don't Tell" policy around immigrant students, which has prevented teachers from fully understanding their students by restricting access to crucial information and making them fearful of engaging in any conversation about national origin or status. For educators who sought to understand their students better, the only accessible data points were often limited to the student's date of entry, place of birth, and English Learner (EL) status. Some federal actions that could support schools in centering knowing and caring for students include:

- **Protect Plyler:** *Plyler v. Doe* has withstood challenges for over forty years. However, one goal of the second Trump administration is to have the Supreme Court reconsider Plyler and rescind the right of undocumented children to have an education. The Heritage Foundation, a right-wing think tank, released a brief encouraging states to pass laws requiring undocumented students to pay tuition with the hope of forcing the issue into the courts.
- **Offer Professional Development and Guidance:** To help educators better know and care for their immigrant students, the US Department of Education should offer professional development highlighting crucial data about immigrant students and provide an overview of the US immigration system, dispelling myths about how people immigrate to the United States. This training should also cover essential educational protections and introduce strategies, like the ones examined in this book, which help foster a sense of belonging and provide holistic academic and social support for newcomers. Federal initiatives should aim to expand teacher training pipelines and enhance the number of teachers who identify as immigrants, speak more than one language, and have first-hand experience with English language learning programs in US public schools.
- **Establish National Newcomer Designation:** A potential policy shift to foster deeper understanding would involve introducing a "Newcomer" designation for any student born outside of the United States and who has been in the country for fewer than four to six years. This designation would differentiate between recent arrivals and long-term or US-born students who are learning English, allowing the Department of Education to gather, study, and disseminate data specific to this population of students. It could also help educators to identify and support students more effectively without violating

Plyler v. Doe since it could be done without inquiring about legal status. While this may not be prudent to do in the current anti-immigrant climate, it should be something we strive for at an appropriate moment.

Policies at the State Level

- **Require Pre-Service Teacher Candidates to Take Courses on Immigration and Language Acquisition:** A deeper understanding of what it takes to learn a new language and culture in a new country could help address pre-service teachers' misunderstandings of their immigrant and English-learning students. Traditionally, only teachers who plan to teach a language other than English or those enrolled in Teaching English to Speakers of Other Languages take courses in language acquisition. The implementation of these courses has been studied in California and Florida. Researchers studying these interventions find that students who take courses on immigration, education, and new language acquisition are better able to see themselves through the experiences of immigrant students, are more compassionate about understanding the lived experiences of immigrant students, and gain cultural awareness.[42] Those of us who prepare future teachers and leaders believe that preparation programs should require all students to take courses in language acquisition designed around students' perceptions of English learners to be able to identify and address misunderstandings students may have from their own foreign language learning journeys in high school or college or from lack of exposure to non-English speaking people.

School Actions

- **Create Space for Undocumented Students and Designate a Point Person:** To effectively support undocumented students and youth in mixed-status families, schools should designate a point person—such as a counselor, teacher, or leader—dedicated to providing guidance, resources, and advocacy for these students. This individual can serve as a trusted ally, ensuring access to legal information, mental health services, and scholarship opportunities while fostering a sense of safety and belonging. Additionally, schools should encourage the formation of student-led clubs where undocumented students, their peers from mixed-status families, and allies can connect, share experiences, and advocate for immigrant rights. These clubs not only raise awareness about immigration issues but also create a supportive community that empowers students to overcome challenges and achieve their goals.[43]

Individual Actions

- **Spend Time with Your Students Outside the Classroom:** Educators can actively engage with students and their families outside the classroom by participating in community events and spaces that are meaningful to them. Attending sporting events, celebrations like quinceañeras, spending time in local parks where families gather, and eating or shopping in students' neighborhoods can help build trust, strengthen relationships, and demonstrate genuine care and respect for their lives beyond school. These efforts foster a deeper understanding of students' cultural backgrounds and lived experiences, creating a bridge between their home and school environments that enriches their education and sense of belonging.
- **Visit Students' Homelands:** Educators should consider visiting the homelands or significant places in their students' journeys to gain a deeper connection to their stories and experiences. One teacher I interviewed shared how she wrote a grant to fund a visit to the refugee camp where her student had lived, and she shared how seeing that part of her student's life gave her a new perspective on their resilience and strength. Immersing yourself in these places not only

fosters empathy but also strengthens the bond between teacher and student. Even beyond specific journeys, travel can open hearts and minds, expanding compassion and understanding that can be brought back into the classroom to create a more supportive and inclusive environment. Reading about immigrant youths' journeys across borders and experiences in school can also be powerful, like in Javier Zamora's memoir, *Solito,* Lauren Markham's *Faraway Brothers,* and Brook Houser's *The New Kids.*

MINDSET SHIFT III: VALUE STABILITY OVER URGENCY

One key mindset difference between IHS and many other newcomer programs is valuing stability over urgency. Rather than working urgently to move students out of newcomer programs in a few short months or years, IHS is designed to provide a stable educational environment for recently arrived immigrant youth throughout their entire high school experience. Schools in the Internationals Network recognize that their immigrant students face far more challenges in high school compared to their US-born peers. In addition to typical academic demands, they must learn a new language, adapt to a new culture, and often reunite with family members after years of separation. Some also grapple with significant educational gaps due to interruptions in their schooling in their home country.

A whole-school model, like IHS and other schools in the Internationals Network, allows more time for growth, learning, and relationship building. Unlike schools that aim to transition students into the general education population within a set timeframe—often based on the assumption that success depends on quickly learning English and assimilating—IHS focuses on insulating students from harmful acculturative policies and practices.

IHS creates opportunities for students to stay in high school for more than four years. The common expectation that students graduate within four years is based on the normative needs of middle-class, US-born students and may not be appropriate for traditionally marginalized groups, such as immigrant students. Given how much more immigrant students need to learn, educators at IHS believe it is reasonable to expect their students to take longer to graduate than their US-born peers. They recognize that students should graduate when they are fully prepared for post-secondary opportunities, not before.

IHS accommodates older and working students, reduces the stigma associated with retention, and ensures that older students feel welcomed and valued. For instance, Milagros and Gonzalo, who graduated in August 2018 after seven and six years of high school, respectively, are now more likely to earn a living wage, contribute to the economy, and raise children who graduate from high school or higher education. IHS counselors work closely with students to highlight the long-term benefits of staying in school until they earn a diploma.

Valuing stability over urgency extends to staffing a school. Developing a stable, racioethnically and linguistically diverse, and culturally conscientious corps of veteran teachers begins with collectively hiring and recruiting educators who empathize with the experiences of recently arrived immigrant students. It is sustained through deliberate and long-term investment in teaching practices that respond to the specific and varied needs of low-income, newly arrived, English-learning immigrant teenagers. Leaders and veteran teachers at IHS actively cultivate a teacher corps that is responsive to the needs of their immigrant student population and collaborative across disciplines and divisions.

The Personnel Committee at IHS seeks to hire new teachers for their ability to be reflective, collaborative, and culturally relevant educators. Many share backgrounds similar to the students they will serve. The school's high teacher retention rate allows for selectivity in hiring. Candidates are vetted through a multistep interview involving leaders, teachers, and students, focusing on their teaching abilities and perceptions of immigrant students. Candidates expressing deficit views of immigrants or other traditionally marginalized groups are not advanced in the process.

The interdisciplinary team that the new teacher will join plays a significant role in the hiring process, as they will work closely with the new hire and help integrate them into the school culture. During this study, new teachers, like their veteran colleagues, often recalled personal experiences of travel or language learning, which helped them understand the challenges that newly arrived immigrant students face.

School leaders should involve teachers in the hiring process to ensure that those collaborating closely have a say in the choice. In addition to considering a candidate's credentials and identity, hiring committees should also consider life experiences, self-reflectiveness, and motivations for working at the school. Involving more teachers in the process ensures that multiple perspectives are considered.

After hiring, new teachers at IHS are integrated into interdisciplinary teams, which they plan, share classrooms with, and spend most of their day in. They are mentored in designing project-based curricula by both their interdisciplinary and discipline-specific team members. School leaders believe this mentorship should span years or as long as it takes for teachers to embrace project-based learning and content and language integration fully. Rather than "training teachers" to adopt and blindly follow a prescribed curriculum, sanctuary schools develop teachers. Over time, the stable teacher collective in a sanctuary school provides developing teachers a buffer to ensure their learning does not negatively impact students. The whole school model, cohorting, and looping of teams of teachers with small groups of students creates a cocoon of protection for both the developing teacher and vulnerable students, ensuring they both have the support they need to be successful. Lara describes this approach as "playing the long game" in service of students.

IHS's investment in teacher development has resulted in a 98 percent teacher attendance rate, a 90 percent teacher retention rate, and a teacher population in which 90 percent have three or more years of experience.

These metrics, consistent over the last ten years, illustrate the impact of diverse, highly engaged, and experienced teachers on school culture. IHS teachers have the time, expertise, and confidence to know their students, build trust with their colleagues, and create project-based, social justice-oriented, and immigrant-specific curricula. They can ensure their immigrant students have access to complex content while using methods of language integration across all classes, including art, physical education, and graphic design.

Actions and Policies That Reflect the Mindset Shift of Stability Over Urgency

Policies at the State and/or District Level

- **Encourage the Development of Whole School Models:** Current accountability structures often discourage districts from adopting whole-school models for newcomers. Stand-alone newcomer schools, which served only recent immigrants like IHS, shuttered across the country in the 1990s and early 2000s when No Child Left Behind high-stakes accountability requirements began disaggregating school data by ethnicity, income, and English learner status, leading to unfair and inaccurate comparisons of newcomer schools.[44] Stand-alone newcomer programs can appear less effective than they truly are when newcomer status is invisible in the data. While accountability approaches have evolved in the decades following NCLB, many districts still opt for a school-within-a-school model for newcomer programs, where a newcomer academy exists within a larger school. This setup allows for the provision of specialized services to newcomers while enabling districts to offset their test scores with those from the broader student population.
- **Prioritize Complex Content Language Integration:** Current accountability policies incentivize schools for newcomers to prioritize accelerating the transition of these programs and back into the general

school population. This process tends to be quick and focused more on achieving adequate test scores than meaningful educational engagement. In newcomer schools where English ability is the main priority, newcomer students may not have access to complex content or be earning course credits. The overarching goal of these programs contrasts sharply with the notion of providing a sanctuary-like environment; instead, they operate more like an assembly line, quickly moving newly arrived immigrant students through the system based on test performance with little emphasis on community building or holistic care. While there are certainly welcoming academies with dedicated educators who positively impact students' lives, the prevalent model does not typically allow teachers sufficient time to truly know their students, nor does it enable students to form stable relationships or adequately adjust to their new environment. The primary focus is still on language acquisition over integrated, content-rich, and thoughtful instruction. This approach results more in pushing students out than nurturing them within a supportive community.

- **Give Newcomer Academies Space to Innovate:** Stand-alone schools also have more autonomy in making collective decisions. For example, all of the International High Schools in New York City have been able to become Progressive Redesign Opportunity Schools for Excellence (PROSE), which allows schools to adopt innovative practices around measuring student achievement and teacher effectiveness.[45]
- **Track Extended-Year Graduation Rates:** For those schools that do adopt a whole-school model, emphasis on the traditional four-year timeline pressures school leaders to push students to graduate before they are fully prepared or discourages students unlikely to graduate in four years from even enrolling in the first place. Recent studies have shown the clear benefits of extending high school beyond four years to better serve students, especially traditionally, systematically, or strategically marginalized students.[46] Policy makers should

increase funding for programs that extend high school specifically for immigrant youth, and researchers should investigate how this approach impacts newcomers specifically. Currently, only thirty-five states include extended-year graduation rates in their accountability and improvement metrics.[47] Sixteen states track only five-year graduation rates, while just nineteen states collect data through the sixth or seventh year of high school. The Every Student Succeeds Act (ESSA), the current iteration of the Elementary and Secondary Education Act (ESEA), provides flexibility for states that want to support students who may not graduate within the standard four years. By working to destigmatize taking more than four years to graduate high school, schools can signal to communities continually disadvantaged by this timeline for graduation that they are welcomed, valued, and seen by the school district.[48] This has already been done in schools in New York City. Early college and career schools, also called "Pathways in Technology Early College High Schools" officially have grades 9–14 and offer a six-year program where students can earn a high school diploma and a no-cost, career-specific Associate's degree, two years of transferable college credits, and learn workplace skills.[49] Finally, by collecting data on extended graduation rates, states can begin to challenge the normative expectation of a four-year graduation timeline and improve outcomes for recently arrived immigrant youth.[50]

- **Teacher Development:** Current protocols for teacher evaluation and feedback are often achievement-focused, short-term, and generalized. Standard evaluation frameworks assume that the principal is the primary supervisor and that teachers can only be "trained" through evaluations, assessments, and improvement conversations. These frameworks also assume that feedback must come from school leaders who may observe a teacher for less than an hour per year. Sanctuary schooling practices at IHS challenge these assumptions by adopting more holistic measures for teacher effectiveness and sustainable practices for development and attrition. This process begins with a different perspective on the relationship between school leadership, the teaching staff, and students. Lara treats teachers as professionals who develop over time rather than being trained through short observations and closed-door meetings. She sees herself as a relationship cultivator rather than an executive or evaluator. This approach is reflected in the use of committees with robust decision-making power. At IHS, teacher development is embedded in the everyday practices of all school community members rather than being driven by a single individual.

- **Develop Teacher Pipeline and Residency Programs:** Districts should collaborate with universities to establish and fund residency programs that prepare teachers to support immigrant students effectively. Programs like Bank Street's TESOL Residency combine coursework, mentoring, and hands-on experience, ensuring educators are equipped to address the academic, linguistic, and emotional needs of immigrant youth. By offering paid apprenticeships and discounted tuition, these programs make teaching more accessible and sustainable, especially for diverse candidates. Graduates emerge as advocates and innovators, integrating culturally sustaining practices and adapting instruction for diverse learning needs. Residency programs build a pipeline of qualified, equity-focused teachers, enhancing student outcomes and retention in high-need schools serving immigrant populations.[51]

School Actions

- **Create Time for Social Emotional Learning in Advisory:** Schools should implement advisory programs to foster a supportive environment where students build meaningful relationships with peers and a trusted adult advisor. These programs promote social–emotional learning by engaging students' self-awareness, social skills, and responsible decision-making. Advisory sessions should not be focused on academics, but rather on goal-setting, organization, and time management, while creating a safe space to explore diverse identities and cultural awareness. Through collaborative activities and discussions, students strengthen communication and teamwork skills, paving the way for personal growth, self-reflection, and a growth mindset essential for their success.

MINDSET SHIFT IV: REEVALUATE THE ROLES THAT IMMIGRANT STUDENTS PLAY IN SCHOOLS

Establishing conditions for sanctuary schooling relies heavily on students being socialized into an often-unfamiliar school culture. Students who come to the sanctuary school have not often had the experience of feeling welcomed, valued, or celebrated in schools. More often than not, students have learned from the hidden global curriculum of traditional schools that docility and silence are rewarded, rules are made to be followed, and they are there to learn by receiving knowledge from experts.[52] Furthermore, they learn that their peers are the competition and that collaboration is cheating. To succeed at school, they must be compliant and work alone. Their success is measured by their ability to pass tests and, particularly for low-income students, if they do not succeed, it is their own fault, rather than the fault of systems and structures.[53]

The sanctuary school recognizes that teachers alone cannot make immigrant students feel welcome in a school. Developing a sense of belonging in school requires strong peer relationships.[54] At IHS, school structures encourage the organic formation of these relationships. For instance, using a cohort model for ninth and tenth graders increases students' opportunities to spend time with one another and build trust, which in turn contributes to a safer learning environment. Additionally, advisory classes allocate daily time for social–emotional support and social-language development. This emphasis on relationships and social–emotional learning helps cultivate a unique set of social values within the school.

When schools prioritize English learning over creating a sense of trust and safety, they miss the opportunity to develop a social climate that enhances learning opportunities for immigrant students. This social climate becomes especially important when the broader sociopolitical environment is hostile toward a particular group or community. At IHS, creating a safe social environment for immigrant students has become even more critical as the political climate toward immigrant communities has grown more hostile.

Educators at sanctuary schools think deeply about how what is displayed on the walls of the school signal to students. What we see in a space orients us to what and who is valued. In schools, what hangs on the walls often celebrates high-achieving students, athletes, and those deemed leaders by their teachers and peers. Immigrant students who are newest to the country often are not represented at all. The message to immigrant students is that they are not essential members of a community. At IHS, educators prominently display student work that showcases the different languages spoken at the school. A welcome poster, for example, might feature the word "welcome" in multiple languages. Student work that includes annotations and translations is common in hallways and classrooms. Language dictionaries are placed on tables where students work, and books in multiple languages are often prominently displayed in classrooms. Displaying student work that reflects the language-learning process helps students feel recognized and represented. Additionally, student work is shown at various stages of development, highlighting the learning process rather than just showcasing the exemplary final products of the highest-achieving students. Student-created art is always on display, from masks showing their inner and outer selves to mural painting to represent mythologies from their home countries. The world flags hanging in the lobby, the mural by the front office (and the cover of this book), and the Sanctuary Now poster in the main office are symbols that orient students and families and explicitly declare them welcomed and valued.

Another essential aspect of sanctuary schooling is recognizing that students are knowledgeable in their own right and that their knowledge is valuable to the school community. Immigrant students often report feeling invisible in schools where institutional structures socially isolate them due to a perceived lack of knowledge, usually of English.[55] For instance, when students are confined to classrooms focused solely on drilling English sight words and grammar, they miss out on fully participating in or contributing to the broader school community. When students fear speaking because they know their knowledge, culture, or identity is not valued, their learning opportunities are significantly diminished. Research has extensively documented how immigrant students are subjected to peer, teacher, and institutionalized acculturation practices that contribute to this marginalization.[56] Protecting immigrant students from harmful acculturative practices is crucial in providing sanctuary and creating better learning opportunities.

At IHS, students are encouraged to use any language skills they possess to communicate orally from their first day in school. Verbal participation is consistently reinforced through group work, presentations, and debates. Students who are more comfortable speaking English often serve as interpreters for others. All students are expected to speak and are supported, respected, and encouraged when their peers are speaking. It is common for students to wait patiently in silence while a classmate tries to communicate what they know or have learned, regardless of the language they are speaking. New language development is further supported with interactive prompts displayed on the walls or printed and taped to tables where students work. Feeling empowered to speak is crucial for students learning a new language, but it is much more common for students learning English to experience fear of ridicule from teachers and peers at school than it is for them to feel safe making mistakes.[57]

Educators at IHS know they can create conditions for empowerment at school but recognize that for students to fully participate in American society after high school, they must also learn to navigate systems and institutions that are not tailored to meet their needs. In the later grades, IHS implements practices that address many of the institutional barriers faced by immigrant students and their families. For example, in eleventh grade, students complete an internship outside the school. Alongside this, they take a class where they develop a resume and cover letter, learn relevant labor market and internship-specific vocabulary, and discuss the cultures of their new workplaces. These experiences introduce immigrant students to the social norms of the US labor market. By helping students develop skills for navigating US institutions, which may be designed to exclude them, IHS provides a form of sanctuary that extends beyond the classroom.

In the sanctuary school, students are not what Freire describes as receptacles for information; instead, they are highly valued members of a community in which their relationships with one another are as important as their relationships with their teachers.[58]

Actions and Policies That Increase Student Standing in Schools

Many of the actions described in previous sections contribute to improving the standing of immigrant students within a school community. The establishment of newcomer academies and International High Schools also raises the profile of immigrant students in the school. In these schools, immigrant students take on all of the leadership roles that are typically reserved for English-dominant, US-born peers. At schools like those in the Internationals Network of Public Schools, which strive to keep students throughout their entire high school journey and operate as whole-school models, immigrant students lead clubs, create the yearbook, and hold student council positions. The valedictorian is always an immigrant, as are the captains of sports teams like soccer, badminton, baseball, and cricket. These activities, as well as clubs and school events, are chosen based on the interests of the immigrant student population, further empowering them and making them central to the school's culture.

Policies at the State Level

- **Ensure Immigrant Student Access to Complex Content and Credit-Bearing Courses:** One imperfect example of what this would look like as a policy action comes from the New York State Education Department's Office of Bilingual Education and World Languages (OBEWL), which recently revised its policy standards to reflect the central guiding principle that every adult in a school district has a responsibility for the success of all English Language Learners (ELLs) and Multilingual Learners (MLLs). The law as it is written calls for teachers across all subjects to work together to support ELLs/MLLs in both content and language development, ensuring they meet the high demands of complex content courses that should be available to all students, regardless of their language learning designation. This policy initiative has the potential to serve as a model for other states. By emphasizing the importance of language support in all subjects and recognizing the diversity of students' linguistic backgrounds, this initiative could help improve the education of recently arrived immigrant students, particularly those learning English in school. Unfortunately, the guidance given to schools following the passage of this law basically said that two teachers in an English class was sufficient.

School Actions

- **Encourage Opportunities for Student Voice:** Give students a chance to talk in school instead of being talked at. This signals that their voices matter. Serving as translators raises their standing at the school since they are able to demonstrate an expertise that their teachers may not have. While this may seem abstract, or an oversimplification, it is a practice that is radical since the silencing of students, particularly those who do not speak English, has been well documented for generations. The literature suggests that the most common practices in schools enforce English language learning and American cultural assimilation in oppressive ways. In many typical schools, immigrants are "not only compelled to speak English, but to speak English *only* as the prerequisite of social acceptance and integration."[59] These "subtractive" schooling practices actively facilitate native language and culture loss.[60] At IHS, demonstrating multilingualism through public translation gives students an opportunity to lead, to participate in the community, and to return a favor done for them when they were ninth graders.

- **Use Cohorts and Teams:** Grouping immigrant students with a shared team of teachers and allowing them to loop grades can help teachers get to know their students and better understand their backgrounds and stories. Finally, teacher preparation programs can better equip pre-service content teachers with knowledge about second-language acquisition, addressing some deficit ideologies and misconceptions about how a new language is learned. These actions humanize immigrant students and increase teachers' awareness, reducing the likelihood that immigrant students will be marginalized in schools.

"UNWELCOME TO AMERICA": THE CURRENT EDUCATIONAL LANDSCAPE

In June 2024, Jo Napolitano, a Pulitzer Prize–nominated journalist and author, published "Unwelcome to America," a scathing report on the hundreds of US high schools that have wrongfully and illegally refused entry to older immigrant students. Over sixteen months, Napolitano tried to register a nineteen-year-old "who spoke little English and whose education had been interrupted" in six hundred schools. Half of the schools denied this young person entry, even in states where the right to enroll extends to age twenty. This report shows a persistent trend in public education that continues despite policy changes meant to make such practices illegal.[61]

Napolitano's article highlights the limitations of policy change and the tenacity of ideological biases. It shows how educators rationalize the marginalization of immigrant youth as an act of service to other students, the school community, or even the older immigrant students themselves. She quotes school leaders, counselors, and registrars asking questions like, "Does he speak good English?" and making dismissive statements such as, "At the end of the day, what is the person doing if they can't get a diploma?" They often prejudged the young person as a hopeless case, stating, "It's going to be a waste of time," "We could babysit him," and "He is 100 percent going to be a dropout."

In an editorial published shortly after the report, Napolitano argues that educational journalists "write and talk about immigrants in a tone that would be unacceptable for any other group." Her report, alongside decades of ethnographic and journalistic work in schools for immigrants, underscores how prevalent deficit perspectives about immigrant youth are in schools. Like journalists, educators often perceive and speak about immigrant students and their families in ways that would be unacceptable for other marginalized and minoritized groups. While we have adopted a child-first language in other fields, we still diminish newcomers to their documentation status and language abilities (if you say "immigrant" when you mean "undocumented," for example).

What is clear from the research and reporting on schools for immigrant students is that immigrant youth continue to struggle in school, and some teachers of immigrants struggle to see them as fully human. When I asked Lara what she hoped readers would take away from this book, she quoted engineer W. Edwards Deming, who said, "Every system is perfectly designed to get the results it gets." Lara believes, based on her decades of experience, that recently arrived immigrant youth are often an afterthought in US public schools and at every policy level. These students, who have seen more of the world than their US-born peers, speak another language, understand another culture, and have demonstrated bravery, tenacity, and ingenuity, are systematically overlooked or treated terribly. The current public school system is perfectly designed to fail immigrant newcomers again and again.

To create sanctuary schools for more immigrant students, systemic changes at every level of governance are necessary to keep this growing population of students front of mind. Most importantly, mindsets about these young people's humanity must change, from pre-service teachers to district leaders and policy makers. This will require a radical shift in how we think about, talk about, engage with, and learn from immigrant youth and their teachers. The Internationals Network of Public Schools has created a framework for sanctuary schooling that demonstrates how by adopting these four radical mindset shifts and the actions and policies that follow, we continue to improve the schooling experiences of immigrant youth, take better care of their families and teachers, and create more equitable policy.

AFTERWORD

I HAVE LONG BEEN an admirer of the Internationals Network, not simply for their model pedagogical approach, but for the socioemotional spaces of belonging they nurture for their students. Their ability to provide an inoculative function against both the stresses of migration—including language acquisition, cultural adjustment, and academic transitions—as well as societal hostilities and discrimination has proven instrumental to their success and represents an approach that other schools should strive to emulate.

Sanctuary School's central argument—that sanctuary must encompass both innovation and protection—resonates deeply with my own research on immigrant students' developmental needs during the fraught transitions brought on by migration. Through rich narratives and careful analysis, Miranda demonstrates how International High School (IHS) cultivates a space of possibility for its newly arrived immigrant students.

What makes IHS stand out is its comprehensive approach to creating belonging beyond mere physical safety. The school's commitment to viewing language as an asset, integrating immigration into the curriculum, cultivating cultural respect, and intentional community-building (to name a few) illustrate how sanctuary practices can nurture students' fundamental sense of belonging for all students, regardless of documentation status. These practices create what I call "psychological sanctuary," where students feel valued and seen for who they are, not defined by their immigration status.

And, of course, *Sanctuary School* could not be timelier. Miranda's deep ethnographic account offers a compelling vision of how schools can move beyond mere protection to create genuine sanctuaries for immigrant youth in an era of unprecedented hostility toward immigrant communities during the 45th Presidential Administration.

The administration's hostile immigration policies provide important lessons about the critical role of schools as safe havens. When IHS faced increased ICE activity and enforcement threats, they demonstrated how schools must move beyond symbolic gestures to create substantive protection. Their response—developing accompaniment plans, providing legal resources, and maintaining unwavering support for vulnerable families—offers a blueprint for schools preparing for potential future challenges.

As students, families, schools, and communities face renewed threats of aggressive anti-immigrant policies, IHS's example becomes even more significant. Their experience during the previous administration—transitioning from treating anti-immigrant rhetoric as distant political discourse to developing concrete protective measures—provides crucial lessons for educators nationwide. The school's ability to maintain academic excellence while providing comprehensive support demonstrates that creating nurturing environments and educational achievement strengthen each other.

The practices documented—from multilingual instruction to community organizing—offer concrete examples of how schools can better serve our immigrant youth, particularly in challenging political times. This book makes a vital contribution to our understanding of how educational institutions can create genuine sanctuaries that protect, nurture, and empower immigrant students, while providing a roadmap for schools nationwide.

Carola Suárez-Orozco, PhD
Professor in Residence
Harvard Graduate School of Education
Director, Immigration Initiative at Harvard

APPENDIX

Notes for Novice Ethnographers

AS A COLLEGE PROFESSOR, I teach qualitative research methods and how to do ethnographic fieldwork in cities and schools. I always begin with lessons and activities on how to talk to strangers. Many of my students, regardless of age or degree, hesitate to pick up the phone to call a stranger or visit someone at their office if their first email goes unanswered. Then, once they have access to a site, they feel uncomfortable asking people to sit with them for an interview because they do not want to ask personal questions or waste their time. I understand these impulses but strongly believe that learning to engage strangers in the process of storytelling is a beautiful and necessary skill, particularly when trying to understand how to make schools more humane, justice-oriented places of possibility, particularly for people who are ostracized, marginalized, and minoritized in the broader society.

I hope that by sharing my approach, I can guide students interested in the deep study of schools on how to prepare for fieldwork, take risks, talk with strangers, navigate discomfort in new and unfamiliar places, and engage in thoughtful reciprocity when people share their space, time, and stories with a researcher, particularly a novice researcher just learning the craft.

DEEP STUDY

Before stepping foot in International High School (IHS), I spent almost two full years reading everything I could find about global migration and education. I read decades of research on how schools have historically worked with immigrant students and how different educational practices have affected their learning and adaptation. I read broadly in different disciplines and consumed media and novels by and about immigrants and refugees to develop a broader understanding of the experience of crossing borders.[1] I read extensively on US immigration history and policy to better understand geopolitics and push and pull factors.[2] Finally, I focused in on how the experiences of immigrant students in schools had been studied across disciplines.[3] This background research helped me identify what had not been explored yet and guided my focus once I started learning about the Internationals Network of Public Schools. I began reading about the Internationals Network and quickly realized how highly regarded they were, attracting attention from prominent scholars such as Michele Fine, Carolina Suarez-Orozco, and Reva Jaffe-Walters. I read every academic book, policy report, and popular press book about International High Schools in the early 2000s to try to learn as much as I could about the history of the Network.[4] Finally, I continued reading as new works were published to stay current in the literature.[5]

Like many novice researchers, I almost abandoned my research entirely, assuming everything there was to write about the schools had been done. Still, my curiosity and excitement drove me to do research in hopeful schools, rather than the heartbreaking schools in countless books and articles, with Angela Valenzuela's *Subtractive Schooling* always serving as the ultimate foil for the type of research I hoped to do.[6] My advisor reminded me that ethnographic research, done at a different point in time by a different researcher, makes for a different study and so I pressed forward.

I approached a well-connected professor with a request to connect me with the Network's key figures. He kindly arranged a meeting with Claire Sylvan, the Executive Director at the time. A few weeks later, I anxiously awaited a meeting with Claire at the Internationals office in downtown Manhattan. Claire generously talked with me for an hour about the Network's history and impact. When I walked out of the building and onto Wall Street, I knew there was still more to uncover about the schools and the Networks that guided them. Claire helped me see that the schools were living laboratories for innovation and that the Network was still evolving. I was eager to begin visiting the schools to see them for myself.

DEALING WITH DISAPPOINTMENT AND DOUBT

I knew I would need approval from a principal to proceed with my research in one of their schools, so I embarked on an intensive outreach campaign, contacting principals through phone and email, starting with those schools nearest to my apartment, knowing proximity to the school would mean I could spend more time observing and less time commuting. Despite my persistent efforts, I faced numerous rejections. Principals at the well-established schools were inundated with research requests from students like me. They also had more established scholars who brought experience, technical skills, and grant money. Again, I considered abandoning my project and starting over.

In a final effort to gain access to an International High School, I called the main office number of International High School, the school furthest from where I lived in a neighborhood I did not know well. When Susan, the now-retired administrative assistant, answered the phone, I delivered my pitch with trepidation. To my surprise, Susan responded by inviting me to an orientation to learn more about the school the following week. This invitation felt like a breakthrough, and I was elated.

NAVIGATING ACCESS

On the day I was invited to visit IHS, I left home early, giving myself two hours to navigate trains and buses, and still almost arrived late to the orientation. I signed in with security and rushed up the stairs to the school's front office before being ushered by Susan into a classroom filled with a half dozen young-looking college students. Bryan began by introducing himself and going through a brief PowerPoint presentation on the mission and design of the school. Given how much time I had invested in learning about the Network and school, I was familiar with the presentation's content. I quickly realized that the orientation was for college students studying secondary education at nearby colleges and needed to observe in a school for one hundred hours before they could start student teaching. I panicked when I realized Susan had mistaken me for one of the students who had actually been invited to the orientation. I was anxious Bryan would think I had finagled my way into the school dishonestly.

Once we were dismissed, I waited until the room cleared to talk to Bryan one-on-one. We still laugh about the awkwardness of this first encounter. He remembers being surprised by how much I knew about the school. I remember just wanting to be invited back. He agreed to let me observe as often as I wanted, and I knew better than to ask if I could do my dissertation research in the school after one short meeting. By that point, I was enrolled in a methods class that had Internal Review Board (IRB) approval, which allowed me to do an ethnographic pilot study of IHS if I did not publish anything from the study. I took full advantage of Bryan's invitation to observe and my class's permission to begin practicing the skills I would need to be able to eventually do an ethnography of a school.

TALKING TO STRANGERS AND IMMERSING MYSELF IN THE SCHOOL

Being an active part of the school community was essential to truly understanding the daily life at IHS and gaining the trust of the teachers, staff, and students with whom I interacted. I quickly immersed myself in the routines and activities of school. This meant not just watching from the back of the classroom but participating in the life of the school—joining classroom instruction, attending committee meetings, chaperoning field trips, and helping with the yearbook.

In the spring of 2015, I spent two to three days each week at the school for about five weeks. After each visit, I would carefully expand my field notes and make a research plan for the following day. While at IHS, I paid close attention to various aspects of school life, asking myself questions like: What is the atmosphere in the hallways during different times of the day? How do students and teachers interact? What are the stories they tell about these interactions? I observed these dynamics in various settings, from classrooms to after-school meetings, which gave me insights into how the school operated internally and within its community.

At the end of the five weeks, I picked up a few dozen donuts and a jug of coffee on my way to visit the school as a thank you to the teachers for letting me observe in their classroom. Then, I asked Bryan and Lara if they would allow me to do my study at the school. Mercifully, they agreed, and I began the process of writing and defending my proposal.

I successfully defended my proposal and received IRB permission from NYU and the DOE to begin fieldwork in September 2016. Being present in the school day in and day out was crucial. Over time, I attended classes, participated in staff meetings, and joined in on school events like talent shows and art gallery openings. I continued volunteering and helping out wherever needed. Usually, this meant working with students one-on-one on PBAT essays in the assistant principal's office or working with a group on a project while sitting at their table. I made copies, graded papers, and organized paperwork. I attended Thanksgiving feasts, school plays, graduations, open houses, parent–teacher conferences, career days, and sporting events. Sometimes, I sat quietly at the middle table of the classroom, observing how students interacted with each other. Other times, I was invited to join discussions, help students with assignments, and sit on PBAT panels. Active participation helped me see how the school operated and understand social dynamics. Being an active participant in the school allowed me to see beyond what was happening in the classroom and curriculum to fully understand the school community and culture. It was not just about watching what happened but having meaningful interactions with school actors and building trusting relationships.

GENERATING DATA THROUGH INTERVIEWS AND FIELDNOTES

Conducting interviews was a key part of my research. I held semi-structured interviews with a wide range of participants, including students, alumni, teachers, staff, and school leaders. These interviews provided invaluable insights into how school policies are developed, disseminated, and implemented, as well as how students experience the school community and the changing political environment. By talking to people from various backgrounds and perspectives, I was able to uncover underlying assumptions and gain a deeper understanding of IHS's culture and practices. Through these interviews, I aimed to create a comfortable space for open conversations and to build trust with the participants. This approach allowed me to gather stories that reflect the complexity of the school environment and the diverse experiences of those who are part of it.

To really understand the life of the school, I had to see things from different angles. In addition to formal interviews, I had many informal conversations in the hallways or over lunch. These discussions created space for personal stories, challenges, and insights into the school's culture. I interviewed veteran teachers who had been at IHS for years and new teachers who were just learning the ropes. I talked to students who had been at the school for a long time and had a deep understanding of its culture and those who had just arrived. The counseling team sat with me for a focus group focused on supporting the social and emotional needs of students. The students, teachers, and leaders whose stories I focus on in this book were interviewed multiple times. These different perspectives helped me piece together a more complete picture of what makes IHS tick.

I was able to interview two administrators, twenty-nine teachers, a paraprofessional, a school aide, a parent coordinator, a community liaison, the administrative assistant, the business manager, two counselors, and a social worker. I was particularly eager to talk with teachers who played leadership roles, such as team leaders or department heads, and those who were active in committees that made decisions about discipline, hiring, and school policies. For the student participants, I focused on those who had moved to the United States between the ages of ten and sixteen, or who had first enrolled in US schools between sixth and tenth grades. This study concentrated on students enrolled during the 2016–2017 academic year who were between the ages of fourteen and twenty-one. I also interviewed two alums who had returned to work at the school.

When I listen to these interviews so many years later, I realize how much I still had to learn about the art of listening and the power of stories. Sometimes, I wish I had asked follow-up questions or dug deeper into a story. This is particularly true of interviews I did in Spanish, where I cringe at my mistakes or the cadence of my voice. Fortunately, I have stayed in touch with teachers at IHS and can text, email, or call as I write this book. This is not always possible, but I am glad I continued to nurture my relationships with teachers at the school not only because it has helped me write a more updated and accurate book but also because I am now a professor with meager but existent grants and students who want to learn from the school in the same way I did, by observing and making themselves useful members of the community, offering mentoring, college counseling, and sitting on portfolio presentations.

Taking detailed notes was crucial in capturing the essence of IHS. These notes included descriptions of the physical environment and social atmosphere, capturing everything from gestures and tone of voice to the interactions between students and teachers. One thing I did not fully grasp as a doctoral student and see my students struggle with now is understanding the value in taking detailed and descriptive fieldnotes. It was not until I started my first round of data analysis in January 2017 that I realized how terrible I was at writing fieldnotes. Details I thought I would remember when jotting down my observation were blurry in my memory. I was constantly backtracking, looking at pictures I took or interviews I had done earlier in the study to jog my memory about a conversation, interaction, or scene. When I finally realized the importance of fieldnotes as data, I began to take breaks in the teacher's lounge during the day to write rich, descriptive notes, using all five senses to try to capture rich details. On days when I did not have time to write notes at the school, I would walk out of the school, turn on my phone's voice memo app, and start describing everything I could remember. Later, I would transcribe these notes. I found that this practice transformed my notes and made the process of writing memos and, eventually, my dissertation, articles, and this book much easier because my notes contained narratives that would become the first draft of a finding section or chapter. Most of the vignettes introducing each chapter were plucked from fieldnotes, and the details I recorded helped me create richer narratives that reflect the daily life at the school, providing a more holistic view of the participants' experiences.

Currently, my students and I use apps like otter.ai and Rev to generate rich, descriptive fieldnotes and reflective journals quickly by using voice-to-text technologies that are constantly improving. These can make the practice of turning observations and jottings from the field into richly detailed fieldnotes faster. Still, it is important to return to those recordings and rough transcripts soon after leaving the field to ensure they capture the scene, atmosphere, and dialogue as accurately as possible.

SHAPING STORIES WITH DOCUMENTS

In addition to conversations and observations, I also gathered hundreds of documents. I collected staff emails, meeting minutes, student work, and curriculum materials. These documents provided a written record of the school's practices and policies, which helped me see how things were done officially. By comparing these documents with what I observed and what people told me, I could see how the official rules lined up with the everyday experiences of the school community. Analyzing documents shed light on how school structures and systems evolved over time.

SITUATING MY SUBJECTIVITY

Understanding and acknowledging my biases was crucial. By consciously setting aside my personal beliefs or assumptions, I was able to better listen to what participants were sharing during interviews or observations. This way, I wasn't trying to force their experiences into any preexisting theories or frameworks. To do this, I maintained a reflective journal to record my personal reactions, thoughts, and challenges throughout the study. This journal helped me stay aware of my biases and subjectivity, acknowledging how my identity and background might influence my interpretations. By documenting my assumptions and the groups I was naturally drawn to, I was able to devise strategies to ensure a diverse range of experiences were represented in my study. This practice allowed me to conduct a more trustworthy study and write an ethnographic account that better represents the lived realities of the participants at IHS.

This process was particularly important after the 2016 election. The political climate at the time was highly charged, and it was easy to let personal emotions and reactions color my understanding of the educational environment for immigrants. At IHS, I made a deliberate effort to listen to the stories of teachers and students with an open mind. By doing this, I could better understand the participants' unique experiences and points of view. It meant approaching their stories with curiosity and without judgment, allowing their voices to speak for themselves. This approach enabled me to gain a clearer, more nuanced understanding of what sanctuary schooling meant for them, based solely on their experiences rather than any preconceived ideas I might have had.

Like all ethnographers, I had to contend with my own ego, gaps in knowledge, and misunderstandings of the community of study. I had many expectations about what I would and would not see at IHS. There were moments when I was shocked, like when I was sitting in a classroom, and a teacher barked at a table of students, "SPEAK ENGLISH!" Since this was so detached from what was typical at the school, even in this teacher's classroom, I wondered in my journal what had happened that day to set the teacher off or if I had missed an inside joke. The students seemed unphased, but my emotional reaction was strong, so I wrote about it. Another example of when I had to situate my subjectivity was in an interview with a Muslim student who told me she hated the school because she had experienced bullying from a boy for wearing a hijab. I wrote later about how sad and disappointed I felt during the interview. I realized I had witnessed her bully being unkind to peers multiple times but framed it differently in my notes. I observed and recorded teacher's meetings about the bully and the interventions counselors were doing with him using restorative justice. I was focused on how the school responded to a student lashing out with deliberate care and kindness. I questioned how I could have missed seeing her hurt and isolation.

Incidents like these would make me doubt my research abilities and the story emerging in most of my data about the school's culture. I grappled with how to represent the school accurately. How could I accurately describe a very human environment where people made mistakes, kids sometimes got into fights, and teachers acted inappropriately, like at any school or place of work, without losing the thread that was so evident in the data that this was a radically different school, particularly for the least likely to find care and success in a school community, like Milagros,

Gonzalo, and the bully? My journal did not answer these questions, but they helped me make sense of what I was feeling and keep it distinct from what I was seeing. Making a deliberate effort to keep these two ways of interpreting the world separate makes the research less messy, creates an audit trail, and keeps me accountable.

MAKING SENSE OF STORIES

The real work of ethnography is in putting pieces of data together in compelling, evidence-based ways to tell a cohesive story. By looking at interview transcripts, fieldnotes, journal entries, and documents over two academic years, I could clearly see through the data how IHS created an environment where immigrant students could thrive. To make sense of the stories I had gathered, I began piecing together the participants' narratives in a way that highlighted the broader themes and patterns that emerged from their stories. I organized these narratives to show how individual incidents were connected and how they reflected the larger culture of the school. The data was clear. The study was not just about the teaching methods or the curriculum; it was about the school's relationships and culture at a particular moment. Teachers and students at IHS interacted in ways that fostered a strong sense of community and belonging. This was crucial for students navigating a new country and education system, even in a crisis and under considerable pressure from outside forces. This process was about more than just identifying patterns; it was about understanding how what was happening in the school differed from previous research on the experiences of immigrant youth and their teachers in US schools.

UNDERSTANDING THE BIGGER PICTURE

The last step in writing a school ethnography is considering the broader social and political context—like immigration policies and educational reforms—and how these factors influence the school's environment. This broader perspective helped me understand not just what was happening at IHS, but why it was happening and what it could mean for other schools and communities. The theme of sanctuary emerged from both inside and outside the school. In a memo in January 2017, I wrote:

> One of the things that I keep coming back to is that this school is amazing but it is so sad that it has to exist at all. That these kids would be made invisible in other schools, that they would be treated like they have a deficit for not speaking English or having an accent, or that we would take the opportunity away from them to learn content and stick them in a room to learn to say "cat" and "dog." It *is* a type of segregation.
>
> In an ideal society, where education is the catalyst for the American Dream, this school should not *have* to exist. Yes, they have created a really special place for kids to be immigrants, but in the society that we are trying to build, this is not the answer. The answer is schools where it is ok to be an immigrant and not have to be segregated and have teachers who understand you and services provided to you because you are a student in a public school in the US and not because you somehow found your way to a sanctuary school. These schools are few and far between. They serve a fraction of the immigrant population. There are many more kids who need what these kids are getting. Do I want to call it a sanctuary school? What does that even mean?

A year later, in January 2018, Lara wrote the following in a weekly newsletter to the staff:

> I was heartened this week to see so many students making progress towards graduation. . . . I am especially thankful for the joy and progress that comes for our students at a time like this one, when so many of our students and families are feeling hopeless and afraid. One of our sister schools had a student picked up by ICE just this past week, the day he turned 18, from his foster home. Families at our "Beyond

> our Rights" workshop last week shared their fears and discussed emergency planning and sanctuary sites. Life and work have changed for our whole community in the year since the inauguration, but I couldn't be prouder of how we continue to strive to create a safe, welcoming and hopeful space for our students, families, and each other.

In the year between my notes and Lara's newsletter, teachers and students tried to make meaningful sense of the concepts of sanctuary cities and sanctuary schools as they managed the daily demands of public schools with the realities of living in a nation hostile to immigrants. I began to see how the stories from the school fit into a larger context. By grounding the lived experiences of students and teachers in these broader realities, I could connect the dots between individual experiences and the larger social and political landscape that shaped those experiences. What emerged was an understanding of sanctuary that was incongruent with how the concept of sanctuary was interpreted in other educational spaces as well as in legal and political realms.

LESSONS LEARNED IN THE FIELD

I wrote this last note on methods with my undergraduate and graduate students in mind—those eager to understand schools, school culture, and the needs of traditionally marginalized and minoritized students. It reflects a journey of risk-taking, relationship-building, and learning from the true experts: immigrant students, New York City school alumni, career educators, school leaders, mental health professionals, social workers, and educational activists dedicated to serving immigrant youth equitably.

NOTES

INTRODUCTION

1. All names are pseudonyms except Lara Evangelista, who elected to use her real name. International High School is one of the fifteen schools in the Internationals Network of Public Schools.
2. In this book, I use terms like "recently arrived immigrant youth," "immigrant teenagers," "immigrant students," and "newcomers" interchangeably to describe the diverse student population at IHS. I made this editorial choice to simplify the narrative and focus on the stories from the school community rather than the terminology. The term "immigrant" is a holistic term to describe people *following multiple patterns of movement between countries.* In academic articles, I often use the terms "im/migrant" and "recently arrived immigrant English learner (RAIEL)" because they are the most inclusive and descriptive terms, but in the context of the book can be distracting to readers and convolute the narrative. I want to emphasize that students at IHS are not a monolith, and they bring considerable cultural and linguistic knowledge to the school community as well as a diversity of pre-migration, migration, and resettlement experiences that depend on their country of origin, geopolitics, family dynamics, premigration and new country socioeconomic status, racism and racialized experiences, gender, sexuality, religion, traumatic experiences, and mental health. Some common terms used in the legal, policy, and institutional realm to describe varied experience of migrant young people include "unaccompanied minors," "Dreamers," "special immigrant juveniles," "transmigrants," "undocumented youth," "asylees," "refugees," "permanent residents," and "citizens." "Immigrant origin youth" is a term used by students who are immigrants themselves or have at least one immigrant parent. This group is further categorized into "first-generation" (born abroad and moved to the United States), "second-generation" (born in the United States to immigrant parents), and "1.5 generation" (born abroad but with significant

formative experiences there). The students at IHS would be considered 1.5 generation by most immigration scholars. Immigrant children and their families navigate complex legal landscapes, which impact their experiences and opportunities in the United States. Finally, the "immigrant paradox or advantage" is a phrase used to describe how some immigrant origin youth perform better in school than their native-born peers. This advantage is not uniform across all immigrant groups and can vary depending on factors such as English proficiency, wealth, and the quality of education received in their home countries. In the conclusion, I include notes on where to read more about the specific experiences of particular im/migrant communities, the plights of refugees and asylum seekers, and the geopolitical histories that impact migration and resettlement patterns today.

3. *New York Times'* Upshot wrote that Mrs. Clinton's chance of losing is about the same as the probability that an N.F.L. kicker misses a 37-yard field goal. https://www.nytimes.com/interactive/2016/upshot/presidential-polls-forecast.html.
4. Naomi Paik, *Bans, Walls, Raids, Sanctuary: Understanding U.S. Immigration for the Twenty-First Century* (University of California Press, 2022).
5. Mark Keierleber, "'Sanctuary Schools' Across America Defy Trump's Immigration Crackdown," *The Guardian*, August 21, 2017, https://www.theguardian.com/us-news/2017/aug/21/american-schools-defy-trump-immigration-crackdown.
6. *Universal Declaration of Human Rights* (United Nations, 1948), https://www.un.org/en/about-us/universal-declaration-of-human-rights; "What Is the Universal Declaration of Human Rights and Why Was it Created?," Amnesty International, https://www.amnesty.org/en/what-we-do/universal-declaration-of-human-rights.
7. Sarah Dryden-Peterson, *Right Where We Belong: How Refugee Teachers and Student are Changing the Future of Education* (Harvard University Press, 2022).
8. Jonathan Blitzer, *Everyone Who Is Gone Is Here* (Penguin, 2024), 68–69.
9. Jim Corbett, *The Sanctuary Church* (Pendle Hill, 1985).
10. Corbett, *The Sanctuary Church.*
11. Elizabeth G. Ferris, *Beyond Borders: Refugees, Migrants, and Human Rights in the Post Cold-War Era* (WCC Publications, 1993); Renny Golden and Michael McConnell, *Sanctuary: The New Underground Railroad* (Orbis, 1986); Gary MacEoin, ed., *Sanctuary: A Resource Guide for Understanding and Participating in the Central American Refugees' Struggle*, 1st ed. (Harper & Row, 1985); Judith McDaniel, *Sanctuary: A Journey* (Firebrand, 1987).
12. Robert Tomsho, *The American Sanctuary Movement* (Texas Monthly Press, 1987).
13. Daniel Corral, "The Relationship Between Immigration Enforcement and Educational Attainment: The Role of Sanctuary Policies," *AERA Open* 7 (2021), https://doi.org/10.1177/23328584211037253; Robert Nott, "SFPS Board Votes to Become 'Sanctuary School District,'" *The Santa Fe New Mexican*, December 7, 2016, https://www.santafenewmexican.com/news/education/sfps-board-

votes-to-become-sanctuary-school-district/article_7e724034-7773-599d-af2e-7b4f8a518d61.html.

14. *Plyler v. Doe* and the Family Educational Rights and Privacy Act (FERPA) provide legal precedent for schools to protect all personal student data from immigration officials.
15. Corral, "The Relationship Between Immigration Enforcement and Educational Attainment."
16. Scholars like Susan Bibler Coutin, A. Naomi Paik, Alexandra Délano Alonso, and Elliott Young argue that the term "sanctuary" has evolved as a symbolic and powerful idea, uniting people in transnational movements of resistance to global power imbalances. Alonso argues "sanctuary has no clear or consistently understood and applied meaning" while Young posits it is an aspirational statement of values. Countin suggests that sanctuary can be understood as a transnational movement that has pursued and achieved different political goals in different geographic locations and sociopolitical contexts. Paik describes it as a radical welcome and judgment-free embrace of anyone. These scholarly interpretations differ from the practical application of the word by institutions to signal a protective stance in preventing the federal government from physically removing undocumented people from the institution's grounds. Alexandra Delano Alonso, "Sanctuary Campus: Resistance and Protection Within and Beyond the University," *Avery Review* 21 (2017): 53–63; Paik, *Bans, Walls, Raids, Sanctuary*; Hector Perla and Susan Bibler Coutin, "Legacies and Origins of the 1980s US–Central American Sanctuary Movement," in *Sanctuary Practices in International Perspectives*, ed. Randy K. Lippert and Sean Rehaag (Routledge, 2012), 73–91; Elliot Young, "On Sanctuary: What Is in a Name?," HuffPost, November 30, 2016, https://www.huffpost.com/entry/on-sanctuary-what-is-in-a-name_b_583f8feae4b0b93e10f8df24.
17. Cory Collins, citing *Plyler v. Doe, Lau v. Nichols,* and the Family Educational Rights and Privacy Act (FERPA), argues, "taken together, these laws and legal precedents paint a clear picture: Sanctuary schools, despite critics' words, are not running afoul of the law; they are upholding it." This sentiment represents the mainstream interpretations of Sanctuary in schools from 2017 to the present day. Another example is the ACLU of California Model Sanctuary School Board Policy (https://www.aclusocal.org/sites/default/files/february_2018_aclu_model_sanctuary_school_board_policy.pdf). While both encourage a welcoming school culture, the guidance they provide to school focuses on protection of students' physical safety while on campus and data privacy. Cory Collins, "School as Sanctuary," *Learning for Justice,* Fall 2020, https://www.learningforjustice.org/magazine/fall-2020/school-as-sanctuary.
18. Barbara Oomen, "Cities of Refuge: Rights, Culture and the Creation of Cosmopolitan Citizenship," in *Cultures, Citizenship and Human Rights,* ed. Rosemarie Buikema et al. (Routledge, 2019), 121–36.

19. The administration attempted to rescind Deferred Action for Childhood Arrivals (DACA); retracted Temporary Protected Status for immigrants from Haiti, Nicaragua, Honduras, and El Salvador; reduced the number of refugees allowed into the United States; forcibly separated almost five thousand children from their families at the southern border; canceled funding for recreational activities in unaccompanied minor shelters; expelled migrant children from other countries into Mexico; and made legal immigration more difficult and naturalization more expensive. Even the Civics exam that immigrants must pass to become naturalized citizens was adapted to reflect the administration's politics and agenda. Immigration Policy Tracking Project, *1,030 Trump-Era Immigration Policies (and Their Current Status)*, August 24, 2023, https://immpolicytracking.org/home.
20. For examples, see Sergio Martínez-Beltrán, "Pushed by Public Opinion Shift, Democrats Adopt Immigration Restrictions," NPR, November 1, 2024, https://www.npr.org/2024/10/29/nx-s1-5171441/democrats-shift-immigration; Luke Garrett, "Vance Defends Spreading Claims That Haitian Migrants Are Eating Pets," NPR, September 15, 2024, https://www.npr.org/2024/09/15/nx-s1-5113140/vance-false-claims-haitian-migrants-pets.
21. "Americans hold complex views on what should happen to undocumented immigrants. As President-elect Donald Trump prepares to ramp up mass deportations, about three-quarters of U.S. adults say they are at least somewhat concerned about the number of immigrants entering the country illegally, and a majority support enforcing mass deportation." Jens Manuel Krogstad and Sahana Mukherjee, "Most Americans Say Undocumented Immigrants Should Be Able to Stay Legally Under Certain Conditions," Pew Research Center, November 22, 2024, https://www.pewresearch.org/short-reads/2024/11/22/most-americans-say-undocumented-immigrants-should-be-able-to-stay-legally-under-certain-conditions.
22. Patricia Gándara and Jongyeon Ee, eds., *Schools Under Siege: The Impact of Immigration Enforcement on Educational Equity* (Harvard Education Press, 2022). A *testimonio* is a first-person, narrative account in which a witness shares their lived experiences of injustice, oppression, or marginalization. Rooted in a collaborative tradition, *testimonios* serve as a means of healing, empowerment, and advocacy, revealing racial, classed, gendered, and nativist injustices. By amplifying personal truths, *testimonios* raise awareness, foster solidarity, and promote social change. See the special issue of *Equity & Excellence in Education* from 2012 on the history of the term and its use as a methodology. In particular, Kathryn Blackmer Reyes and Julia E. Curry Rodríguez, "Testimonio: Origins, Terms, and Resources," *Equity & Excellence in Education* 45, no. 3 (2012): 525–38 is very helpful.
23. Muzaffar Chishti and Kathleen Bush-Joseph, *In the Twilight Zone: Record Number of U.S. Immigrants Are in Limbo Statuses* (MPI, 2023), https://www.migrationpolicy.org/article/twilight-immigration-status.

24. Ninety-five percent have English Language Learner (ELL) accommodations.
25. Students with Interrupted Formal Education (SIFE). The acronym SLIFE is also used to specify cases of *limited* formal education. The SIFE or SLIFE label is generally applied to recently arrived immigrant youth whose formal education was interrupted during migration, in their home country, or in a previous country of residence. See Chris K. Chang-Bacon, "Generation Interrupted: Rethinking 'Students with Interrupted Formal Education' (SIFE) in the Wake of a Pandemic," *Educational Researcher* 50, no. 3 (2021): 187–96.
26. Reva Jaffe-Walter, "Negotiating Mandates and Memory: Inside a Small Schools Network for Immigrant Youth," *Teachers College Record* 110 (2008): 2040–66.
27. Thea Renda Abu El-Haj, *Unsettled Belonging: Educating Palestinian American Youth After 9/11* (University of Chicago Press, 2015); Reva Jaffe-Walter, *Coercive Concern: Nationalism, Liberalism, and the Schooling of Muslim Youth* (Stanford University Press, 2016); Stacy J. Lee, *Up Against Whiteness: Race, School, and Immigrant Youth* (Teachers College Press, 2005); Laurie Olsen, *Made in America: Immigrant Students in Our Public Schools* (New Press, 1997); Angela Valenzuela, *Subtractive Schooling: US-Mexican Youth and the Politics of Caring* (State University of New York Press, 1999).
28. Clifford Geertz, *The Interpretation of Cultures* (Basic Books, 1973).
29. *Palanca* directly translates to "lever," but is a word that means having or using connections, or to explain a culture of nepotism that is profoundly powerful in most parts of Colombia, particularly in the large cities where wealth is concentrated.
30. People do not realize that the impact of the Biden administrative action to allow spouses of US citizens to parole in place will keep families together.

CHAPTER 1

1. Field Notes, February 2017.
2. Dara Lind, "Trump on Deported Immigrants: 'They're Not People. They're Animals,'" *VOX*, May 17, 2018, https://www.vox.com/2018/5/16/17362870/trump-immigrants-animals-ms-13-illegal; Erin McCann and Jonah Engel Bromwich, "'Nasty Woman' and 'Bad Hombres': The Real Debate Winners?," *New York Times*, October 20, 2016, https://www.nytimes.com/2016/10/21/us/politics/nasty-woman-and-bad-hombres-the-real-debate-winners.html; Amber Phillips, "'They're Rapists.' President Trump's Campaign Launch Speech Two Years Later, Annotated," *Washington Post*, June 16, 2017, https://www.washingtonpost.com/news/the-fix/wp/2017/06/16/theyre-rapists-presidents-trump-campaign-launch-speech-two-years-later-annotated.
3. Ran Abramitzky et al., "Law-Abiding Immigrants: The Incarceration Gap Between Immigrants and the US-Born, 1870–2020," National Bureau of Economic Research, March 2024, https://www.nber.org/papers/w31440.

4. Steve Drummond, "Politics in the Classroom: How Much is Too Much?," NPR, August 6, 2015, https://www.npr.org/sections/ed/2015/08/06/415498760/the-role-of-politics-in-the-classroom; Javier C. Hernandez, "Judge Says No to Teachers' Campaign Buttons, but Yes to Certain Politicking," *New York Times* 158, no. 54467 (2008): A20-L; Andrew Jones, "From Brexit to Trump: Should Teachers Talk Politics in the Classroom?," *The Guardian*, January 11, 2017, https://www.theguardian.com/teacher-network/2017/jan/11/brexit-trump-teaching-politics-classroom; Denisha Jones, Deena Khalil, and R. Davis Dixon, "Teacher-Advocates Respond to ESSA: 'Support the Good Parts—Resist the Bad Parts,'" *Peabody Journal of Education* 92, no. 4 (2017): 445–65, https://doi.org/10.1080/0161956X.2017.1349479.
5. Approximately 17.6 million US children under age 18 lived with at least one immigrant parent in 2022. They accounted for 26 percent of all 68.6 million children under age 18, up from 24 percent in 2010, 19 percent in 2000, and 13 percent in 1990. Jeanne Batalova, "Frequently Requested Statistics on Immigrants and Immigration in the United States," Migration Policy Institute, March 13, 2024, https://www.migrationpolicy.org/article/frequently-requested-statistics-immigrants-and-immigration-united-states-2024#children-immigrants.
6. Lilyana Ortega et al., "Outcomes of a Restorative Circles Program in a High School Setting," *Psychology of Violence* 6, no. 3 (2016): 459.
7. Pete Railand, "Sanctuary Cities Now," Just Seeds, January 2020, https://justseeds.org/product/sanctuary-cities-now-3.
8. Mackenzie Mays, "Fresno County Board of Education Urges Local Districts to Support Undocumented Students," *The Fresno Bee*, February 22, 2017, https://www.fresnobee.com/news/local/education-lab/article134077694.html.
9. Cassi Feldman, "Despite Trump Immigration Crackdown, City Tells Students and Families: 'We Stand with You,'" Chalkbeat New York, January 30, 2017, https://www.chalkbeat.org/newyork/2017/1/30/21102944/despite-trump-immigration-crackdown-city-tells-students-and-families-we-stand-with-you; Lee V. Gains, "Evanston School District 202 Adopts 'Haven' Resolution for Some Immigrant Students," *Chicago Tribune*, January 18, 2017, http://www.chicagotribune.com/suburbs/evanston/news/ct-evr-evanston-school-district-202-adopts-haven-policy-tl-0126-20170118-story.html; Kyra Gurney, "Miami Schools Vote to Protect Undocumented Immigrants, Refugees," *Miami Herald*, March 15, 2017, https://www.miamiherald.com/news/local/education/article138758253.html; Saint Paul Public Schools, "Resolution Regarding District Practices Related to Immigration and Customs Enforcement," 2017, https://worldwithoutgenocide.org/wp-content/uploads/2019/03/St.-Paul-School-District-Resolution.pdf.
10. Andrea Salcedo, "Workshops Help Teachers Cope with Students' Immigration Fears," *Chicago Sun Times*, March 19, 2017, http://chicago.suntimes.com/news/workshops-help-teachers-cope-with-students-immigration-fears.

11. Claudia Rowe, "Navigating Minefield of Student-Immigration Questions, Widely Honored Teacher to Host Town Hall," *Seattle Times*, February 23, 2017, https://www.seattletimes.com/education-lab/navigating-minefield-of-student-immigration-questions-widely-honored-teacher-to-host-town-hall.
12. A. Naomi Paik, *Bans, Walls, Raids, Sanctuary: Understanding U.S. Immigration for the 21st Century* (University of California Press, 2018), 102.
13. Paik, *Bans, Walls, Raids, Sanctuary*, 106.
14. Immigrants Rising, Understanding the Sanctuary School & Safe Zone Movement; Cory Collins, "Toolkit For 'School as Sanctuary,'" *Learning for Justice* 65 (Fall 2020), https://www.learningforjustice.org/magazine/fall-2020/toolkit-for-school-as-sanctuary.

CHAPTER 2

1. Paulo Coelho, *The Alchemist* (HarperCollins, 1993).
2. Valeria Luiselli, *Tell Me How It Ends: An Essay in 40 Questions* (Coffee House Press, 2017).
3. Óscar Martínez, *The Beast: Riding the Rails and Dodging Narcos on the Migrant Trail* (Verso, 2014).
4. Brian Resnick and National Journal, "Why We Don't Immediately Send the Border Kids Back," *The Atlantic*, July 8, 2014, https://www.theatlantic.com/politics/archive/2014/07/why-we-dont-immediately-send-the-border-kids-back/453345/.
5. Muzaffar Chishti and Faye Hipsman, "Dramatic Surge in the Arrival of Unaccompanied Children Has Deep Roots and No Simple Solutions," Migration Policy Institute, June 13, 2014, https://www.migrationpolicy.org/article/dramatic-surge-arrival-unaccompanied-children-has-deep-roots-and-no-simple-solutions.
6. Eric Nadelstern, "The International High School at LaGuardia Community College: Bridging the Gap," paper presented at the Annual Meeting of the Teachers of English to Speakers of Other Languages (20th, Anaheim, CA, March 3–8, 1986).
7. Lesley Bartlett and Ofelia García, *Additive Schooling in Subtractive Times: Dominican Immigrant Youth in the Heights* (Vanderbilt University Press, 2011); Monisha Bajaj et al., *Humanizing Education for Immigrant and Refugee Youth: 20 Strategies for the Classroom and Beyond* (Teachers College Press, 2022); Michelle Fine and Reva Jaffe-Walter, "Swimming on Oxygen: Resistance and Possibility for Immigrant Youth Under Siege," *Anthropology & Education Quarterly* 38, no. 1 (2007): 76–96.
8. Michael Elsen-Rooney, "They Thought Graduation Was Near. Instead, Several Immigrant Students Were Pressured to Transfer," Chalkbeat New York, May 20, 2024, https://www.chalkbeat.org/newyork/2024/05/20/nyc-high-school-principal-push-out-immigrant-students-staff-families-say/; Benjamin

Mueller, "Westbury Schools Agree to Alter Enrollment Policies for Immigrants," *New York Times*, March 1, 2016, https://www.nytimes.com/2016/03/02/nyregion/westbury-schools-agree-to-alter-enrollment-policies-for-immigrants.html.

9. Marguerite Lukes, *Latino Immigrant Youth and Interrupted Schooling: Dropouts, Dreamers and Alternative Pathways to College* (Multilingual Matters, 2015).
10. National Center for Education Statistics, "High School Graduation Rates," Condition of Education, US Department of Education, Institute of Education Sciences, 2024, https://nces.ed.gov/programs/coe/indicator/coi.
11. Jeffrey S. Passel and Jens Manuel Krogstad, "What We Know About Unauthorized Immigrants Living in the U.S.," Pew Research Center, November 16, 2023, https://www.pewresearch.org/short-reads/2023/11/16/what-we-know-about-unauthorized-immigrants-living-in-the-us/.
12. Jeanne Batalova, "Frequently Requested Statistics on Immigrants and Immigration in the United States," Migration Policy Institute, March 13, 2024, https://www.migrationpolicy.org/article/frequently-requested-statistics-immigrants-and-immigration-united-states-2024#children-immigrants.
13. Hirokazu Yoshikawa, *Immigrants Raising Citizens: Undocumented Parents and Their Children* (Russell Sage Foundation, 2011).
14. Kelly Allen et al., "What Schools Need to Know About Fostering School Belonging: A Meta-Analysis," *Educational Psychology Review* 30 (2018): 1–34; Leon Grinberg and Rebeca Grinberg, *Psychoanalytic Perspectives on Migration and Exile* (Yale University Press, 1989).
15. Roberto G. Gonzales, Luisa L. Heredia, and Genevieve Negrón-Gonzales, "Untangling Plyler's Legacy: Undocumented Students, Schools, and Citizenship," *Harvard Educational Review* 85, no. 3 (2015): 318–41; Luisa Laura Heredia, "Lives in Limbo: Undocumented and Coming of Age in America," *NACLA Report on the Americas* 48, no. 4 (2016): 410.
16. *Plyler v. Doe*, 457 US 202 (1982), United States Supreme Court, No. 80-1538, paragraph 3.
17. Kalyn Belsha, "Think Tank with Ties to Trump Lays Out Plan to Deny Free Education to Undocumented Students," Chalkbeat, April 9, 2024, https://www.chalkbeat.org/2024/04/09/plyler-protects-undocumented-students-heritage-foundation-seeks-challenge/.
18. Farah Z. Ahmad and Ulrich Boser, "America's Leaky Pipeline for Teachers of Color: Getting More Teachers of Color into the Classroom," *Center for American Progress*, 2014, https://cdn.americanprogress.org/wp-content/uploads/2014/05/TeachersOfColor-report.pdf; Hua-Yu Sebastian Cherng and Peter F. Halpin, "The Importance of Minority Teachers: Student Perceptions of Minority Versus White Teachers," *Educational Researcher* 45, no. 7 (2016):

407–20; Hua-Yu Sebastian Cherng, "If They Think I Can: Teacher Bias and Youth of Color Expectations and Achievement," *Social Science Research* 66 (2017): 170–86; Seth Gershenson, Stephen B. Holt, and Nicholas W. Papageorge, "Who Believes in Me? The Effect of Student–Teacher Demographic Match on Teacher Expectations," *Economics of Education Review* 52 (2016): 209–24.

CHAPTER 3

1. Sheila M. Fram and Ellyn M. Dickmann, "How the School Built Environment Exacerbates Bullying and Peer Harassment," *Children, Youth and Environments* 22, no. 1 (2012): 227–49; Paul Horton, Camilla Forsberg, and Robert Thornberg, "Places and Spaces: Exploring Interconnections Between School Environment, Resources and Social Relations," *Educational Research* 65, no. 4 (2023): 462–77.
2. Kara D. Brown, "Estonian Schoolscapes and the Marginalization of Regional Identity in Education," *European Education* 37, no. 3 (2005): 78–89.
3. "Flushing Asphalt Schoolyard to be Transformed into Green Playground," NYC Department of Environmental Protection, https://www.nyc.gov/html/dep/html/press_releases/17-071pr.shtml.
4. Clifford Geertz, *The Interpretations of Cultures* (Basic Books, 1973).
5. Kristina F. Brezicha and Chandler Patton Miranda, "Actions Speak Louder Than Words: Examining School Practices That Support Immigrant Students' Feelings of Belonging," *Equity & Excellence in Education* 55, no. 1–2 (2022): 133–47; Laurie Olsen, *Made in America* (New Press, 1997), 37–57; Carola Suarez-Orozco and Marcelo Suarez-Orozco, *Children of Immigration* (Harvard University Press, 2001); Carola Suarez-Orozco, Marcelo Suarez-Orozco, and Irena Todorova, *Learning in a New Land* (Harvard University Press, 2008), 79–84.
6. Hua-Yu Sebastian Cherng, "Social Isolation Among Racial/Ethnic Minority Immigrant Youth," *Sociology Compass* 9, no. 6 (2015): 509–18; Ernest V. E. Hodges et al., "The Power of Friendship: Protection Against an Escalating Cycle of Peer Victimization," *Developmental Psychology* 35, no. 1 (1999): 94–101.
7. Jongyeon Ee and Patricia Gándara, "The Impact of Immigration Enforcement on the Nation's Schools," *American Educational Research Journal* 57, no. 2 (2020): 840–71.
8. Angela Valenzuela, *Subtractive Schooling: US-Mexican Youth and the Politics of Caring* (State University of New York Press, 2010).
9. Students who enroll at any of the Internationals Network of Public Schools in New York must score at Entering, Emerging, or Transitioning on the NYSESLAT exam and have been in the United States for less than four years when they start ninth grade. "About Us," https://www.IHSnyc.org/about_us.

10. Rebecca M. Callahan, "Tracking and High School English Learners: Limiting Opportunity to Learn," *American Educational Research Journal* 42, no. 2 (2005): 305–28; Rebecca M. Callahan, Lauren Schudde, and Kimberly Pack-Cosme, "Moving the Needle for Ever-ELs? Advanced Math Course Taking and College Enrollment," *International Multilingual Research Journal* 18, no. 2 (2024): 173–95.
11. "High School Graduation Rates for English Learners," Office of English Language Acquisition, US Department of Education (NCELA, 2020), https://ncela.ed.gov/sites/default/files/legacy/files/fast_facts/20200916-ELGraduationRatesFactSheet-508.pdf.
12. Looping describes when students stay with the same teacher for over a year. Andrew J. Hill and Daniel B. Jones, "A Teacher Who Knows Me: The Academic Benefits of Repeat Student-Teacher Matches," *Economics of Education Review* 64 (2018): 1–12; NaYoung Hwang, Brian Kisida, and Cory Koedel, "A Familiar Face: Student-Teacher Rematches and Student Achievement," *Economics of Education Review* 85 (2021): 102194.
13. Marjorie Faulstich Orellana, *Translating Childhoods: Immigrant Youth, Language, and Culture* (Rutgers University Press, 2009), 68.
14. Andrew J. Martin, "Holding Back and Holding Behind: Grade Retention and Students' Non-Academic and Academic Outcomes," *British Educational Research Journal* 37, no. 5 (2011): 739–63.
15. Mieke Goos, Joana Pipa, and Francisco Peixoto, "Effectiveness of Grade Retention: A Systematic Review and Meta-Analysis," *Educational Research Review* 34 (2021): 100401.
16. Studies consistently find that, while the role is vague and school-dependent, most assistant principals report that they spend most of their time managing discipline. Rinat Cohen and Chen Schechter, "Becoming an Assistant Principal: Mapping Factors That Facilitate or Hinder Entering the Role," *International Journal of Educational Leadership Preparation* 14, no. 1 (2019): 99–112; Charles Hausman et al., "The Worklife of the Assistant Principal," *Journal of Educational Administration* 40, no. 2 (2002): 136–57.
17. Reva Jaffe-Walter and Chandler Patton Miranda, "Segregation or Sanctuary? Examining the Educational Possibilities of Counterpublics for Immigrant English Learners," *Leadership and Policy in Schools* 19, no. 1 (2020): 104–22.
18. Amy Zimmer, "How to Help Struggling Students? NYC's Comfort Dog Program Might Unleash Some Answers," Chalkbeat New York, May 5, 2022, https://www.chalkbeat.org/newyork/2022/5/5/23059236/nyc-schools-comfort-dog-program-mental-health-literacy/.
19. Rachel Garver and Pedro Noguera, "Supported and Unsafe: The Impact of Educational Structures for Immigrant Students on School Safety," *Youth Violence and Juvenile Justice* 13, no. 4 (2015): 323–44; Stacey J. Lee, *Up Against Whiteness: Race, School, and Immigrant Youth* (Teachers College Press, 2005).

CHAPTER 4

1. The original waiver was granted in 1995 to a small number of schools as a direct result of advocacy from Deborah Meier, a New York City principal, and Steve Phillips, superintendent of the alternative superintendency in New York City, at the time. Thomas Sobel, the state commissioner who was working to de-bureaucratize the state education department and better support schools serving urban populations, granted the waiver after recognizing several small schools for their innovative assessment practices. In the same year, however, Sobel quit in frustration with the growing bureaucracy under the new governor, George Pataki. The next commissioner, Richard Mills, ushered in a new focus on standardization and testing. Commissioner Mills revoked the waiver in 1999 after his appointed panel argued that tests were the only appropriate form of assessment. However, because the system was never studied as was called for in the original waiver, the following five years were marked by lawsuits and advocacy from educators, students, and parents as well as education researchers and experts. As a result, despite NCLB testing policies, the waiver was granted an extension and reinstated in 2004. One school in the Internationals Network was included in the original waiver. The other fourteen schools in the network were added to this waiver in 2013.
2. Richard Ingersoll et al., "The Demographic Transformation of the Teaching Force in the United States," *Education Sciences* 11, no. 5 (2021): 234.
3. Katherine Schaeffer, "America's Public School Teachers Are Far Less Racially and Ethnically Diverse Than Their Students," Pew Research Center, December 10, 2021, https://www.pewresearch.org/short-reads/2021/12/10/americas-public-school-teachers-are-far-less-racially-and-ethnically-diverse-than-their-students/.
4. "The Internationals Approach," Internationals Network of Public Schools, https://www.internationalsnetwork.org/about/#intls-approach.
5. I am using "accent" in this context to refer to a manner of pronunciation that may differ from the local variety of English in a way that impacts both speakers and listeners. Accent is a highly subjective construct. What one person might consider accented speech could be seen as perfectly standard by another. Arguably, everyone and no one has an accent, and the word "accent" has been used as a cover-up for racism and other kinds of discrimination. I am using it here to demonstrate the expansiveness of diversity in the IHS teaching force and the celebration of difference. Accent discrimination and bias are also a well-documented global phenomenon in the labor market, and in schools and universities specifically. See Tracey M. Derwing and Murray J. Munro, "Putting Accent in Its Place: Rethinking Obstacles to Communication," *Language Teaching* 42, no. 4 (2009): 476–90; Pierre W. Orelus, "Other People's English Accents Matter: Challenging Standard English Accent Hegemony," *Excellence in Education Journal* 9, no. 1 (2020): 120–48.

6. Patricia Lavon Hanna and Ann Allen, "Educator Assessment: Accent as a Measure of Fluency in Arizona," *Educational Policy* 27, no. 4 (2013): 711–38; Erez Levon, Devyani Sharma, and Christian Ilbury, "Speaking Up: Accents and Social Mobility," Sutton Trust, 2022, https://eric.ed.gov/?id=ED625661; Tarık Uzun, "Foreign Accent, Identity and Accent Discrimination: A Literature Review," *International Journal of Language Academy* 11, no. 2 (2023), https://doi.org/10.29228/ijla.69110.
7. I am not arguing that travel abroad is the equivalent of what students experience as im/migrants to the United States. There is a dramatic differential in power and privilege between an expat or tourist and someone forced to leave their homeland. However, since fewer than half of all US citizens have passports (up from 3 percent in 1989), and 80 percent are monolingual English speakers, having traveled and/or attempted to learn a new language is an unusual experience for a large portion of the teaching force in the United States. For the teachers at IHS, living abroad, learning a new language, or even having immigrant in-laws seemed to impact how teachers thought of their students and how students thought about their teachers. Additionally, research in psychology and organizational theory points to shared or similar experiences as a way to promote socialization and bonding. It may be valuable for teacher education programs to encourage students to cross geographic, cultural, linguistic, and social borders, to build their capacity for compassion and expand their world view before they enter the classroom. As it currently stands, in an effort to graduate "highly qualified teachers," many teacher candidates are discouraged from study abroad since they have so much course work to complete before student teaching in their senior year of college.
8. Katherine Schaeffer, "A Dwindling Number of New U.S. College Graduates Have a Degree in Education," Pew Research Center, September 27, 2022, https://www.pewresearch.org/short-reads/2022/09/27/a-dwindling-number-of-new-u-s-college-graduates-have-a-degree-in-education.
9. Lucy C. Sorensen and Helen F. Ladd, "The Hidden Costs of Teacher Turnover," *Aera Open* 6, no. 1 (2020), https://doi.org/10.1177/233285842090581; "What's the Cost of Teacher Turnover?," Learning Policy Institute, https://learningpolicyinstitute.org/product/the-cost-of-teacher-turnover.
10. Matthew A. Kraft, William H. Marinell, and Darrick Shen-Wei Yee, "School Organizational Contexts, Teacher Turnover, and Student Achievement: Evidence from Panel Data," *American Educational Research Journal* 53, no. 5 (2016): 1411–49.
11. Richard M. Ingersoll and Michael Strong, "The Impact of Induction and Mentoring Programs for Beginning Teachers: A Critical Review of the Research," *Review of Educational Research* 81, no. 2 (2011): 201–33.
12. Norm Fruchter, "New York City's Affinity District (Part 1): What Is It?," Metropolitan Center for Research on Equity and the Transformation of Schools, June 16, 2020.

13. Daniel Walsh et al., "Strategy 9: Adopt Intentional Staffing," in *Humanizing Education for Immigrant and Refugee Youth: 20 Strategies for the Classroom and Beyond*, ed. Monisha Bajaj et al. (Teachers College Press, 2022).
14. Hua-Yu Sebastian Cherng and Peter F. Halpin, "The Importance of Minority Teachers: Student Perceptions of Minority Versus White Teachers," *Educational Researcher* 45, no. 7 (2016): 407–20; Ana Maria Villegas and Jacqueline Jordan Irvine, "Diversifying the Teaching Force: An Examination of Major Arguments," *Urban Review* 42 (2010): 175–92.
15. Roozbeh Shirazi, "Decentering Americanness: Transnational Youth Experiences of Recognition and Belonging in Two US High Schools," *Anthropology & Education Quarterly* 49, no. 2 (2018): 111–28.
16. Eric A. Hanushek, "The Economic Value of Higher Teacher Quality," *Economics of Education Review* 30, no. 3 (2011): 466–79.

CHAPTER 5

1. The HELLO model, also known as the International Approach, is an anacronym for the five core principles that all network schools share: heterogeneity and collaboration, experiential learning, language and content integration, localized autonomy and responsibility, one learning model for all. See "The Internationals Approach," https://www.internationalsnetwork.org/about.
2. According to Claire, the initial funding for the partnership that eventually became the Internationals Network of Public Schools came from Title VII Academic Excellence grant, first written by a founding teacher to disseminate the practices of the original school. This evolved into an approach where both the new and existing schools learned from one another, growing one school at a time. That grant was renewed at least once. The second source of funding came from the Annenberg Foundation through its "Networks for School Renewal" initiative, which required new small schools in New York City to form networks in order to access that funding. Debbie Meier was involved in that work, and networks like Renaissance, School for the Physical City, and El Puente formed three-school collaborations. Of all the networks formed back then, the only one still standing today is the Internationals.
3. ACLY of New York, "Legislative Memo: Alternative Assessments to Regents Exams," February, 26, 2007, https://www.nyclu.org/resources/policy/legislations/legislative-memo-alternative-assessments-regents-exams.
4. The first waiver in 1995 exempted students from all Regents exams. In 2008, with the renewal of the waiver, the consortium was granted the right to replace schools that had either (1) closed or (2) no longer wanted the waiver (CPESS) and agreed to the requirement of passing the English exam. No existing International High School—all opened between 2000 and 2008—were admitted. In 2013, the Consortium's variance was again extended and two International High Schools were admitted. A second, ELL pilot waiver was granted to the

remaining International High Schools. This waiver required students to take both a math and English Regents exam.

5. New York State Education Department, "New York Performance Standards Consortium ('Consortium Schools')," July 17, 2013, https://www.regents.nysed.gov/sites/regents/files/713brca12.pdf.
6. I am counting the thirty-eight schools recognized on the Performance Standards Consortium website, which includes International High School at LaGuardia, Brooklyn International High School, Manhattan International High School, Bronx International High School, International Community High School as well as the other twelve International High Schools included in the ELL waiver, which are Lafayette International Community High School, International Community High School, Claremont International High School, Crotona International High School, ELLIS Preparatory Academy, Pan American International High School at Monroe, International High School at Prospect Heights, International High School at Lafayette, International High School at Union Square, International High School for Health Sciences, Pan American International High School at Elmhurst, and International High School. See Performance Standards Consortium, "Our Schools," https://www.performanceassessment.org/member-schools-22.
7. According to Claire, the Native Language (NL) project was agreed upon as part of the requirements for all International High Schools in the 1990s, although some schools ended that requirement with the advent of Regent exams. The original argument to include the NL was to make sure students felt that their native languages were assets and valued by the school.
8. The "One Model for All" principle ensures that everyone in the school community, both students and educators, engages in the same collaborative, hands-on learning approach. However, this is complemented by "Localized Autonomy," which allows schools to tailor these practices to meet their unique needs and perspectives.
9. The research they cite in the guide is J. Michael O'Malley and Lorraine Valdez Pierce, *Authentic Assessment for English Language Learners: Practical Approaches for Teachers* (Addison-Wesley, 1996).
10. Intervisitations have been part of the professional development practice at Internationals Network Schools for many years and continue today. Different themes are taken up depending on the school's focus or the work of other networkwide committees with the support of Internationals Network staff.
11. "Teaching to the test" is a colloquial phrase that describes an educational approach that focuses on preparing students for standardized tests by having students complete worksheets with multiple choice questions, write formulaic essays, memorize facts, and analyze short reading passages. This type of instruction is common in classrooms where students are learning English. See Kate Menken, "Teaching to the Test: How No Child Left Behind Impacts

Language Policy, Curriculum, and Instruction for English Language Learners," *Bilingual Research Journal* 30, no. 2 (2006): 521–46.

12. New York State Education Department, "Appeals, Safety Nets, and Superintendent Determination," https://www.nysed.gov/standards-instruction/appeals-safety-nets-and-superintendent-determination#TraditionalAppeals.
13. Richard Spencer is an American neo-Nazi, antisemitic conspiracy theorist, and white supremacist.
14. New York State Education Department, "Blue Ribbon Commission on Graduation Measures," November 2023, https://www.nysed.gov/sites/default/files/programs/grad-measures/nys-blue-ribbon-commission-graduation-measures-report.pdf.
15. Troy Closson, "Regents Exams May Become Optional for High School Graduation in New York," *New York Times*, November 13, 2023, https://www.nytimes.com/2023/11/13/nyregion/regents-exams-new-york.html; Sunisa Nuonsy, "NY Is Poised to Phase out Regents Exam Requirements. For English Learners, Especially, It's Past Time," *Chalkbeat New York*, June 14, 2024, https://www.chalkbeat.org/newyork/2024/06/14/ny-plans-to-end-regents-requirements-for-english-learners-its-past-time.

CONCLUSION

1. The most compelling history I have read about US involvement in geopolitics that continue to have broad implication for modern migration from Central America is Jonathan Blitzer, *Everyone Who Is Gone Is Here: The United States, Central America, and the Making of a Crisis* (Penguin, 2024). I also recommend Greg Grandin, *The End of the Myth: From the Frontier to the Border Wall in the Mind of America* (Metropolitan, 2019); Julia Rose Kraut, *Threat of Dissent: A History of Ideological Exclusion and Deportation in the United States* (Harvard University Press, 2020); Daniel Okrent, *The Guarded Gate: Bigotry, Eugenics, and the Law That Kept Two Generations of Jews, Italians, and Other European Immigrants out of America* (Scribner, 2019).
2. Project 2025 proposals include eliminating T and U visas, which provide critical protections for trafficking and crime victims, while restricting avenues for relief. It seeks to rescind ICE "sensitive zones" policies, removing safeguards in vulnerable locations, and repeals Temporary Protected Status (TPS), stripping humanitarian protections for those fleeing crises. For unaccompanied minors, the plan includes repealing or severely amending the TVPRA, allowing for the expedited deportation of children regardless of nationality, dismantling the Flores Settlement Agreement's protections, and permitting large-scale use of temporary detention facilities. Additionally, it transfers child custody from HHS to DHS, prioritizing enforcement over care. Collectively, these measures undermine the safety and dignity of children, exacerbating their vulnerability and disregarding their basic human rights.

3. Project 2025, 142, https://static.project2025.org/2025_MandateForLeadership_FULL.pdf.
4. Ran Abramitzky and Leah Boustan, *Streets of Gold: America's Untold Story of Immigrant Success* (PublicAffairs, 2022) provides a wonderful history of how we have come to misunderstand immigration. The National Institute of Justice's recent study, "Undocumented Immigrant Offending Rate Lower Than U.S.-Born Citizen Rate" (https://nij.ojp.gov/topics/articles/undocumented-immigrant-offending-rate-lower-us-born-citizen-rate) and the Brennan Center for Justice, "Debunking the Myth of the 'Migrant Crime Wave'" (https://www.brennancenter.org/our-work/analysis-opinion/debunking-myth-migrant-crime-wave) address untruths about immigration and criminality. For school enrollment numbers and impact, see Libby Stanford, "A More Complete Picture of Immigration's Impact on U.S. Public Schools," *Education Week*, June 6, 2024, https://www.edweek.org/policy-politics/a-more-complete-picture-of-immigrations-impact-on-u-s-public-schools/2024/06.
5. Heba Gowayed, *Refuge: How the State Shapes Human Potential* (Princeton University Press, 2022), 3.
6. Thea Renda Abu El-Haj, *Elusive Justice: Wrestling with Difference and Educational Equity in Everyday Practice* (Routledge, 2012), 200.
7. Helen Thorpe, *The Newcomers: Finding Refuge, Friendship, and Hope in an American Classroom* (Simon & Schuster, 2017), 77.
8. Andrea Dyrness and Enrique Sepúlveda III, *Border Thinking: Latinx Youth Decolonizing Citizenship* (University of Minnesota Press, 2020), 35.
9. Chandler Patton Miranda, "Checks, Balances, and Resistance: The Impact of an Anti-Immigrant Federal Administration on a School for Immigrant Teenagers," *Anthropology & Education Quarterly* 48, no. 4 (2017): 376–85; Chandler Patton Miranda and Hua-Yu Sebastian Cherng, "Accountability Reform and Responsive Assessment for Immigrant Youth," *Theory Into Practice* 57, no. 2 (2018): 119–26; Chandler Patton Miranda, "Justice-Oriented Assessment in Immigrant Serving Schools: A Critical Ethnographic Case Study of the Elements of Performance Assessment," *International Journal of Qualitative Studies in Education* (2024): 1–18.
10. Kristina F. Brezicha and Chandler Patton Miranda, "Actions Speak Louder Than Words: Examining School Practices That Support Immigrant Students' Feelings of Belonging," *Equity & Excellence in Education* 55, no. 1–2 (2022): 133–47; Reva Jaffe-Walter and Chandler Patton Miranda, "Segregation or Sanctuary? Examining the Educational Possibilities of Counterpublics for Immigrant English Learners," *Leadership and Policy in Schools* 19, no. 1 (2020): 104–22.
11. Suzanne Gamboa, "Congress Has Failed for More Than Two Decades to Reform Immigration — Here's a Timeline," *NBC News*, January 7, 2023, https://www.nbcnews.com/news/latino/immigration-reform-failure-congress-timeline-rcna64467.

12. Ariel G. Ruiz Soto, Julia Gelatt, and Jennifer Van Hook, *Diverse Flows Drive Increase in U.S. Unauthorized Immigrant Population* (Migration Policy Institute, 2024), https://www.migrationpolicy.org/news/us-unauthorized-population-diversifying.
13. Susan Bibler Coutin, Jennifer M. Chacón, and Stephen Lee, *Legal Phantoms: Executive Action and the Haunting Failures of Immigration Law* (Stanford University Press, 2024).
14. American Immigration Council, "Tending to America's Food Supply: The Essential Role of Immigrants in America's Meat and Dairy Industries," https://www.americanimmigrationcouncil.org/research/tending-americas-food-supply-meat-dairy-industries; Troy Closson, "Migrants Have Been a 'Godsend,' New York Schools Chief Says," *New York Times*, September 11, 2024, https://www.nytimes.com/2024/09/05/nyregion/banks-migrants-nyc-schools.html; Katia Savchuk, "A New Look at Immigrants' Outsize Contribution to Innovation in the U.S.," Stanford Business, March 13, 2023, https://www.gsb.stanford.edu/insights/new-look-immigrants-outsize-contribution-innovation-us.
15. Fighting Hate & Bias Resources, *Cause for Concern 2024: The State of Hate* (Leadership Conference Education Fund, 2024).
16. Julia Gelatt, Valerie Lacarte, and Joshua Rodriguez, *A Profile of Low-Income Immigrants in the United States* (Migration Policy Institute, 2022), https://www.migrationpolicy.org/sites/default/files/publications/mpi_low-income-immigrants-factsheet_final.pdf.
17. Rebecca M. Callahan, "Tracking and High School English Learners: Limiting Opportunity to Learn," *American Educational Research Journal* 42, no. 2 (2005): 305–28; Rebecca Callahan, Lindsey Wilkinson, and Chandra Muller, "Academic Achievement and Course Taking Among Language Minority Youth in U.S. Schools: Effects of ESL Placement," *Educational Evaluation and Policy Analysis* 32, no. 1 (2010): 84–117.
18. Julie Sugarman, *The Impacts on English Learners of Key State High School Policies and Graduation Requirements* (Migration Policy Institute, 2021), https://www.migrationpolicy.org/sites/default/files/publications/high-school-policies-els-2021_final.pdf.
19. Sugarman, *The Impacts on English Learners of Key State High School Policies and Graduation Requirements.*
20. DACA recipients must have come to the United States before their sixteenth birthday, be under thirty-one on June 15, 2012, and have been residing in the United States continuously from June 15, 2007, to the present. Recipients must be currently enrolled in school, completed high school, or be an honorably discharged veteran. Based on these criteria, most DACA-eligible people are between the ages of seventeen and forty. Of currently undocumented college students, fewer than four out of six are DACA-eligible, with that number dropping each year. For those who want to pursue education but are ineligible for

DACA, there is no current pathway to certification. For this reason, advocates and scholars have begun to differentiate between DACAmented and undocumented immigrants in policy conversations. There are an estimated 15,000 teachers who are DACAmented. Andrene J. Castro, "Teachers of Color and Precarious Work: The Inequality of Job Security," *Labor Studies Journal* 47, no. 4 (2022): 359–82, https://doi.org/10.1177/0160449X221128050; José García, "'Lo que yo en realidad quería hacer': Rationales of Latina/o DACA Recipients for Pursuing Careers as Teachers," *Urban Review* 52, no. 5 (2020): 830–52.

21. Kate Menken and Cristian Solorza, "No Child Left Bilingual: Accountability and the Elimination of Bilingual Education Programs in New York City Schools," *Educational Policy* 28, no. 1 (2014): 96–125.
22. For example, legislation, see Migration Policy Institute, "Side-by-Side Comparison of 2013 Senate Immigration Bill with 2006 and 2007 Senate Legislation," April 2013, https://www.migrationpolicy.org/research/side-side-comparison-2013-senate-immigration-bill-2006-and-2007-senate-legislation; H.R. 3194-US Citizenship Act, https://www.congress.gov/bill/118th-congress/house-bill/3194.
23. "Population Projections," Pew Research Center, https://www.pewresearch.org/race-and-ethnicity/2008/02/11/ii-population-projections.
24. Leslie Villegas, "California Will Start Disaggregating English Learner Academic Data," New America, October 3, 2022, https://www.newamerica.org/education-policy/edcentral/california-will-start-disaggregating-english-learner-academic-data/.
25. Reema Amin, "After COVID Paused Regents Exams, Graduation Rates for NYC's English Language Learners Surged," Chalkbeat, January 19, 2023, https://www.chalkbeat.org/newyork/2023/1/19/23562593/ny-english-language-learners-regents-exams-graduation-rate-immigrant-students.
26. Harry Feder, "Press Release: Massachusetts & New York Reject Graduation Exam Requirements; Only Six States Maintain Mandatory Exit Tests for Diploma," Fairtest, November 13, 2024, https://fairtest.org/massachusetts-only-six-states-maintain-mandatory-exit-tests-for-diploma-voters-and-policy-makers-see-education-and-equity-benefits-from-multiple-measur.
27. Jo Napolitano, "In Pursuit of a Better Democracy or Something Else: Oklahoma Latest State to Require High Schoolers to Pass Citizenship Test," The 74, July 11, 2021, https://www.the74million.org/article/in-pursuit-of-a-better-democracy-or-something-else-oklahoma-latest-state-to-require-high-schoolers-to-pass-citizenship-test.
28. There seem to be many rationales given by politicians about these bills but they are immigrant blind at best and dangerous at worst. I fear they will be used to identify and/or target undocumented students depending on the state and the opt-out options given to families. Bill DeBaun, "Four More States

Adopt Universal FAFSA; Total Climbs to 12," National College Attainment Network, August 8, 2023, https://www.ncan.org/news/648074/Four-More-States-Adopt-Universal-FAFSA-Total-Climbs-to-12.htm.

29. "Florida Educators and Students Challenge State's Discriminatory 'Stop WOKE' Act," https://www.naacpldf.org/press-release/florida-educators-and-students-challenge-floridas-discriminatory-stop-woke-act.
30. See Miriam Jordan, "Students, Legal Scholars Push California Universities to Hire Undocumented Students," *New York Times*, October 19, 2022, https://www.nytimes.com/2022/10/19/us/daca-dreamers-university-of-california.html?ref=oembed; Undocumented Student Led Network, "The Opportunity for All (O4A) Campaign," https://undocstudentnetwork.org/home/opportunity-for-all/; Silvia Vazquez, "Assemblymember David Alvarez Introduces Assembly Bill 2586 to Open Employment Opportunities to Undocumented Students on UC, CSU and Community College Campuses," *UCLA Labor Center*, February, 15, 2024, https://labor.ucla.edu/press-release/assemblymember-david-alvarez-introduces-assembly-bill-2586-to-open-employment-opportunities-to-undocumented-students-on-uc-csu-and-community-college-campuses/.
31. Rebecca C. Lewis, "New York Looks at Options for State Work Authorization for Asylum-Seekers," City & State New York, September 13, 2023, https://www.cityandstateny.com/policy/2023/09/new-york-looks-options-state-work-authorization-asylum-seekers/390273.
32. Danila Alulema, "Opinion: To Solve Teacher Shortages, Let's Open Pathways for Immigrants So They Can Become Educators and Role Models," *The Hechinger Report*, November 14, 2023, https://hechingerreport.org/opinion-to-solve-teacher-shortages-lets-open-pathways-for-immigrants-so-they-can-become-educators-and-role-models/.
33. Oakland Unified School District, "Sanctuary District," https://www.ousd.org/about-us/sanctuary-district.
34. ACLU of Southern California, "Sanctuary Schools Campaign," https://www.aclusocal.org/en/sanctuary-toolkit; Immigrants Rising, "Understanding the Sanctuary School & Safe Zone Movement," https://immigrantsrising.org/wp-content/uploads/Immigrants-Rising_Understanding-the-Sanctuary-School-and-Safe-Zone-Movement.pdf.
35. NYC Public Schools, "Immigration Guidance for Principals," https://infohub.nyced.org/in-our-schools/policies/immigration-guidance-for-schools.
36. Mobilization for Justice, https://mobilizationforjustice.org.
37. Immigrant Legal Resource Center, https://www.ilrc.org/red-cards.
38. Jenna Queenan et al., "Learning from Our History: The Role of the New York Collective of Radical Educators in Movements for Educational Justice," *Radical Teacher* 128 (2024).
39. Thorpe, *The Newcomers*, 77.

40. The "your story is your ticket" phenomenon is illustrated by participants by Andrea Flores, *The Succeeders: How Immigrant Youth Are Transforming What It Means to Belong in America* (University of California Press, 2021), 95.
41. Children, even from a very young age, are "intentional about how to disclose immigration status," as highlighted by Ariana Mangual Figueroa, *Knowing Silence: How Children Talk About Immigration Status in School* (University of Minnesota Press, 2020), 71.
42. Deborah Busch, "Pre-Service Teacher Beliefs About Language Learning: The Second Language Acquisition Course as an Agent for Change," *Language Teaching Research* 14, no. 3 (2010): 318–37, https://doi.org/10.1177/1362168810365239; Clarisse Halpern, Joseph Trunfio, and Hasan Aydin, "'We Learned to Be Compassionate': Pre-Service Teachers' Perceptions of Teaching Immigrant Children," *Journal of Multilingual and Multicultural Development* 45, no. 4 (2024): 1004–16.
43. Immigrant Rising, "A Guide to Building On-Campus Undocumented Student Programs," https://immigrantsrising.org/resource/a-guide-to-building-on-campus-undocumented-student-programs.
44. Deborah J. Short and Beverly A. Boyson, *Helping Newcomer Students Succeed in Secondary Schools and Beyond*, vol. 78 (Center for Applied Linguistics, 2012).
45. Kevin Close, Audrey Amrein-Beardsley, and Clarin Collins, "Putting Teacher Evaluation Systems on the Map: An Overview of State's Teacher Evaluation Systems Post-Every Student Succeeds Act," *Education Policy Analysis Archives* 28, no. 58 (2020).
46. Recent studies have shown the clear benefits of extending high school beyond four years to better serve students, especially traditionally marginalized students. Sugarman, *The Impacts on English Learners of Key State High School Policies and Graduation Requirements*, 12; Julie Sugarman, *The Unintended Consequences for English Learners of Using the Four-Year Graduation Rate for School Accountability* (Migration Policy Institute, 2019), https://www.migrationpolicy.org/research/english-learners-four-year-graduation-rate-school-accountability.
47. Stephen Kostyo, Jessica Cardichon, Linda Darling Hammond, *Implementing an Extended-Year Graduation Rate Making ESSA's Equity Promise Real: State Strategies to Close the Opportunity Gap* (Learning Policy Institute, 2018), https://learningpolicyinstitute.org/product/essa-equity-promise-extended-year-grad-brief.
48. Nakia M. Gray-Nicolas, "College Readiness and Critical Structural Capital: Mediating the Dual Meanings of Readiness at a Transfer Community High School," *International Journal of Qualitative Studies in Education* (2023): 1–15.
49. Rana Foroohar, "The School That Is Changing American Education," *Time*, February 13, 2014, https://time.com/10038/the-school-that-is-changing-american-education.

50. Sugarman, *The Unintended Consequences for English Learners of Using the Four-Year Graduation Rate for School Accountability.*
51. See also Roneeta Guha, Maria E. Hyler, Linda Darling-Hammond, "The Teacher Residency," *American Educator*, Spring 2017, https://www.aft.org/ae/spring2017/guha_hyler_darling-hammond; Tim Silva et al., *Teaching Residency Programs: A Multisite Look at a New Model to Prepare Teachers for High-Need Schools. NCEE 2015-4002* (National Center for Education Evaluation and Regional Assistance, 2014).
52. Jean Anyon, "Social Class and the Hidden Curriculum of Work," in *Childhood Socialization* (Routledge, 2017), 369–94.
53. Erin B. Godfrey, Carlos E. Santos, and Esther Burson, "For Better or Worse? System-Justifying Beliefs in Sixth-Grade Predict Trajectories of Self-Esteem and Behavior Across Early Adolescence," *Child Development* 90, no. 1 (2019): 180–95.
54. Kristina Brezicha and Megan Hopkins, "Shifting the Zone of Mediation in a Suburban New Immigrant Destination: Community Boundary Spanners and School District Policymaking," *Peabody Journal of Education* 91, no. 3 (2016): 366–82, https://doi.org/10.1080/0161956X.2016.1184945; S. Garnett Russell and Paula Mantilla-Blanco, "Belonging and Not Belonging: The Case of Newcomers in Diverse U.S. Schools," *American Journal of Education* 128, no. 4 (2022): 617–45; Carola Suárez-Orozco, "The Diverse Immigrant Student Experience: What Does It Mean for Teaching?," *Educational Studies* 53, no. 5 (2017): 522–34; Carola Suárez-Orozco, Adam Strom, and Rosalinda Larios, "A Culturally Responsive Approach to Understanding Immigrant Origin Children," *Re-Imagining Migration* (2018); Margary Martin and Carola Suárez-Orozco, "What It Takes: Promising Practices for Immigrant Origin Adolescent Newcomers," *Theory Into Practice* 57, no. 2 (2018): 82–90.
55. Jorge Ruiz-de-Velasco and Michael Fix, *Overlooked & Underserved: Immigrant Students in US Secondary School* (Center for Applied Linguistics, 2000); Felecia S. Russell and Alonso R. Reyna Rivarola, "What Does It Mean to Be UndocuBlack? Exploring the Double Invisibility of Black Undocumented Immigrant Students in US Colleges and Universities," *New Directions for Higher Education* 2023, no. 203 (2023): 61–76.
56. Hua-Yu Sebastian Cherng, "If They Think I Can: Teacher Bias and Youth of Color Expectations and Achievement," *Social Science Research* 66, no. 2017 (2017): 170–86.
57. Guadalupe Valdés, *Learning and Not Learning English: Latino Students in American Schools* (Teachers College Press, 2004).
58. Paulo Freire, *Pedagogy of the Oppressed* (Seabury, 1968).
59. Alejandro Portes and Rubén G. Rumbaut, *Immigrant America: A Portrait* (University of California Press, 2024), 196.

60. Angela Valenzuela, "Subtractive Schooling, Caring Relations, and Social Capital in the Schooling of US-Mexican Youth," *Beyond Silenced Voices: Class, Race, and Gender in United States Schools* (2005): 83–94.
61. Jo Napolitano, "From New Mexico to Michigan, States Take Action After 74 Investigation Reveals Rampant Enrollment Discrimination," The 74, August 8, 2024, https://www.the74million.org/article/from-new-mexico-to-michigan-states-take-action-after-74-investigation-reveals-rampant-enrollment-discrimination.

APPENDIX

1. The novels I read included Chimamanda Ngozi Adichie, *The Thing Around Your Neck* (Knopf, 2009); Chimamanda Ngozi Adichie, *Purple Hibiscus* (Algonquin, 2003); Julia Alvarez, *How the García Girls Lost Their Accents* (Algonquin, 1991); May-Lee Chai, *Useful Phrases for Immigrants* (Blair, 2018); Sandra Cisneros, *The House on Mango Street* (Vintage, 1991); Mohsin Hamid, *Exit West* (Riverhead, 2017); Jhumpa Lahiri, *The Namesake* (Houghton Mifflin Harcourt, 2003); Jhumpa Lahiri, *Interpreter of Maladies* (Houghton Mifflin Harcourt, 1999); Viet Thanh Nguyen, *The Refugees* (Grove, 2017). Non-fiction books included Valeria Luiselli, *Tell Me How It Ends: An Essay in 40 Questions* (Coffee House Press, 2017); Viet Thanh Nguyen, *The Displaced: Refugee Writers on Refugee Lives* (Abrams, 2018); Javier Zamora, *Solito, a Memoir* (Hogarth, 2022). I also read books that I saw students reading in class including Elizabeth Acevedo, *The Poet X* (HarperTeen, 2018); Mawi Asgedom, *Of Beetles and Angels* (Little, Brown, 2002); Deborah Ellis, *The Breadwinner* (Groundwood, 2001); Nicola Yoon, *The Sun Is Also a Star* (Delacorte, 2016); Malala Yousafzai, *I Am Malala: The Girl Who Stood Up for Education and Was Shot by the Taliban* (Little, Brown, 2013).
2. To learn more about the history and mythology of immigration to the United States, I recommend reading Ran Abramitzky and Leah Boustan, *Streets of Gold: America's Untold Story of Immigrant Success* (Public Affairs, 2022); Harsha Walia, *Border and Rule: Global Migration, Capitalism, and the Rise of Racist Nationalism* (Haymarket, 2021). On family separation and reunification, I read Ko-lin Chin, *Smuggled Chinese: Clandestine Immigration to the United States* (Temple University Press, 1999); Gabrielle Oliveira, *Motherhood Across Borders: Immigrant Families and Their Children in Mexico and New York* (New York University Press, 2018); Jacob Soboroff, *Separated: Inside an American Tragedy* (Harper, 2020).
3. Nancy Foner, Rubén G. Rumbaut, and Steven J. Gold, eds., *Immigration Research for a New Century: Multidisciplinary Perspectives* (Russell Sage Foundation, 2000); Carola Suárez-Orozco et al., "Academic Trajectories of Newcomer Immigrant Youth," *Developmental Psychology* 46, no. 3 (2010): 602; Carola Suárez-Orozco and Marcelo M. Suárez-Orozco, *Children of Immigration* (Harvard University Press, 2009); Carola Suárez-Orozco, Marcelo M. Suárez-Orozco, and

Irina Todorova, *Learning a New Land: Immigrant Students in American Society* (Harvard University Press, 2008).

4. This is not an exhaustive list of research on Internationals but these are the books and articles I returned to again and again to better understand what I was seeing in my research. Lesley Bartlett and Ofelia García, *Additive Schooling in Subtractive Times: Dominican Immigrant Youth in the Heights* (Vanderbilt University Press, 2011); Brooke Hauser, *The New Kids: Big Dreams and Brave Journeys at a High School for Immigrant Teens* (Simon & Schuster, 2011); Lauren Markham, *The Far Away Brothers: Two Young Migrants and the Making of an American Life* (Crown, 2018); Mary Mendenhall, Lesley Bartlett, and Ameena Ghaffar-Kucher, "'If You Need Help, They Are Always There for Us': Education for Refugees in an International High School in NYC," *Urban Review* 49 (2017): 1–25.
5. The books that came out between my dissertation and this book that I found helpful included Jordan Corson, *Reconceptualizing Education for Newcomer Students: Valuing Learning Experiences Inside and Outside of School* (Teachers College Press, 2023); Ariana Mangual Figueroa, *Knowing Silence: How Children Talk About Immigration Status in School* (University of Minnesota Press, 2024).
6. Angela Valenzuela, *Subtractive Schooling: US-Mexican Youth and the Politics of Caring* (State University of New York Press, 2010).

ACKNOWLEDGMENTS

THIS BOOK WOULD NOT have been possible without the cooperation, support, and encouragement of the students and educators at International High School. I am forever grateful for what I have learned from the amazing people in this community about the power of relationships, collaboration, compassion, and the love of teaching. The warmth of my welcome and the transparency of the school staff made truly understanding the culture of the school a real possibility. Few researchers enjoy unrestricted access to a school, and even fewer get to do research at schools that are true beacons of hope for young people. Mil gracias, చాల కృతజ్ఞతలు, 非常感谢, جزيل شكرا, mèsi anpil, অনকে ধন্যবাদ, 많은 감사.

Lara Evangelista has become my friend and collaborator through the writing of this book. She is the humblest person I have ever met who is fully committed to the work of supporting immigrant children, their families, and the educators who serve them. It has been a great honor to learn from her and watch her lead International High School, and now the Internationals Network of Public Schools, with conviction. It is a joy to talk to Lara because she has such a clear vision of what immigrant students need. She knows because she has learned from a long list of radical activist educators that came before her like Sara Newman, Claire Sylvan, Eric Nadelstern, Deborah Meier, Cecilia Cunningham, Janet Lieberman, and many more. I hope to continue to write about her approach to building authentic relationships to facilitate radical change in this particular educational space. You've learned so much about Lara's call to do this work in the preceding chapters and how she thinks about schools and people with genuine love. I can honestly say I have never met someone quite like her or an educator I believe in so completely.

This book would also never have been possible without the constant support and guidance of my tireless advisor, dissertation chair, and mentor, Colleen L. Larson. Colleen has been at once my biggest cheerleader and most honest critic. She has pushed me further intellectually and emotionally than I thought possible. She has helped me see myself as belonging in academia and has believed this study to be important and insightful, even when I doubted myself. As my advisor, she read every word of every draft of every paper, transcript, and memo I turned in to her. I hope to be as present as an advisor and chair to my students as she has been to me.

Reva Jaffe-Walter, whose work I read and admired long before we met for lunch almost a decade ago, saw this study as a book long before I could envision that possibility. Our first lunch led to a mentorship that has resulted in countless conference papers, publications, and collaborations. She taught me to write for an academic audience and introduced me to her village of educational anthropologists, many of whom have become mentors and friends. Most of this book was revised or written on Reva's farm, miles away from my chaotic life in Brooklyn. Reva provided constant encouragement and a peaceful sanctuary, both of which helped quiet my mind and rediscover my voice as a writer, one I felt I lost to motherhood and a barrage of pandemic-era rejections from the academy.

Mary Patton, my mother, also read every draft of every paper, dissertation chapter, and conference paper that I have written in the last decade, offering both critical feedback and positive affirmations. Everyone in academia should have an editor as particular and uplifting as she is. Her guidance has helped me hone my writing and craft my analysis in ways that are solutions focused. My father, the English major, has also pointed out my many grammatical errors and is my on-call thesaurus. He is also great for a pep talk whenever I doubt my ability to finish something I start.

I am forever indebted to *mi media naranja*, Luis Gabriel Miranda, who left his country, family, and everything he knew so that I could do this study and write this book. His adaptability and fierce resilience amaze me daily. He has been my inspiration for trying to understand the plight of new immigrants and has given me hope that the United States can still be a land of opportunity for newly arrived immigrants if the right public policies and school practices are in place. Because of Luis, I am a better researcher, educator, and human. We have become parents to Gabriel and Martina, who continue to amaze us daily with their ability to navigate their bilingual, binational identities. As people who learned a second language as adults and studied language acquisition in our graduate programs, watching them learn Spanish and English simultaneously has been mind-boggling!

The incredible cover art for this book was painted by Angel Garcia, a Mexican-American artist based in New York City. His family was among the many who immigrated to Sunset Park in the 1990s, a Brooklyn neighborhood known for its large community of migrants from Puebla. Growing up in Brooklyn, Angel was immersed in the city's rich cultural tapestry, which, along with his Mexican heritage, shaped his identity and later became central to his art. He first encountered art and muralism in high school through after-school programs—similar to the community-engaged public art projects he now leads. The "Our Roots" mural he painted at IHS was one of his first. More of his studio work and community murals can be found at www.angelgarcia-art.com or on Instagram @angelgarciaart. I am so grateful he allowed his work to grace the cover of this book.

I want to acknowledge a community of educators beyond International High School that have also helped me understand the work of the Internationals Network within the context of New York City Public Schools, including Natalia Ortiz, Nedda de Castro, Melissa de Leon, and many others. I am very grateful for the guidance, wisdom, and accountability imparted to me by a number of academic mentors and colleagues, including Thea Abu El-Haj, Noel Anderson, Hua-Yu Sebastian Cherng, Rebecca Callahan, Ginetta Candelaria, Cecilia Silva, Andrea Dyrness, Alex Freidus, Erika Kitzmiller, Mary Rocco, Adriana Villavicencio, and Molly Weinburgh, all of whom have guided me in my career and on the publication of this book. There have also been other scholars and writers whose work has had a particularly strong impact on my thinking, including Monisha Bajaj, Lesley Bartlett, Ofelia Garcia, Maria Hantzopoulos, Lauren Markham, Eric Nadelstern, Jo Napolitano, Laurie Olson, A. Naiomi Pak, Rosa L. Rivera-McCutchen, Sophia Rodriquez, Enrique Sepúlveda III, Claire Sylvan, and Daniel Walsh. A special thanks to Angela Valenzuela for her paradigm-changing work, which has brought so many of us to the field. Finally, I want to acknowledge Laura Portwood-Stacer, whose proposal development program helped me articulate the goals for this book in new and exciting ways.

I am grateful to the many students who have worked with me throughout the years so that I could teach and mother during some very challenging years and still be able to write and do the research I care about so much. Yasmin Naji was a constant force pushing my writing forward through COVID-19, pregnancy, and maternity leave in her kind and highly organized way. I also want to thank Orubba Almansouri and Lana Kalfas for their insights and collaboration.

Thank you to Amanda Matthews and Katina Peron for reading early drafts and to Lucy Bennett for guidance on how to articulate my message on social media. I am so lucky to have such smart and generous friends. And a huge thank you to my scholar family, Nakia Gray-Nicolas, Aisha Haynes, Chy McGee, Fawziah Qadir, Tatiana Bacigalupe, and Rachel Throop, for support and inspiration (and baby-holding) at all stages of this process.

Finally, I am grateful for the people who have helped me grow as an educator and thinker. Thank you to my former students, fellow teachers, and school leaders with whom I have worked throughout my teaching career. You have helped me truly understand the importance of school culture. Finally, thank you to my current colleagues who have been my cheerleaders from my first day at Molloy when this book was still in its early stages: Tricia Kress, Carolyne Ali-Khan, Warren Whitaker, Allison Roda, Joanna Alcruz, Denise Smith, Cindy Vaupel, Denise Hughes, Joanne O'Brian, Melissa McCardle, Audry Cohan, and the entire Education Summit.

ABOUT THE AUTHOR

CHANDLER PATTON MIRANDA, PHD, is a scholar, educator, and community organizer whose work centers on the experiences of immigrant youth and their teachers in urban public high schools. Her research primarily focuses on schools within the Internationals Network of Public Schools, which she considers innovation hubs for discovering effective ways to support recently arrived immigrant students. Her work has been published in *Harvard Educational Review*, *Anthropology & Education Quarterly*, *Leadership and Policy in Schools*, and *Equity & Excellence in Education*. She currently serves as an Assistant Professor of Education at Molloy University.

Before transitioning to higher education, Chandler spent seven years teaching high school science in San Benito, Texas, as well as in Barranquilla and Bogotá, Colombia. She has also volunteered as a child advocate for the Young Center for Immigrant Children's Rights and is actively involved in community organizing with mutual aid and neighborhood community defense. On weekends, she coaches soccer in Brooklyn, where she lives with her husband, Luis, and their two children, Gabriel and Martina.

INDEX